A COLLECTOR'S ITEM

New award winners and more photos than ever!

HISTORY OF THE

ACADEMY

AWARD

WINNERS

1974 EDITION

The entire history from 1927 - More than 250 rare photographs - Biographies of all winners!

ace books

A Division of Charter Communications Inc.
1120 Avenue of the Americas
New York, N.Y. 10036

acknowledgments

Written by Nathalie Fredrik and Auriel Douglas
Editorial Supervisor: Lawrence Sloan
1974 photos by Tony Rizzo

NOTE: *"History of the Academy Award Winners" is not a publication of the Academy of Motion Picture Arts and Sciences.*

46th annual academy awards April 2, 1974

...n emotion-choked Jack Lemmon ...bilantly accepts his Oscar for ...est Actor. Best Actress winner ...lenda Jackson was not on hand ...o accept her award.

Tatum O'Neal, after receiving her Best Supporting Actress award, poses with grandfather Charles O'Neal.

...rnest Borgnine and Cybill Shepherd present Best Supporting Actor award to ...ohn Houseman ("The Paper Chase").

Katharine Hepburn, appearing at an Academy Award ceremony for the first time, presents the Irving G. Thalberg award to her old and good friend, producer Lawrence Weingarten.

Sven Nykvist accepts his Cinematography award for "Cries and Whispers" from Cicely Tyson. ⟶

James Caan and Raquel Welch give the Best Documentary award to Keith Merrill for "The Great American Cowboy."

Ex-Beatle Paul McCartney arrives with his wife, Linda.

Burt Reynolds, one of
the 1974 hosts.

Ann-Margret is astonished at Marvin
Hamlisch's three Oscars. He won for
Best Song, "The Way We Were;"
Best Score and Best Adaptation,
"The Sting."

Peter Falk and Twiggy congratulate Edith Head on winning
her eighth Costume Design Oscar, this time for "The Sting."

Alfred Hitchcock, with MCA's Lew Wasserman, who received the Jean Hersholt Humanitarian Award.

Yul Brynner presents Francois Truffaut's Oscar for Best Foreign Language Film ("Day For Night").

Paul Newman and Joanne Woodward with their daughter, Nell, chat with Shirley MacLaine before the Awards.

Dani Greco and David
Janssen arriving at L.A.
Music Center for the
Award ceremony.

Debbie Reynolds and
Donald O'Connor.

Liza Minnelli and Elizabeth Taylor are happy with David S. Ward's win for
Best Original Story and Screenplay ("The Sting"). Just before their appearance, a nude "streaker" ran across the stage - fulfilling a rumor that had
circulated all day about the latest American fad.

Michael Wilding Jr., and his mother, Elizabeth Taylor, backstage at the Music Center

Groucho Marx accepts an honorary award from Jack Lemmon for the comedy geniuses known as The Marx Brothers. "I wish Harpo and Chico were here to see this," he commented

Glamorous Cher, recently separated from husband Sonny Bono, is shown with her date, David Geffen.

contents

NOTE: Number beside name denotes a multiple winner and number of Oscars won.

YEAR	PICTURE	ACTOR	ACTRESS	SUPPORTING PLAYERS	PAGE
1927/28	Wings	Emil Jannings The Last Command; The Way of All Flesh	Janet Gaynor Seventh Heaven; Street Angel; Sunrise	Not awarded until 1936	13
1928/29	Broadway Melody	Warner Baxter In Old Arizona	Mary Pickford Coquette		16
1929/30	All Quiet On the Western Front	George Arliss Disraeli	Norma Shearer The Divorcee		19
1930/31	Cimarron	Lionel Barrymore A Free Soul	Marie Dressler Min and Bill		22
1931/32	Grand Hotel	Fredric March (2) Dr. Jekyll and Mr. Hyde Wallace Beery The Champ	Helen Hayes (2) The Sin of Madelon Claudet		25
1932/33	Cavalcade	Charles Laughton The Private Life of Henry VIII	Katharine Hepburn (3) Morning Glory		29
1934	It Happened One Night	Clark Gable It Happened One Night	Claudette Colbert It Happened One Night		32
1935	Mutiny On the Bounty	Victor McLaglen The Informer	Bette Davis (2) Dangerous		35
1936	The Great Ziegfeld	Paul Muni The Story of Louis Pasteur	Luise Rainer (2) The Great Ziegfeld	Walter Brennan (3) Gale Sondergaard	38
1937	The Life of Emile Zola	Spencer Tracy (2) Captains Courageous	Luise Rainer (2) The Good Earth	Joseph Schildkraut Alice Brady	42
1938	You Can't Take It With You	Spencer Tracy (2) Boys Town	Bette Davis (2) Jezebel	Walter Brennan (3) Fay Bainter	51
1939	Gone With the Wind	Robert Donat Goodbye, Mr. Chips	Vivien Leigh (2) Gone with the Wind	Thomas Mitchell Hattie McDaniel	55
1940	Rebecca	James Stewart The Philadelphia Story	Ginger Rogers Kitty Foyle	Walter Brennan (3) Jane Darwell	59
1941	How Green Was My Valley	Gary Cooper (2) Sergeant York	Joan Fontaine Suspicion	Donald Crisp Mary Astor	63
1942	Mrs. Miniver	James Cagney Yankee Doodle Dandy	Greer Garson Mrs. Miniver	Van Heflin Teresa Wright	67
1943	Casablanca	Paul Lukas Watch on the Rhine	Jennifer Jones Song of Bernadette	Charles Coburn Katina Paxinou	71
1944	Going My Way	Bing Crosby Going My Way	Ingrid Bergman (2) Gaslight	Barry Fitzgerald Ethel Barrymore	75
1945	The Lost Weekend	Ray Milland The Lost Weekend	Joan Crawford Mildred Pierce	James Dunn Anne Revere	79
1946	The Best Years of Our Lives	Fredric March (2) The Best Years of Our Lives	Olivia de Havilland (2) To Each His Own	Harold Russell Anne Baxter	83
1947	Gentleman's Agreement	Ronald Colman A Double Life	Loretta Young The Farmer's Daughter	Edmund Gwenn Celeste Holm	87
1948	Hamlet	Laurence Olivier Hamlet	Jane Wyman Johnny Belinda	Walter Huston Claire Trevor	99
1949	All the King's Men	Broderick Crawford All the King's Men	Olivia de Havilland (2) The Heiress	Dean Jagger Mercedes McCambridge	103
1950	All About Eve	Jose Ferrer Cyrano de Bergerac	Judy Holliday Born Yesterday	George Sanders Josephine Hull	107

year by year

YEAR	PICTURE	ACTOR	ACTRESS	SUPPORTING PLAYERS	PAGE
1951	An American In Paris	Humphrey Bogart The African Queen	Vivien Leigh (2) A Streetcar Named Desire	Karl Malden Kim Hunter	111
1952	The Greatest Show On Earth	Gary Cooper (2) High Noon	Shirley Booth Come Back, Little Sheba	Anthony Quinn (2) Gloria Grahame	115
1953	From Here To Eternity	William Holden Stalag 17	Audrey Hepburn Roman Holiday	Frank Sinatra Donna Reed	119
1954	On the Waterfront	Marlon Brando On the Waterfront	Grace Kelly The Country Girl	Edmond O'Brien Eva Marie Saint	123
1955	Marty	Ernest Borgnine Marty	Anna Magnani The Rose Tattoo	Jack Lemmon Jo Van Fleet	127
1956	Around the World In 80 Days	Yul Brynner The King and I	Ingrid Bergman (2) Anastasia	Anthony Quinn (2) Dorothy Malone	131
1957	The Bridge on the River Kwai	Alec Guinness The Bridge on the River Kwai	Joanne Woodward The Three Faces of Eve	Red Buttons Miyoshi Umeki	135
1958	Gigi	David Niven Separate Tables	Susan Hayward I Want to Live!	Burl Ives Wendy Hiller	148
1959	Ben-Hur	Charlton Heston Ben-Hur	Simone Signoret Room at the Top	Hugh Griffith Shelley Winters (2)	152
1960	The Apartment	Burt Lancaster Elmer Gantry	Elizabeth Taylor (2) Butterfield 8	Peter Ustinov (2) Shirley Jones	156
1961	West Side Story	Maximilian Schell Judgment at Nuremberg	Sophia Loren Two Women	George Chakiris Rita Moreno	160
1962	Lawrence of Arabia	Gregory Peck To Kill a Mockingbird	Anne Bancroft The Miracle Worker	Ed Begley Patty Duke	164
1963	Tom Jones	Sidney Poitier Lilies of the Field	Patricia Neal Hud	Melvyn Douglas Margaret Rutherford	168
1964	My Fair Lady	Rex Harrison My Fair Lady	Julie Andrews Mary Poppins	Peter Ustinov (2) Lila Kedrova	172
1965	The Sound of Music	Lee Marvin Cat Ballou	Julie Christie Darling	Martin Balsam Shelley Winters (2)	176
1966	A Man for All Seasons	Paul Scofield A Man for All Seasons	Elizabeth Taylor (2) Who's Afraid of Virginia Woolf?	Walter Matthau Sandy Dennis	180
1967	In the Heat of the Night	Rod Steiger In the Heat of the Night	Katharine Hepburn (3) Guess Who's Coming to Dinner	George Kennedy Estelle Parsons	184
1968	Oliver!	Cliff Robertson Charly	Katharine Hepburn (3) The Lion in Winter Barbra Streisand Funny Girl	Jack Albertson Ruth Gordon	195
1969	Midnight Cowboy	John Wayne True Grit	Maggie Smith The Prime of Miss Jean Brodie	Gig Young Goldie Hawn	200
1970	Patton	George C. Scott Patton	Glenda Jackson Women in Love	John Mills Helen Hayes (2)	204
1971	The French Connection	Gene Hackman The French Connection	Jane Fonda Klute	Ben Johnson Cloris Leachman	208
1972	The Godfather	Marlon Brando (2) The Godfather	Liza Minnelli Cabaret	Joel Grey Eileen Heckart	212
1973	The Sting	Jack Lemmon (2) Save The Tiger	Glenda Jackson (2) A Touch of Class	John Houseman Tatum O'Neal	216

1968-73 oscar winners in other categories

1968

DIRECTOR
CAROL REED, Oliver!

WRITING
THE LION IN WINTER, James Goldman (Best Screenplay—based on material from another medium)
THE PRODUCERS, Mel Brooks (Best Story and Screenplay—written directly for the screen)

CINEMATOGRAPHY
ROMEO & JULIET, Pasqualino De Santis

ART DIRECTION-SET DIRECTION
OLIVER!, John Box, Terence Marsh, Vernon Dixon, Ken Muggleston

SOUND
OLIVER!, Shepperton Studio Sound Dept.

SHORT SUBJECTS
ROBERT KENNEDY REMEMBERED, National General (Live Action Subjects)
WINNIE THE POOH AND THE BLUSTERY DAY, Walt Disney Productions (Cartoon)

DOCUMENTARY
JOURNEY INTO SELF, Western Behavioral Sciences Institute (Features)
WHY MAN CREATES, Saul Bass & Associates (Short Subjects)

MUSIC
THE WINDMILLS OF YOUR MIND (The Thomas Crown Affair) Music, Michel LeGrand; Lyrics, Alan and Marilyn Bergman (Song)
THE LION IN WINTER, John Barry (Best Original Score—not a musical
OLIVER!, John Green (Scoring of a Musical Picture)

FILM EDITING
BULLITT, Frank P. Keller

SPECIAL EFFECTS
2001: A SPACE ODYSSEY, Stanley Kubrick

COSTUME DESIGN
ROMEO & JULIET, Danilo Donati

FOREIGN LANGUAGE FILM AWARD
WAR AND PEACE (Russia)

JEAN HERSHOLT HUMANITARIAN AWARD
MARTHA RAYE

SPECIAL AWARD
JOHN CHAMBERS, for makeup for Planet of the Apes
ONNA WHITE, for choreographing Oliver!

SCIENTIFIC OR TECHNICAL

CLASS I
PHILIP V. PALMQUIST, DR. HERBERT MEYER, CHARLES STAFFEL; EASTMAN KODAK

CLASS II
DONALD NORWOOD; EASTMAN KODAK & PRODUCERS SERVICE CO.; EDMUND M. DIGIULIO, NIELS G. PETERSON, NORMAN S. HUGHES; OPTICAL COATING LABORATORIES; PANAVISION; TODD-A-O CO.; MITCHELL CAMERA CO.

CLASS III
CARL W. HAUGE, EDWARD H. REICHARD, E. MICHAEL MEAHL, ROY J. RIDENOUR; EASTMAN KODAK, CONSOLIDATED FILM INDUSTRIES

1969

DIRECTOR
JOHN SCHLESINGER, Midnight Cowboy

WRITING
MIDNIGHT COWBOY, Waldo Salt (Best Screenplay based on material from another medium)
BUTCH CASSIDY AND THE SUNDANCE KID, William Goldman (Best Story and Screenplay based on material not previously published or produced)

CINEMATOGRAPHY
BUTCH CASSIDY AND THE SUNDANCE KID, Conrad Hall

ART DIRECTION-SET DECORATION
HELLO, DOLLY!, John DeCuir, Jack Martin Smith, Herman Blumenthal; Walter M. Scott, George Hopkins, Raphael Bretton

SOUND
HELLO, DOLLY!, Jack Solomon, Murray Spivack

SHORT SUBJECTS
THE MAGIC MACHINES, Fly-by-Night Productions (Live Action Subjects)
IT'S TOUGH TO BE A BIRD, Walt Disney Production (Cartoons)

DOCUMENTARY
ARTHUR RUBINSTEIN—THE LOVE OF LIFE, A Midem Production (Features)
CZECHOSLOVAKIA 1968, Sanders Fresco Film Makers for U.S. Information Agency (Short Subjects)

MUSIC
RAINDROPS KEEP FALLIN' ON MY HEAD (Butch Cassidy and the Sundance Kid) Music, Burt Bacharach; Lyrics, Hal David (Song)
HELLO, DOLLY!, music adapted by Lennie Hayton and Lionel Newman (Scoring of a Musical Picture)
BUTCH CASSIDY AND THE SUNDANCE KID, Burt Bacharach (Best Original Score, not a Musical)

FILM EDITING
Z, Francoise Bonnot

SPECIAL VISUAL EFFECTS
MAROONED, Robbie Robertson

COSTUME DESIGN
ANNE OF THE THOUSAND DAYS, Margaret Furse
FOREIGN LANGUAGE FILM AWARD
Z (Algeria)

JEAN HERSHOLT HUMANITARIAN AWARD
GEORGE JESSEL

SPECIAL AWARD
CARY GRANT

SCIENTIFIC OR TECHNICAL

CLASS II
HAZELTINE CORP.; FOUAD SAID; JUAN DE LA CIERVA, DYNASCIENCES CORP.

CLASS III
OTTO POPELKA, MAGNA-TECH ELECTRONICS CO.; FENTON HAMILTON, MGM STUDIOS; PANAVISION INC.; ROBERT M. FLYNN, RUSSELL HESSY, UNIVERSAL CITY STUDIOS, INC.

1970

DIRECTOR
FRANKLIN J. SCHAFFNER, Patton

WRITING
M*A*S*H, Ring Lardner, Jr. (Best Screen Play based on material from another medium)
PATTON, Francis Ford Coppola, Edmund H. North (Best Story and Screenplay based on factual material or material not previously published)

CINEMATOGRAPHY
RYAN'S DAUGHTER, Freddie Young

ART DIRECTION-SET DIRECTION
PATTON, Urie McCleary, Gil Parrondo; Antonio Mateos, Pierre-Louis Thevenet

SOUND
PATTON, Douglas Williams, Don Bassman

SHORT SUBJECTS
THE RESURRECTION OF BRONCHO BILLY, University of Southern California, Dept. of Cinema (Live Action Subjects)
IS IT ALWAYS RIGHT TO BE RIGHT?, Stephen Bosustow Productions (Cartoons)

DOCUMENTARY
WOODSTOCK, A Wadleigh-Maurice Ltd. Production (Features)
INTERVIEWS WITH MY LAI VETERANS, Laser Film Productions (Short Subjects)

MUSIC
FOR ALL WE KNOW (Lovers and Other Strangers) Music, Fred Karlin; Lyrics, Robb Wilson, Arthur James (Best Song, original for the picture)
LOVE STORY, Francis Lai (Best Original Score)
LET IT BE, Music and Lyrics, The Beatles (Best Original Song Score)

FILM EDITING
PATTON, Hugh S. Fowler

SPECIAL VISUAL EFFECTS
TORA! TORA! TORA!, A. D. Flowers, L. B. Abbott

COSTUME DESIGN
CROMWELL, Nino Novarese

FOREIGN LANGUAGE FILM AWARD
INVESTIGATION OF A CITIZEN ABOVE SUSPICION (Italy)

JEAN HERSHOLT HUMANITARIAN AWARD
Frank Sinatra

IRVING G. THALBERG MEMORIAL AWARD
Ingmar Bergman

SPECIAL AWARD
Lillian Gish, Orson Welles

SCIENTIFIC OR TECHNICAL

CLASS II
LEONARD SOKOLOW and EDWARD H. REICHARD, CONSOLIDATED FILM INDUSTRIES

CLASS III
SYLVANIA ELECTRIC PRODUCTS INC.; B. J. LOSMANDY; EASTMAN KODAK CO. and PHOTO ELECTRONICS CORP.; ELECTRO SOUND INC.

1971

DIRECTOR
WILLIAM FRIEDKIN, The French Connection

WRITING
THE FRENCH CONNECTION, Ernest Tidyman (Best Screenplay — based on material from another medium)
THE HOSPITAL, Paddy Chayefsky (Best Story and Screenplay — based on material not previously published or produced)

CINEMATOGRAPHY
FIDDLER ON THE ROOF, Oswald Morris

1968-73 cont'd.

ART DIRECTION-SET DIRECTION
NICHOLAS AND ALEXANDRA,
John Box, Ernest Archer,
Jack Maxsted, Gil Parrondo;
Vernon Dixon

SOUND
FIDDLER ON THE ROOF,
Gordon K. McCallum,
David Hildyard

SHORT SUBJECTS
SENTINELS OF SILENCE,
Manuel Arango, Robert Amram
(Live Action)
THE CRUNCH BIRD,
Ted Petok (Cartoon)

DOCUMENTARY
THE HELLSTROM CHRONICLE,
David Wolper Productions
(Features)
SENTINELS OF SILENCE,
Manuel Arango, Robert Amran
(Short Subjects)

MUSIC
SUMMER OF '42, Michel Legrand
(Best Original Dramatic Score)
FIDDLER ON THE ROOF,
John Williams (Adaptation and
Original Song Score)
THEME FROM SHAFT, Music and
Lyrics, Isaac Hayes (Song)

FILM EDITING
THE FRENCH CONNECTION,
Jerry Greenberg

SPECIAL VISUAL EFFECTS
BEDKNOBS AND BROOMSTICKS,
Alan Maley, Eustace Lycett,
Danny Lee

COSTUME DESIGN
NICHOLAS AND ALEXANDRA,
Yvonne Blake

FOREIGN-LANGUAGE FILM
THE GARDEN OF THE
FINZI-CONTINIS (Italy)

SPECIAL AWARD
CHARLES CHAPLIN, for the
incalculable effect he has had
in making motion pictures the
art form of this century.

SCIENTIFIC OR TECHNICAL
CLASS II
John N. Williamson,
Optical Radiation Corp.

CLASS III
THOMAS JEFFERSON HUTCHINSON,
JAMES ROCHESTER and FENTON
HAMILTON; PHOTO RESEARCH
DIVISION OF KOLLMORGEN
CORP.; ROBERT D. AUGUSTE and
CINEMA PRODUCTS CORP.;
PRODUCERS SERVICE CORP.
CONSOLIDATED FILM
INDUSTRIES: CINEMA RESEARCH
CORP. and RESEARCH PRODUCTS,
INC.; CINEMA PRODUCTS CO.

1972

DIRECTOR
BOB FOSSE, Cabaret

WRITING
THE GODFATHER
Mario Puzo and Francis
Ford Coppola (Best Screenplay
based on material from another
medium)

THE CANDIDATE, Jeremy
Larner. (Best Story and
Screenplay   based on material
not previously published or
produced'

CINEMATOGRAPHY
CABARET
Geoffrey Unsworth

ART DIRECTION — SET DIRECTION
CABARET
Rolf Zehetbauer, Jurgen Kiebach,
Herbert Strabel

SOUND
CABARET
Robert Knudson,
David Hildyard

SHORT SUBJECTS
NORMAN ROCKWELL'S WORLD
AN AMERICAN DREAM
Concepts Unlimited
(Live Action)

A CHRISTMAS CAROL
Richard Williams Productions
(Cartoon)

DOCUMENTARY
MARJOE
Cinema X
(Features)

THIS TINY WORLD
Charles Huguenot van der Linden
Productions
(Short Subjects)

MUSIC
LIMELIGHT, Charles Chaplin,
Raymond Rasch, Larry Russell
(Best Original Dramatic Score)
CABARET, Ralph Burns (Adaptation
and Original Song Score'
THE MORNING AFTER, Music and
Lyrics, Al Kasha and Joel Hirschhorn
(Song)

FILM EDITING
CABARET
David Bretherton

SPECIAL VISUAL EFFECTS
THE POSEIDON ADVENTURE
L. B. Abbott, A. D. Flowers

COSTUME DESIGN
TRAVELS WITH MY AUNT
Anthony Powell

FOREIGN-LANGUAGE FILM
THE DISCREET CHARM OF THE
BOURGEOISIE (France)

JEAN HERSHOLT
HUMANITARIAN AWARD
ROSALIND RUSSELL

SPECIAL AWARD
CHARLES BOREN (for his
long service to the industry
as chief executive for the
Association of Motion Picture and
Television Producers
EDWARD G. ROBINSON, posthumous, for
his contributions to the art of motion
pictures.

SCIENTIFIC OR TECHNICAL
CLASS II
JOSEPH E. BLUTH
EDWARD H. REICHARD and
HOWARD T. LAZARE
CONSOLIDATED FILM INDUSTRIES
PANAVISION, INC.

CLASS III
PHOTO RESEARCH DIVISION OF
KOLLMORGEN CORP. and PRODUCERS
SERVICE; CARTER EQUIPMENT CO.
INC. and RAMTRONICS; DAVID
DEGENKOLB, HARRY LARSON,
MANFRED MICHELSON, FRED SCOBEY,
DELUXE GENERAL INC.; JIRO
MUKAI, RYUSHO HIROSE, CANON
INC. and WILTON R. HOLM, AMPTP
MOTION PICTURE AND TELEVISION
RESEARCH CENTER; PHILIP V.
PALMQUIST, LEONARD L. OLSON,
3M CO. and FRANK P. CLARK,
AMPTP-MPTRC; E H GEISSLER,
G. M. BERGGREN, WIL KIN INC.

1973

DIRECTOR
GEORGE ROY HILL, The Sting

WRITING
THE EXORCIST
William Peter Blatty (Best
Screenplay — based on
material from another medium)

THE STING
David S. Ward (Best Story and
Screenplay — original)

CINEMATOGRAPHY
CRIES AND WHISPERS
Sven Nykvist

ART DIRECTION — SET DIRECTION
THE STING
Henry Bumstead, James Payne

SOUND
THE EXORCIST
Robert Knudson
Chris Newman

SHORT SUBJECTS
THE BOLERO
Allan Miller Production
(Live Action)

FRANK FILM
Frank Mouris Production
(Cartoon)

DOCUMENTARY
GREAT AMERICAN COWBOY
Keith Merrill Associates —
Rodeo Film Productions
(Features)

PRINCETON: A SEARCH FOR ANSWERS
Kranin-Sage Productions
(Short Subjects)

MUSIC
THE WAY WE WERE, Rastar Productions,
Columbia, Marvin Hamlisch
(Best Original Dramatic Score)
THE STING, Marvin Hamlisch
(Adaptation and Original Song Score)
THE WAY WE WERE, Music by Marvin
Hamlisch, Lyrics by Alan and
Marilyn Bergman (Song)

FILM EDITING
THE STING
William Reynolds

COSTUME DESIGN
THE STING
Edith Head

FOREIGN-LANGUAGE FILM
DAY FOR NIGHT (France)

JEAN HERSHOLT
HUMANITARIAN AWARD
LEW R. WASSERMAN

IRVING G. THALBERG
MEMORIAL AWARD
LAWRENCE WEINGARTEN

HONORARY AWARDS
GROUCHO MARX (in recognition of his
"brilliant creativity and for the
unequalled achievements of the Marx
Brothers in the art of motion picture
comedy."
HENRI LANGLOIS (for his "untiring
devotion to the art of the film; for
his measure contributions towards
preserving its historical past; and
his unswerving faith in its
future.")

SCIENTIFIC OR TECHNICAL
CLASS II
JOACHIM GERB and ERICH KASTNER,
ARNOLD & RICHTER, CO.; MAGNA-
TECH ELECTRONIC CO. INC.;
WILLIAM W. VALLIANT, PSC
TECHNOLOGY INC.; HOWARD F.
OTT, EASTMAN KODAK CO.; GERRY
DIEBOLD, RICHMARK CAMERA
SERVICE INC.; HAROLD A. SCHEIB,
CLIFFORD H. ELLIS, ROGER W.
BANKS, RESEARCH PRODUCTS INC.

CLASS III
ROSCO LABORATORIES INC.; RICHARD
H. VETTER, TODD-AO CORP.

7

birth of the oscar

THE AWARDS given out by the Academy of Motion Picture Arts and Sciences are only one of many honors bestowed throughout the world yearly for outstanding excellence in various areas of the motion picture. But the little golden statuette known as "Oscar" is the supreme accolade, the acknowledged king of them all, the most courted.

Only in its first year of existence was it awarded for achievements in silent films. The birth of the figurine — 13½ inches tall, 6¾ pounds in weight, and made of a combination of metals coated in 10-karat gold—coincided almost exactly with the arrival of talking pictures.

The year was 1927, the movie industry's coffers, already fat, were still swelling most gratifyingly.

But the leaders of the industry were unhappy that its reputation was not all it should be. Censorship threatened, the church was often antagonistic.

Films needed a new, more dignified image and 36 of the field's leaders put their heads together over dinner one night to ponder what could be done.

Their answer was to organize the Academy of Motion Picture Arts and Sciences, a non-profit organization dedicated to the ideal of improving the artistic quality of the film medium.

Louis B. Mayer, one of filmdom's giants and a founding father of the industry, came up with the suggestion that a yearly awards program would be one way to focus attention on outstanding achievements in films.

The others liked the idea, art director Cedric Gibbons quickly sketched the figure that became the Awards symbol, and sculptor George Stanley molded it. Over the years, new categories for which the little statuette was given have been added many times, some categories have been scrapped. But the Oscar, a strong man holding a crusader's sword and standing on a reel of film, remained unchanged except for adding some weight. He's 8½ pounds now.

how "oscar" got his name

When it was awarded for the first time at the initial Academy Awards banquet, May 16, 1929, to honor achievements for the year 1928/ 1929, the figure was nameless. It remained "the statuette" officially until 1931, when Margaret Herrick, today the Academy's executive director, inadvertently christened it "Oscar."

One of the Academy's many lesser publicized activities is its library, a top source of information on movies and the people who make them. Miss Herrick was a new, young librarian there when she caught her first glimpse of the Awards symbol. "Why, it looks like my Uncle Oscar!" she exclaimed.

A newspaperman happened to be

there at the time and overheard Miss Herrick, the remark hit print, and "Oscar" it has been since then.

how the winners are chosen

The Motion Picture Academy of Arts and Sciences is divided into various craft branches—acting, directing, cinematography, etc.

In selecting nominees for the Best Picture Award, the entire Academy membership (now numbering 3,197) is polled and the five films receiving the greatest number of votes are designated as the nominees.

In the case of all other regular Oscar categories, only the members of each branch receive ballots for the initial selection of nominees in their particular category—actors vote for actors; writers, for writers, etc.

No more than five nominees per category are allowed (in some past years there were more), and the five top vote-getters in each division are designated the nominees.

Once the nominees are set, the next step is to vote for the Oscar winners themselves. In this voting for the finalists, the entire Academy membership participates. Each member receives a ballot which then goes, unopened, to Price Waterhouse & Company, the international public accounting firm which totals and verifies the votes. The name of the winner in each classification is placed in a sealed envelope not to be opened until that category comes up on Oscar night.

In the Academy's early days, this secrecy did not hold and winners knew in advance that they had been chosen. In 1940, however, the 1939 winners' names were released prematurely by the press, leaving little interest in the actual event, and the sealed-envelope system was adopted the following year.

honorary and special awards

This voting procedure does not hold so far as the various honorary awards and the Irving G. Thalberg Memorial Award and Jean Hersholt Humanitarian Award are concerned. Winners in these categories are selected by the Academy's Board of Governors, and each award is not necessarily given every year.

Awards for Scientific or Technical Achievement are made by the Board of Governors, at the recommendation of their appointed Scientific or Technical Committee, made up of outstanding representatives of the motion picture and technical fields.

The three classifications in this category cover basic achievements in engineering and other technical aspects, first used within the Awards' year, which have a definite influence upon the advancement of the industry.

These various special awards may be in the form of an Oscar, a plaque, or a certificate.

1927/28-37
introduction to the first decade

Oscar Night began modestly when a couple of hundred Hollywood people—stars, directors, writers, and others prominent in the film world—attended a banquet at the Hollywood Roosevelt Hotel, May 16, 1929, to see 15 of the brand-new golden statuettes given out.

In his first six years of existence, Oscar was not on a calendar basis. Instead, the Awards year ran from August 1 through July 31. The initial vote counting was slow, so the Oscars that went to *Wings,* Emil Jannings and Janet Gaynor were for the year 1927-28. The winners' names had been announced in February, after the votes were tallied, so no element of suspense existed.

For that year only, Awards were given for multiple, rather than single, achievements. Jannings' Oscar covered two films; Janet Gaynor got hers for three.

The Oscar citations were the talk of the industry, and by the second presentation night, April 3, 1930 (for 1928-29), interest ran so high that a Los Angeles radio station did an hour's on-the-spot broadcast. Oscar has been on the air ever since, as much a star in his own right as any he honors.

The Academy opened the sound era in awards by declaring a musical, *The Broadway Melody,* the picture of the year. Acting honors were captured by Warner Baxter (*In Old Arizona*) and Mary Pickford (*Coquette*). "America's Sweetheart" was the first of many winners to weep with joy.

During its third year, the Oscar

Mary Pickford and Warner Baxter get their 1928-29 Oscars from Academy President William C. DeMille.

Lionel Barrymore presents Wallace Beery with the 1931-32 Best Actor Oscar for his performance in ''The Champ,'' as Conrad Nagel looks on.

Stan Laurel, Producer Hal Roach and Oliver Hardy admire the award for their comedy "The Music Box", Best Short Subject of the year 1931/32.

In 1934, Shirley Temple, all of six, received the first honorary Juvenile Award, a miniature Oscar given child performers for outstanding work. Presenter was humorist Irvin S. Cobb.

presentations became so important nationally that Vice President Charles Curtis came from Washington to convey President Herbert Hoover's greetings and his own. The top honorees on this illustrious occasion were *All Quiet on the Western Front,* George Arliss (*Disraeli*) and Norma Shearer (*The Divorcee*).

The following year, Jackie Cooper, ten at the time, was a nominee in the male category, for *Skippy,* and was fast asleep on Marie Dressler's friendly shoulder when fellow-nominee Lionel Barrymore was announced as the winner, for *A Free Soul.* When Marie Dressler had to pick up an Oscar herself (*Min and Bill*) she gently eased young Jackie onto his mother's lap before rising. The picture that year was *Cimarron.*

The highlight of the 1931-1932 awards was the first tie in the history of the Academy Awards. (The second was in 1968 when Katherine Hepburn and Barbra Streisand shared Best Actress honors.) Frederic March (*Dr. Jekyll and Mr. Hyde*) and Wallace Beery (*The Champ*) shared the men's acting honors and each got an Oscar. *Grand Hotel* and Helen Hayes (*The Sin of Madelon Claudet*) were the other winners.

That, year, too, the Short Subjects category was added, and the late Walt Disney, the all-time Oscar champion, collected the first of his 24 regular trophies, for the year's best cartoon. Over the years he also won six honorary Oscars, for a grand total of 30.

Henry VIII's Charles Laughton had yet to set foot on American soil, and Katherine Hepburn (*Morning Glory*) was also among the absentees at the 1934 presentations when their names came up for Oscars for 1933. Movie of the year was *Cavalcade.*

It Happened One Night made a clean sweep when 1934's achievements were honored, the picture, its co-stars (Clark Gable, Claudette

11

Bette Davis, a winner the year before, extends best wishes to Paul Muni for his 1936 victory. Jack L. Warner is at right.

Colbert) and director Frank Capra all walking off with statuettes.

This was also the year the accounting firm of Price Waterhouse & Co. was retained to count ballots and assure secrecy of the results.

When the 1935 accolades were distributed, *Mutiny on the Bounty*, Victor McLaglen (*The Informer*) and Bette Davis (*Dangerous*) were the Oscared.

The 1937 show was highlighted by the addition of supporting players to the roster of awards, with Walter Brennan (*Come and Get It*) and Gale Sondergaard (*Anthony Adverse*) carrying off the first Best Supporting Actor and Best Supporting Actress trophies. Front-runners

in the top three classifications were *The Great Ziegfeld* and its feminine star, Luise Rainer, and Paul Muni (*The Story of Louis Pasteur*).

The newly established Irving G. Thalberg Memorial Award, to recognize consistent high quality of production, went to Darryl F. Zanuck.

In the closing year of Oscar's first decade, Luise Rainer (*The Good Earth*) became the first player to win two Oscars and the only female star to win twice in a row until 1968. Oscars went also to *The Life of Emile Zola* and Spencer Tracy (*Captains Courageous*).

Oscar was at his eleventh birthday, a big boy now with a high standard to maintain.

Clark Gable, right, makes way for Victor McLaglen who rushes toward the podium to accept the 1935 Best Actor award for "The Informer." At left is Louis B. Mayer, M-G-M studio chief.

1927/28
best picture

Wings
PARAMOUNT

CAST: Charles "Buddy" Rogers, Clara Bow, Richard Arlen, El Brendel, Richard Tucker, Gary Cooper, Jobyna Ralston
CREDITS: Producer, Lucien Hubbard; Director, William A. Wellman; Screenplay, Hope Loring, Louis D. Lighton, from a story by John Monk Saunders; Cinematographer, Harry Perry

THE FIRST FILM to carry the Academy's Best Picture tag was also the only silent to do so. By the time the next Awards date rolled around, movies were talking.

Wings was also one of the earliest films about men who make war in the air, and it still ranks as one of the best.

Wings' war is World War I, and its slight story hardly gets in the way of its real thrills—the air battles and other spectacular sky scenes. What plot there is, revolves around two buddies who go into the U.S. Air Force together. One is captured by the Germans and manages to steal a plane and make his escape, only to be shot down unknowingly by his buddy.

The pals from boyhood were Charles "Buddy" Rogers and Richard Arlen. Rogers, a big favorite of the day, was one of the stars who did not survive the advent of sound very long. Later, he became the husband of Mary Pickford. "It" girl Clara Bow, the Marilyn Monroe of her time, was the feminine lead. She, too, was a sound dropout. But a long, lean minor player who attracted considerable attention became one of the talkies' biggest stars. He was Gary Cooper.

Rudimentary color—blue and red—was used in some of the air battles, and a recording of various sound effects and music, but no speech, was available for theatres with the equipment to handle it.

Over and above everything were the grand sweep of air battles, the massive bombing raids and the spectacular crashes at a time when the air era was just opening up.

OTHER NOMINEES (All Silents):
THE LAST COMMAND, Paramount
THE RACKET, Paramount
SEVENTH HEAVEN, Fox
THE WAY OF ALL FLESH, Paramount

Charles "Buddy" Rogers, Clara Bow, and Richard Arlen

1927/28
best actor

Emil Jannings
THE LAST COMMAND, THE WAY OF THE ALL FLESH

THE FIRST Best Actor awardee, Emil Jannings, was also the first to be absent on presentation night.

German-actor Jannings, a massive bear of a man, had collected his Oscar in advance and was on his way back to the fatherland with it when the Oscars were given out officially for the first time.

Janning's Oscar was a joint tribute to his first two American-made pictures—*The Way of All Flesh* and *The Last Command.*

In the first, he was a respected bank clerk and happy family man who gets entangled in an extra-marital relationship and winds up as a homeless bum. In the second, he was an arrogant ex-Czarist general reduced to leading a movie army as a $7.50-a-day extra in a film directed by a man he had once

Emil Jannings in "The Last Command"

whipped brutally in his days of power.

Jannings himself had come to Hollywood with one of the most prestigeous reputations in Europe. In pre-Nazi days, Germany's film industry was of the best, and Jannings, a former stage player trained by the legendary Max Reinhardt, was its top male star. His *Variety* and *The Last Laugh* were as popular in the U.S. as in Germany, and they led to Paramount bringing him to Hollywood.

Three years later, when sound revolutionized the industry, Jannings saw the handwriting large and clear on the wall.

He was born in Brooklyn, but taken to Germany as an infant when his parents returned there and his English was limited, his accent gutteral. Neither were bars in silent films, but he knew both would be effective barriers to success in English-language talkies.

Besides, Propaganda Minister Joseph Goebbels was pleading with him to come home and help in the Nazification of the German film industry. Jannings grabbed the offer, and despite having had a Jewish mother, he was to make some of Nazi Germany's most vicious propaganda films, including the notorious *Ohm Krugger.*

His first assignment on his return to the homeland was notable for a much pleasanter reason. It was *The Blue Angel,* which introduced a promising screen newcomer, a sultry-voiced blonde named Marlene Dietrich.

Jannings' American films were few: the two pictures for which he received the Oscar; plus *The Patriot* and *Sins of the Fathers.*

OTHER NOMINEES:
RICHARD BARTHELMESS, The Noose
RICHARD BARTHELMESS, The Patent Leather Kid
CHARLES CHAPLIN, The Circus

1927/28
best actress

Janet Gaynor
SEVENTH HEAVEN, STREET ANGEL, SUNRISE

Charles Farrell and Janet Gaynor in "Seventh Heaven"

IN ITS INITIAL YEAR, the Academy gave its Awards on the basis of an actor's yearly output, instead of for a single performance. So when Janet Gaynor—22 years old, tiny and wide-eyed—became the first recipient of the Best Actress designation, it was for three films—*Seventh Heaven, Street Angel, Sunrise.* All were silents.

Seventh Heaven ranks as one of the all-time great movie romances, and box-office queues were long wherever it played. In it, Janet Gaynor was Diane, a Montmartre waif who takes sanctuary from a shrewish older sister in a sewerman's seventh-floor walkup. The sewer cleaner with the soul of a poet was Charles Farrell. They became one of the movies most popular romantic teams, and were to make 11 more films.

Sunrise is considered a silent screen classic, a somber story of a trusting young wife whose husband plots to do away with her.

Street Angel, which again paired Gaynor with Farrell, was pure soap opera, set in Italy. Arrested for prostitution when she makes a desperate try for money to help her gravely ill mother, she escapes from prison, becomes a circus performer and has a touching romance with a young artist. It was her last silent film.

Janet Gaynor was one of the lucky handful of silent players able to survive sound, and she remained a top star for another decade. In 1937, she was again nominated for an Oscar, this time for *A Star Is Born,* which still rates as one of the best films Hollywood ever made about Hollywood. In it, she was an actress on the way up, crossing paths with Fredric March, a once-great star on whose career the sun is setting.

The two Gaynor films that followed—*Three Loves Has Nancy* and *The Young in Heart*—were both box-office disappointments. Gaynor, married to the famed motion-picture couturier Gilbert Adrian, decided it was time to take up the pleasures of domesticity.

She made a one-film comeback, nineteen years later, in *Bernardine,* in 1957, and two years later, on TV's General Electric Theatre, made her last acting appearance.

Some other popular Gaynor films: *Sunny Side Up, Happy Days* (both with Farrell), *Daddy Long Legs, State Fair, The Farmer Takes a Wife.*

OTHER NOMINEES:
LOUISE DRESSER, A Ship Comes In
GLORIA SWANSON, Sadie Thompson

1928/29
best picture

The Broadway Melody
M-G-M

CAST: Bessie Love, Anita Page, Charles King, Jed Prouty, Kenneth Thomson, Edward Dillon
CREDITS: Director, Harry Beaumont; Screenplay, Sarah Y. Mason, from a story by Edmund Goulding; Art Director, Cedric Gibbons

BY TODAY'S STANDARDS, *The Broadway Melody*, the first musical to receive an Oscar, lacked much. But it was a milestone in its day.

Sound was new, and every studio rushed onto the musical band wagon. M-G-M threw all its vast resources into the biggest musical of them all—*The Broadway Melody*.

The story line was simple, just a peg on which to hand the lilting Arthur Freed-John Nacio Brown songs such as *You Were Meant for Me* and *Broadway Melody*. It concerned two stage-struck sisters from the hinterlands who come to Broadway and both fall for the same charming song-and-dance man.

Like sound, color was also in its infancy. The Technicolor camera could pick up only red, blue and green then, and its use was limited. But to a public used to black and white only, this crude color was an eye-filling novelty, as used in the big production number, *The Wedding of the Painted Doll*.

The movie was a personal triumph for silent screen star Bessie Love, as one of the sisters. Anita Page was the other, and the object of their mutual adoration was popular singer-dancer Charles King.

The Broadway Melody, which cost less than a half-million dollars to make, brought the public flocking to New York's Capital Theatre, where it was first shown. The theatre upped the tab to $2.00, a record-breaker in those Depression days, and the eager fans cheerfully dug into their pockets to pay it.

Bessie Love and Anita Page vie for Charles King's affections.

OTHER NOMINEES:
ALIBI, UA
HOLLYWOOD REVUE, M-G-M
IN OLD ARIZONA, Fox
THE PATRIOT, Paramount (Silent)

1928/29
best actor
Warner Baxter
IN OLD ARIZONA

Edmund Lowe and Warner Baxter

WARNER BAXTER got his first crack at playing The Cisco Kid by accident. The year was 1929, and Raoul Walsh was scheduled to both direct *In Old Arizona* (based on O. Henry's *Caballero's Way*) and play its dashing Mexican outlaw-hero as well.

Unfortunately for Walsh, he met with a bad accident just prior to the picture's start, and Baxter was called in to play The Kid.

In Old Arizona was not only to bring him an Oscar, but it revitalized his career, which was temporarily in the doldrums.

Dark, dashing and handsome, with a pencil moustache, Baxter was again the guitar-playing Mexican in *The Arizona Kid* in 1930, and *The Cisco Kid* in 1931. Some eight years later, after several Westerns along similar lines, he made *Return of the Cisco Kid*.

Baxter was born in Ohio, raised in California and after a brief excursion into the selling field after high school, he turned to acting as a way to make a living. He broke in via a Dallas stock company, moved onto Broadway around 1910, and was back in California six years later.

Well established as a silent star, he carried his popularity over into sound.

Daddy Long Legs, Paddy, The Next Best Thing, The King of Burlesque, and *42nd Street* were just some of the bigtime favorites that sent his salary zooming to the point where he was one of the highest paid players of the latter half of the 1930s.

No longer so young or quite as dashing, he made *The Crime Doctor* in 1943, a B picture that did bonanza business and became the first of a long series in which he played Dr. Robert Ordway.

Plagued by arthritis, Baxter retired in 1950. He died a year later, a bachelor despite the women who had swooned over him.

Some other popular Baxter films: *Robin Hood of El Dorado, Wife, Doctor and Nurse, Slave Ship, Kidnaped, Wife, Husband and Friend, Adam Had Four Sons.*

OTHER NOMINEES:
GEORGE BANCROFT, Thunderbolt
CHESTER MORRIS, Alibi
PAUL MUNI, The Valiant
LEWIS STONE, The Patriot

17

1928/29
best actress
Mary Pickford
COQUETTE

Johnny Mack Brown and Mary Pickford

A LEGEND in her own time, the curly-headed, wide-eyed ingenue known as "America's Sweetheart" was, unquestionably, the most popular movie star ever.

By the time she gave her Oscar-winning portrayal of a Southern small-town flirt in *Coquette,* her first talkie, she was a household name for some 20 years. Even today, after a 35-year retirement, her name brings instant recognition and her fabulous Beverly Hills estate, Pickfair, is still a top tourist attraction.

Born Gladys Smith in Toronto, Canada, in 1893, she was an actress from the age of five and made her movie debut in the days when its players were not even identified by name. And long before she emerged as "Mary Pickford," movie-goers knew her as "The Biograph Girl" and eagerly watched for her pictures, often as many as ten in a season.

Such favorites as *Tess of the Storm Country, Rebecca of Sunnybrook Farm, Daddy Long Legs* and countless others made her a very rich woman at a very young age. In 1919, she held a contract that paid her over a million dollars for three pictures—an unheard of sum in those days.

A shrewd businesswoman as well as an actress, Mary Pickford became her own boss in 1920, at the age of 27. She, Douglas Fairbanks (her husband at the time), Charlie Chaplin and D. W. Griffith formed United Artists, which is still in business, though under different management.

With *Coquette,* a more sophisticated Mary Pickford emerged. Her hair short and shingled in the fashion of the day, *Coquette's* heroine let herself in for a variety of compromising and uncompromising situations an earlier Pickford had always side-stepped. Mary's fans loved the "new" Pickford as much as the old, and she followed *Coquette* with *The Taming of the Shrew,* with Fairbanks as the tamer. After two more talkies—*Kiki* and *Secrets* (with Leslie Howard)—she retired.

In the early 1950's, she toyed with the idea of making a comeback, but was advised against it. Today, long married to Buddy Rogers, her leading man in 1927 in *My Best Girl,* she keeps a sharp eye on her many business ventures and philanthropies.

Some Pickford "silent" successes: *Romance of the Redwoods, The Little American* (both for Cecil B. DeMille), *The Little Princess, Dorothy Vernon of Hadden Hall, Little Annie Rooney.*

OTHER NOMINEES:
RUTH CHATTERTON, Madame X
BETTY COMPSON, The Barker
JEANNE EAGELS, The Letter
BESSIE LOVE, The Broadway Melody

1929/30
best picture

All Quiet On The Western Front
UNIVERSAL

CAST: Lew Ayres, Louis Wolheim, John Wray, Slim Summerville, Raymond Griffith, Russell Gleason, Ben Alexander, William Bakewell, Beryl Mercer, Edmund Breese
CREDITS: Producer, Carl Laemmle, Jr.; Director, Lewis Milestone; Screenplay, Del Andrews, Maxwell Anderson, George Abbott, from the novel by Erich Maria Remarque; Cinematographer, Arthur Edeson

MADE FROM Erich Maria Remarque's great anti-war novel, *All Quiet on the Western Front* remains, to today, the most uncompromising anti-war film ever made. Germany banned it until the 1960s.

Never once did director Lewis Milestone let the slightest hint of glorification of war creep into his grim World War I film, one of the first talkies made. Its chief focus is on one German schoolboy. His burning enthusiasm and desire to serve the Fatherland evaporates into war-weary disillusion as he sloughs through the filth and gore of war, lives with starvation, and murders an enemy combatant in a shell-hole. In a frenzy of fear, he then must spend a remorse-wracked night with the corpse.

Finally, there is the heart-breaking incident of his death — just a boy, eagerly reaching out for a butterfly, a bright bit of loveliness amid the horrors of war, at the moment a shot rings out. War, that insatiable devourer of youth, has snuffed out another life.

Lew Ayres played the schoolboy with a poignancy that was almost unbearable. He was sensitive, he had dreams, but was robbed of his chance to live.

It gave an enormous boost to the career of the young actor who was later to become a conscientious objector in World War II, then serve with distinction as a non-combatant hospital corpsman. Louis Wolheim and Slim Summerville also owed much to their chance to be in it.

OTHER NOMINEES:
THE BIG HOUSE, M-G-M
DISRAELI, Warner Bros.
THE DIVORCEE, M-G-M
THE LOVE PARADE, Paramount

Louis Wolheim dresses down Lew Ayres. Slim Summerville is at right.

A weary young soldier (Lew Ayres) enjoys a brief respite from war.

1929/30
best actor

George Arliss
DISRAELI

Florence Arliss played her husband's screen wife in "Disraeli."

WHEN GEORGE ARLISS won his Oscar as *Disraeli,* it was his third time around as England's great Prime Minister, the confidant of Queen Victoria, and the most famous Jew of his time.

Arliss had made his initial hit as the occupant of No. 10 Downing Street in 1911 in the theatre. Between the stage *Disraeli* and sound-screen one had come his silent movie version in 1921.

The actor who scored so resoundingly in one of the earliest biographical sound films, and later in *The House of Rothschild* and *Cardinal Richelieu,* was tall and gaunt, with a prominent, high-bridged nose; he wore a monocle, and he was no longer young.

Hardly the movie-star type, one would have said, except that Arliss had other things going for him. His personality was commanding, his voice one of the most beautiful of his time, his talent outstanding.

He was born in England in 1868, and was a stage star on both sides of the Atlantic when he made his first silent movie, *The Devil,* in 1921. He did so warily, as many legitimate players of stature looked down on films as almost the equivalent of slumming.

They fascinated Arliss and he was soon one of the screen's most prestigeous stars. Sound, naturally, represented no problems to this stage veteran. It simply gave him the chance to use his magnificent voice, too. He brought two more of his stage hits to the screen: *Hamilton,* and *The Green Goddess,* which he made both as a silent film and a talkie.

The Man Who Played God, made in 1932, served as the big break for a spirited young actress who held her own against his formidable presence and for whom he had both affection and respect. Her name was Bette Davis.

Arliss often served as his own screen writer and was a playwright and director as well. In the 12 years between his retirement in 1936 and his death in 1948, he published two volumes of autobiography: *Up the Years from Bloomsbury,* about his stage career, and *My Ten Years in the Studios,* covering his Hollywood experiences.

Some Arliss sound films: *Old English, The Millionaire, A Successful Calamity, Voltaire, The Iron Duke, Dr. Syn.*

OTHER NOMINEES:
GEORGE ARLISS, The Green Goddess
WALLACE BEERY, The Big House
MAURICE CHEVALIER, The Love Parade
MAURICE CHEVALIER, The Big Pond
RONALD COLMAN, Bulldog Drummond
RONALD COLMAN, Condemned
LAWRENCE TIBBETT, The Rogue Song

1929/30
best actress

Norma Shearer
THE DIVORCEE

REGAL IN MANNER and strikingly beautiful of face, Norma Shearer ranks as one of the all-time great ladies of the screen, a silent star who remained a top favorite after the sound revolution, and the undisputed queen of the M-G-M lot in her day.

She was as adept at comedy as tragedy and has six nominations and one Oscar to prove it. (The Academy still invites her to the yearly Oscar presentations, but, like Garbo, she always says no.)

She didn't think too much of the picture that gave her an Oscar, a melodramatic tear-jerker, *The Divorcee,* based on Ursula Parrott's sensational novel, *Ex-Wife.*

Her other nominations were for *Their Own Desire* (actually a second nomination simultaneously with *The Divorcee), A Free Soul* (1931), *The Barretts of Wimpole Street* (1934), *Romeo and Juliet* (1936), *Marie Antoinette* (1938). Her own favorite among them is said to have been *The Barretts,* with Fredric March as Robert Barrett Browning to her Elizabeth.

An interesting footnote to the Shearer Juliet is that Leslie Howard was her Romeo, while John Barrymore, America's greatest stage Romeo, had the subordinate role of Mercutio. It is interesting that he never won a nomination.

Shearer had first pick of all M-G-M scripts, not because she was the wife of Irving Thalberg, M-G-M "boy wonder" vice president, but because her world-wide box-office standing rated it. She refused both Scarlett O'Hara and Mrs. Miniver as roles for herself.

She also had her pick of male co-stars, from Clark Gable, with whom she made several films, including *Strange Interlude* and *Idiot's Delight,* to matinee idol Tyrone Power.

Widowed in 1936, when Irving Thalberg died at a too-young age, she was still a star to conjecture with when she retired, at 38, in 1942, after a wartime public had found her last two films too frothy for its taste. They were Noel Coward's *We Were Dancing,* and *Her Cardboard Lover.*

OTHER NOMINEES:
NANCY CARROLL, The Devil's Holiday
RUTH CHATTERTON, Sarah and Son
GRETA GARBO, Anna Christie
GRETA GARBO, Romance
NORMA SHEARER, Their Own Desire
GLORIA SWANSON, The Trespasser

1930/31
best picture

Cimarron
RKO-RADIO

CAST: Richard Dix, Irene Dunne, Estelle Taylor, William Collier, Jr., Nance O'Neill, Edna May Oliver, Roscoe Ates, George E. Stone
CREDITS: Director, Wesley Ruggles; Screenplay, Howard Estabrook, from the novel by Edna Ferber; Cinematographer, Eddie Cronjager

THAT PROLIFIC DIGGER into Americana, the late Edna Ferber, wrote the novel on which *Cimarron* was based. The picture made from her sprawling, exciting best seller on Oklahoma, from its settlement by homesteaders to the time it becomes a State, is the only Western that ever won an Academy Award.

The story takes the Cravats through some 40 years of marriage. They are among the hordes of eager would-be settlers drawn to Oklahoma by the government's announcement that the territory is being opened up to homesteaders. Theirs is one of the thousands of wagons careening over the virgin land to establish a claim to some of it. They get their land and endure the vicissitudes of pioneer life only to lose it in the end. But he winds up as a newspaper editor and a man of consequence in the state, helped along by the courage and resourcefulness of his wife.

Richard Dix, a great star in his day, was Yancy Cravat, the restless man-of-action. Irene Dunne was his staunch wife, and nominations went to both.

Irene Dunne was a comparative newcomer when she was chosen to play Sabra Cravat. She went on to become one of the screen's brightest lights.

The scene of masses of people racing crazily over millions of acres of rough terrain — in wagons, on horseback, and by shank's mare — each out for a bit of land to call his own, was a standout.

OTHER NOMINEES:
EAST LYNNE, Fox
THE FRONT PAGE, UA
SKIPPY, Paramount
TRADER HORN, M-G-M

As Yancy Cravat, Richard Dix holds a jury spellbound.

1930/31
best actor
Lionel Barrymore
A FREE SOUL

BROTHER JOHN, "the great profile," was flashier, and both John and sister Ethel were greater stage stars, but Lionel was the Barrymore best known on the screen.

A Free Soul was made at about the mid-way point in his 40-year movie career, and with it, he became the first Barrymore to win an acting Oscar.

The picture itself was not that good. But Barrymore was superb as the somewhat dissolute lawyer who keeps the noose from the neck of a gambler (Clark Gable) only to have Gable become involved with his daughter (Norma Shearer) and have to defend her fiancé (Leslie Howard) when he kills Gable.

Barrymore had won an earlier Oscar nomination, but not in the acting category. From time to time, he directed, and in 1929 he received an Oscar bid for his direction of *Madame X*.

In 1932, the three Barrymores made their only joint film appearance. The picture was *Rasputin and the Empress*.

In 1938, Barrymore played Dr. Gillespie for the first time, in *Young Dr. Kildare,* with Lew Ayres as Kildare.

The picture grew into one of the movies' most popular series. In the 14 more pictures that followed, Barrymore was always Gillespie, though the Kildares changed from time to time.

He was also the first Judge Hardy (*A Family Affair),* but Lewis Stone was to play the character from then on.

When an accident put him on crutches for sometime, then ultimately confined him to a wheelchair, Barrymore kept right on making movies. So long as he could "wiggle," he said, he intended to do so. His final starring film was in 1952, as Andrew Jackson in *Lone Star.*

A year later, he and Ethel Barrymore "guest-starred" in *Main Street to Broadway.* The following year, he was dead, at the age of 76.

Some other Barrymore successes: *Grand Hotel, Dinner at Eight, Treasure Island, David Copperfield, Ah, Wilderness, You Can't Take It With You, It's a Wonderful Life, Down to the Sea in Ships.*

OTHER NOMINEES:
JACKIE COOPER, Skippy
RICHARD DIX, Cimarron
FREDRIC MARCH, The Royal Family of Broadway
ADOLPHE MENJOU, The Front Page

23

1930/31
best actress
Marie Dressler
MIN AND BILL

MARIE DRESSLER is the supreme proof that an actress need not be beautiful or young to become a star —so long as she has talent enough.

Though ungainly in appearance, she was one of the best loved screen stars of all time. She herself chose to title her autobiography, *The Life of an Ugly Duckling.*

She was also the actress who, in 1932 and 1933, was the nation's number one box-office performer. Her Oscar-winning *Min and Bill* and *Tugboat Annie,* both in tandem with Wallace Beery, were pure gold at the till.

Marie Dressler was 62 when she played Min, the outwardly tough operator of a waterfront hotel, who liked her nip or two and had a heart of gold.

Behind her was a career of ups and downs. She started in a road company in 1886; became a Broadway favorite in Ziegfeld's *Higgledy-Piggledy, Tillie's Nightmare,* and other Great White Way hits when the 20th Century was young.

In 1914, when Mack Sennett decided to make *Tillie's Nightmare* into his first feature-length movie, it also served as Dressler's screen debut. Two more films in the same vein followed, but with the end of World War I, her career went into a decline.

She was 58 and pretty much on her uppers when Frances Marion, a noted screen writer and her friend, talked M-G-M into teaming her up with long, lanky Polly Moran in *The Callahans and the Murphys.* With it, her career zoomed again, though she was seen sometimes in supporting roles now, as in Rudy Vallee's *The Vagabond Lover,* and Norma Shearer's *Let Us Be Gay.*

In 1930 *Anna Christie* was not only the Great Garbo's first talkie, but Dressler's, too. Two years later, she was to be honored with an Oscar, an accolade that had always escaped Garbo.

She was again Oscar-nominated in 1932, for *Emma,* but time was running out for her. She made just three more films—*Tugboat Annie, Dinner at Eight, Christopher Bean* —before death claimed her in 1934.

Other Dressler "talkies": *The Girl Said No, Chasing Rainbows, Reducing and Politics.*

OTHER NOMINEES:
MARLENE DIETRICH, Morocco
IRENE DUNNE, Cimarron
ANN HARDING, Holiday
NORMA SHEARER, A Free Soul

1931/32
best picture
Grand Hotel
M-G-M

CAST: Greta Garbo, John Barrymore, Joan Crawford, Lionel Barrymore, Wallace Beery, Jean Hersholt, Lewis Stone

CREDITS: Director, Edmund Goulding; from the novel and play by Vicki Baum; Art Director, Cedric Gibbons; Cinematographer, William Daniels

IN GRAND HOTEL, Garbo first spoke those famous words that have become part of the Garbo mystique —"I want to be alone."

M-G-M dug deep into its impressive line-up of stars for the slick, glossy picture, based on Vicki Baum's best seller of the day. It was the first big, all-star talkie and it proved so popular that the "Grand Hotel" formula has been a movie staple ever since.

The formula is to bring a group of unrelated people from diverse stations in life together in some common setting (Berlin's glamorous Grand Hotel; an airport, as in *The VIP*'s, etc.) and interweave their lives dramatically for a brief span of time, allowing equal importance to each of the featured characters.

In *Grand Hotel,* Greta Garbo was an aging and bored-with-life ballerina pursued by an impoverished baron-reduced-to-jewel thief (John Barrymore) in the mistaken belief she is very rich.

As the hotel's public stenographer, Joan Crawford gave the first real indication that she could develop into an actress worth watching, instead of just a vivid personality. Lionel Barrymore was the touching, doomed bookkeeper; Wallace Beery, with a clipped Prussian haircut and a moustache, an industrialist not above using shady methods to gain his ends.

Overall, the critics approved the picture, the public loved it, and the Academy designated it the year's Best Picture. But not a single one of its illustrious battery of stars received an individual nomination.

Greta Garbo portrayed the aging ballerina; John Barrymore, the man after her jewels.

OTHER NOMINEES:
ARROWSMITH, UA
BAD GIRL, Fox
THE CHAMP, M-G-M
FIVE STAR FINAL, First National
ONE HOUR WITH YOU, Paramount
SHANGHAI EXPRESS, Paramount
SMILING LIEUTENANT, Paramount

1931/32
best actor

Wallace Beery
THE CHAMP

HE LOOKED like a roughneck, yet beneath that unprepossessing exterior was an actor of sensitivity and considerable range.

His *The Champ* was Beery at his best, and his best was Oscar quality. There was just one vote difference between Fredric March's *Dr. Jekyll and Mr. Hyde* and Beery's boozy, broken-down ex-prizefighter deluding himself with comeback dreams, so the Academy called it a draw. Both were given Best Actor Oscars.

Young Jackie Cooper was excellent in *The Champ,* too, as Beery's blindly worshiping kid, and they

were paired together again in *Treasure Island* and *O'Shaughnessy's Boy.*

Beery had been Oscar-nominated once before, in 1930, in the pull-no-punches prison story, *The Big House.*

Born in Kansas City, Missouri, in 1889, Beery left school to become an elephant boy in a circus, then quit the sawdust for a Broadway chorus line. At 18, he was a featured player.

In 1913, Chicago's Essaney Films signed him, and despite his claim that he always played himself, he was destined to become one of the biggest stars in pictures.

He co-starred with Marie Dressler (*Min and Bill, Tugboat Annie*) and comics Raymond Hatton and Marjorie Main. But he also played opposite a battery of glamour girls of the silent and talking films: Pola Negri, Norma Talmadge, Jean Harlow (*The Secret Six,* in 1931; *Dinner at Eight,* in 1933).

At one time, he was married to one of the all-time movie glamour queens, Gloria Swanson.

Though he consistently belittled his own acting abilities, the public disagreed with him for over 20 years where it counts the most—at the box office. He made his last important picture, a big musical, *A Date with Judy,* in 1947, just two years before he died. In it he was Carmen Miranda's romantic interest and Jane Powell's father. His last film, *Big Jack,* was released posthumously.

Some other Beery hits: *The Bowery, Viva Villa, Message to Garcia, Stablemates, Twenty Mule Team, Salute to the Marines.*

1931/32
best actor
Fredric March
DR. JEKYLL AND MR. HYDE

FREDRIC MARCH, one of the screen's top matinee idols in the 1930s and 1940s never let his talent be overshadowed by his extraordinary good looks.

Born in Racine, Wisconsin, in 1897 (real name, Frederick Bickel), March became a model after picking up his sheepskin at the University of Wisconsin, and made his stage debut in 1920. In 1929, when the movies were raiding the theatre for actors who could speak lines as well as turn a handsome profile, he made his first film, *The Dummy*.

A year later, he received his first Academy nomination, for his take-off of John Barrymore (to whom he bore a striking resemblance) in *The Royal Family of Broadway*. Two years later, he earned the Oscar for *Dr. Jekyll and Mr. Hyde*, in a tie win with Wallace Beery.

As Robert Louis Stevenson's doctor with the split personality, March not only did a magnificent job, but as Mr. Hyde he wore one of the most horrendous makeups ever to hit the screen.

In 1937, he was again nominated by the Academy *(A Star Is Born)*, and with *The Best Years of Our Lives*, in 1946, he became one of three actors to date to win two Best Actor Oscars (the others: Spencer Tracy, Gary Cooper).

In the years between his two Oscars, March turned out an average of two movies a year. Most were of superior quality, such as *Death Takes a Holiday, The Barretts of Wimpole Street, Mary of Scotland*. For March is an actor of impeccable taste as well as talent and chooses his pictures carefully.

He appeared with almost every top-ranking feminine luminary of the time, from Clara Bow to Garbo.

March and his wife of many years, actress Florence Eldridge, are both "theatre-mad," and even at the height of his screen popularity, he returned to Broadway from time to time, cheerfully taking the necessary salary cut for the pleasure of appearing live on the stage. Most of his stage plays included his wife. Their *Skin of Our Teeth* was the hit of New York in 1942.

Some pre-1946 March film successes: *Design for Living, The Dark Angel, Anthony Adverse, Nothing Sacred, I Married a Witch, Tomorrow the World*.

OTHER NOMINEE:
ALFRED LUNT, The Guardsman

27

1931/32
best actress

Helen Hayes
THE SIN OF MADELON CLAUDET

The Sin of Madelon Claudet was such an unabashed tear-jerker that just making its heroine bearable seemed an almost impossible task. And Helen Hayes, new to the movies but a stage favorite for some 15 years, proved that if the thespian is good enough, no part is impossible.

The story was based on a Broadway play of the 1920's, *The Lullaby,* and even playwright Charles MacArthur, Helen Hayes's husband, couldn't do much with a story that pulled all the emotional stops.

Madelon Claudet's sin was to bear a child outside of wedlock. She atoned for it through a lifetime of devotion to that child, and by making any sacrifice necessary. To send him through medical school, she willingly took the downward path, as she aged, from B-girl, to prostitute, to charwoman.

What Helen Hayes did with that hoary old yarn was a screen miracle, and the Academy recognized her performance as such.

Her next film won no Oscars, but today, some 30-odd years later, it still rates as a masterpiece. It was Ernest Hemingway's *A Farewell to Arms,* with Gary Cooper opposite her.

In 1935, after a couple of bad films, she became discouraged and finally returned to her real love, the New York stage, to score one of her greatest triumphs, in *Victoria Regina.*

Thirty-nine years later, Helen Hayes — born in 1900 in Washington, D.C.

— was again reaping kudos on Broadway in the *Harvey* revival, after which she went to Hollywood, to make *Airport.* Her first movie in 14 years won her a second Oscar.

Other Hayes' pictures : *Arrowsmith, The White Sister, Another Language, Night Flight, Main Street to Broadway, My Son John, Anastasia.*

OTHER NOMINEES:
MARIE DRESSLER, Emma
LYNN FONTANNE, The Guardsman

28

1932/33
best picture

Cavalcade
FOX

CAST: Diana Wynyard, Clive Brook, Ursula Jeans, Herbert Mundin, Una O'Connor, Beryl Mercer, Merle Tottenham, Margaret Lindsay, Frank Lawton, Irene Brown, Bonita Granville

CREDITS: Producer, Winfield Sheehan; Director, Frank Lloyd; Screenplay, Reginald Berkeley, from a play by Noel Coward; Cinematographer, Ernest Palmer

BASED ON THE PLAY by that awesome theatrical talent, Noel Coward, *Cavalcade* was so much a love song to Britain that it seems almost odd that an American film company should have made it. But when Fox did, it saw to it that the cast and most of the production people were tight-little-Islanders, and the story was handled with impeccable taste and dignity.

Cavalcade begins and ends with a New Year's Eve celebration. The first takes place in 1899, the second, 33 years later. In the decades between, Britain's course of history was eventful. There was the Boer War; Queen Victoria had died; the "unsinkable" *Titanic* had sunk with an appalling loss of life, and World War I had siphoned off the flower of England's youth. The story is told in terms of the effect of each event on one particular upper-class British family, the Marryots.

Clive Brooks, a popular star of the day, was the Robert Marryot who winds up with a "Sir" in front of his name. A lesser-known, but lovely British import, Diana Wynyard, was his wife and the only member of the cast to be Oscar-nominated. Young Frank Lawton played their son who died a war hero.

The picture had the grand sweep of history in the making, yet it never lost sight of the individuals whose lives were so shaped and altered by the events of the day.

An American public took all these British goings-on so much to its heart that when *Cavalcade* premiered in New York, the audience stood up and cheered.

The Marryots of "Cavalcade"—Diana Wynyard (second from left) and Clive Brook (center)

OTHER NOMINEES:
A FAREWELL TO ARMS,
   Paramount
FORTY-SECOND STREET,
   Warner Bros.
I AM A FUGITIVE FROM A
   CHAIN GANG, Warner Bros.
LADY FOR A DAY,
   Columbia
LITTLE WOMEN,
   RKO Radio
THE PRIVATE LIFE OF
   'HENRY VIII, UA
SHE DONE HIM WRONG,
   Paramount
SMILIN' THRU,
   M-G-M
STATE FAIR, Fox

1932/33
best actor
Charles Laughton
THE PRIVATE LIFE OF HENRY VIII

His WIVES numbered six, his table manners were unspeakable, he tore England out of the grip of the Catholic church—he was Henry VIII of the House of Tudor.

He was also Charles Laughton, an actor with both the talent and the physique to bring the high-living, autocratic monarch roaringly alive. His portrayal is still talked about, some 35 years after it was first revealed on the screen.

He took home an Oscar for it, and he was to be nominated twice more—as the loathsome Captain Bligh in *Mutiny on the Bounty* in 1935, and for *Witness for the Prosecution* in 1957.

He was born in Scarborough, England in 1899 and served in the British army in World War I. After he was mustered out, acting became his whole life.

He studied at the Royal Academy of Dramatic Arts, played on the English stage, and made his Broadway bow in 1931 in *Payment Deferred*. The picture adapted from the play served as his introduction to the American screen—he made one British picture before—and with it he was to begin a screen career that covered close to 30 years and made him internationally known.

In 1929 he married Elsa Lanchester, another dedicated thespian. She made a great hit in *Henry VIII*, as the wife he divorced, Anne of Cleves, and they appeared together in many films, including *The Beachcomber* and *Witness for the Prosecution* (she got a "supporting" category nomination for the latter).

Whether on the stage, making movies, giving a dramatic reading (with Cedric Hardwicke, Agnes Moorehead and Charles Boyer) of the rarely played *Don Juan in Hell* scene of G. B. Shaw's *Man and Superman,* or touring the country reading selections from the Bible, Laughton was one thing above all else— a total man of the theatre, to the day he died, in 1962.

Some Laughton hit films: *The Barretts of Wimpole Street, Ruggles of Red Gap, Rembrandt, The Hunchback of Notre Dame, Tales of Manhattan, The Paradine Case, The Big Clock, Young Bess, Spartacus, Advise and Consent.*

OTHER NOMINEES:
LESLIE HOWARD, Berkeley Square
PAUL MUNI, I Am A Fugitive from a Chain Gang

1932/33
best actress
Katharine Hepburn
MORNING GLORY

THE 24-year-old actress who won the first of her three Oscars in the Awards' sixth year, as *Morning Glory*'s shining young thespian with king-sized career dreams, was a very different type for Hollywood.

Wand-thin, with a clipped, cultured voice and from a socialite background, she was not beautiful, but projected an exciting, yet well-bred, sexuality that was never allowed to get out of hand.

Hepburn had come to Hollywood from Broadway some two years before her Oscar win. She thought so little of her first film, *A Bill of Divorcement*, in which she was John Barrymore's daughter, that she was en route to Europe when it was previewed. Despite her low opinion of it, the picture and she were sensations.

Connecticut-born "Katie" Hepburn came naturally by the breezy, spirited career-girl image that was to become her trademark. Her mother was a pioneer of civic causes at a time when woman's place was in the home. Her doctor father was also an individualist.

A Bryn Mawr graduate, Katharine Hepburn inherited that independence of mind and spirit. When, less than ten years after her auspicious start, her studio, RKO, labeled her "box office poison," undaunted, she took off for Broadway.

Hollywood could not help but take notice of her rave reviews in *The Philadelphia Story*, which proved one of the great hits of the 1939 season. The next year, she was back in Hollywood, to transfer its bright, brittle Mainline socialite onto film. The picture proved as big a box-office draw as the play; co-star James Stewart got an Oscar for it, Hepburn another nomination.

Two years later, she and Spencer Tracy teamed up for *Woman of the Year,* which brought her another Oscar bid. It also marked the first of a series the pair was to make together between 1941 and 1957. The others were: *Keeper of the Flame, Without Love, Sea of Grass, State of the Union, Pat and Mike, The Desk Set.*

Hepburn won six other nominations up to 1962, when she went into a five-year period of retirement —for *Alice Adams,* in 1935, *The African Queen* (with Humphrey Bogart), in 1951, *Summertime,* in 1955, *The Rainmaker,* in 1956, *Suddenly Last Summer,* in 1959 and *Long Day's Journey into Night,* in 1962.

OTHER NOMINEES:
MAY ROBSON, Lady for a Day
DIANA WYNYARD, Cavalcade

1934
best picture
It Happened One Night
COLUMBIA

Hitchhikers Clark Gable and Claudette Colbert

CAST: Claudette Colbert, Clark Gable, Walter Connolly, Roscoe Karns, Jameson Thomas, Alan Hale, Ward Bond
CREDITS: Producer, Harry Cohn; Director, Frank Capra; Screenplay, Robert Riskin, from a story by Samuel Hopkins Adams; Cinematographer, Joseph Walker

IF YOU CATCH *It Happened One Night* on the late, late show, it is still fresh and funny. The picture was one of the biggest hits of its day, and deservedly so.

Broke, a reporter latches onto a spoiled rich girl running away from home, in the hopes of collecting the reward being offered for her return. Predictably, he falls in love with her instead.

That is the story's framework, and it hardly seems to add up to material for an Oscar-winner.

But the dialogue sparkled, the film had a good-natured, healthy sophistication, and its co-stars, Clark Gable and Claudette Colbert, proved an inspired combination.

It Happened was studded with memorable scenes. Claudette Colbert flirtatiously lifting her skirt to secure them an immediate lift, after Gable's vaunted thumb-jerking failed to stop a single car, was one of those moments.

The tumbling of "the Walls of Jericho" was another, and it remains one of the most talked-about of movie climaxes. "The Walls" was a blanket, decorously dividing in two—but not for long—a motel room where Colbert and Gable had once sought refuge in a storm.

The reporter was Gable's first try at a comedy role, and the picture was one of those breaks that boosts a young star to the top of the ladder where the exalted of filmdom perch.

Gable, Colbert, director Frank Capra and scenarist Robert Riskin all took home Oscars for their part in making *It Happened* happen.

OTHER NOMINEES:
THE BARRETTS OF WIMPOLE STREET, M-G-M
CLEOPATRA, Paramount
FLIRTATION WALK, First National
THE GAY DIVORCEE, RKO Radio
HERE COMES THE NAVY, Warner Bros.
THE HOUSE OF ROTHSCHILD, 20th Century-UA
IMITATION OF LIFE, Universal
ONE NIGHT OF LOVE, Columbia
THE THIN MAN, M-G-M
VIVA VILLA, M-G-M
THE WHITE PARADE, Fox

1934
best actor
Clark Gable
IT HAPPENED ONE NIGHT

FOR SOME THREE DECADES, with time out to become a World War II hero, Clark Gable was the nation's number one movie idol. Since his passing in 1960, the interest in "The King" has remained lively.

Before his Oscar win, in *It Happened One Night,* Gable had already been the romantic hero to such leading feminine lights as Joan Crawford, and Greta Garbo.

After his thumb-jerking reporter, going along with Claudette Colbert for the hitchhike, and bringing down "the Walls of Jericho" in the climactic scene of the year's Best Picture, Gable could do no wrong.

The following year he won another nomination, for his Fletcher Christian who had the spunk to stand up to the terrible Captain Bligh in *Mutiny on the Bounty.*

By the time David O. Selznick

was ready to cast *Gone with the Wind,* the public clamour for Gable as Rhett Butler was so overwhelming that Selznick agreed to give up 50 per cent of the picture's profits to M-G-M, Gable's home studio, to get him. Predictably, Gable was the perfect Rhett Butler, and was nominated, but didn't win.

Every inch the dominating, overpowering male, Gable brought the girls to the box offices in droves, and men liked him, too. Yet his movie career almost ended after he made three silent films, in 1925. Some "far-sighted" executive decided the Gable ears were just too prominent for him to be star material. But after the Ohio-born young actor made a resounding splash on Broadway in *Machinal,* in 1928, Hollywood couldn't get him back fast enough.

The King's private life was as flashy as his screen presence. He was married five times, and the public grieved with him when his third wife, screen-star Carole Lombard, was killed in a plane crash while making a war-bond tour. Gable went into the Air Force shortly after her death.

His post-war films were never of the quality of the earlier ones, but his public remained loyal. *Mogambo,* a remake with Ava Gardner, of *Red Dust,* his 1932 film with Jean Harlow, and a routine Western, *The Tall Men,* were box-office standouts.

His last picture, *The Misfits* (with Marilyn Monroe) was finished only weeks before a heart attack killed him at 59. Three months after his death, his fourth wife, Kay Spreckles, gave birth to his only child, a son.

Some other Gable hits: *San Francisco, Saratoga, Too Hot to Handle, Idiot's Delight, Boom Town, Honky Tonk, The Hucksters, Command Decision.*

OTHER NOMINEES:
FRANK MORGAN, Affairs of Cellini
WILLIAM POWELL, The Thin Man

1934
best actress
Claudette Colbert
IT HAPPENED ONE NIGHT

THE FRENCH-BORN ACTRESS who made her mark playing bright, breezy American girls, usually in bright, breezy comedies, grabbed her Oscar, said, "I'm happy enough to cry but can't take the time to do it. A taxi is waiting outside with the engine running," and departed as breathlessly as she had arrived.

That famous moment in Academy history came about because Claudette Colbert had been so sure she wouldn't win an Oscar for *It Happened One Night* that she was boarding a train when her name was called and had to be whisked off it. Even more, by some application of Hollywood magic, Santa Fe officials had been induced to hold the New York-bound train for her return.

Not only did the so-sure-she-wouldn't-win Miss Colbert do so, but today she and Gable remain the only co-starring team to have won Oscars at the same time.

The girl from Paris with the creamy skin, dark hair and moon-sized eyes had come to the U.S. at the age of three and made her debut in silent films in 1927.

Unlike the many who fell by the wayside when the movies began to talk, Claudette Colbert made the grade easily, thanks to a low, throaty voice and a stage background.

In 1934, when she won her Oscar, two other films she made in the same year were also up for Best Picture—*Cleopatra* and *Imitation of Life*, the Fanny Hurst excursion into race relations and a daring film for its time. They, with *Private*

Worlds and *Since You Went Away*, which netted her two more nominations, represented some of her rare breaks out of comedy.

A series of bad pictures sent her box-office rating tumbling in the mid-fifties, so Colbert returned to Broadway, made several still remembered TV appearances, then came back to filmland in 1961 for one last film fling, in *Parrish*.

Now in her 60s, a widow and still beautiful, she lives in Southern California, but is no longer part of the Hollywood scene.

Among her biggest box-office hits were *Boom Town*, which re-united her with Gable. Also: *The Smiling Lieutenant* (with fellow Frenchman Maurice Chevalier); *Three-Cornered Moon, The Gilded Lily, Tovarish, I Met Him in Paris, The Egg and I.*

OTHER NOMINEES:
GRACE MOORE, One Night of Love
NORMA SHEARER, The Barretts of Wimpole Street

1935
best picture
Mutiny On The Bounty
M-G-M

CAST: Charles Laughton, Clark Gable, Franchot Tone, Herbert Mundin, Eddie Quillan, Dudley Digges, Movita, Donald Crisp
CREDITS: Producer-Director, Frank Lloyd, Screenplay, Jules Furthman, Talbot Jennings, Carey Wilson, from a novel by Charles Nordhoff, James Norman Hall; Cinematographer, Arthur Edeson

FOR THE SECOND YEAR in a row, Clark Gable was one of the stars in the picture of the year. This time, he headed a mutiny.

A sea adventure on the grand scale, *Mutiny on the Bounty* was made from the popular Charles Nordhoff-James Hall novel, which in turn had its genesis in one of the British Navy's most famous mutinies, the Bounty affair in 1787.

Charles Laughton was the Bounty's sadistic Captain Bligh, and he ran his Tahiti-bound ship with such iron-fisted discipline and disregard of his crew that they were driven to mutiny. The Bounty's mate, Fletcher Christian (Gable), was the spearhead and leader of the revolt.

Bligh and the few faithful to him were forced off the Bounty into a small boat and miraculously found their way across thousands of miles of water to the Dutch West Indies.

The mutineers sought sanctuary on Pitcairn Island, a mere dot in the vastness of the South Seas. The descendants of the sailors and the Polynesian girls they married still live on Pitcairn.

Laughton's Captain Bligh was a masterpiece of villainy. He, Gable, and Franchot Tone—who was a mutineer who returned to England and was court-martialed—all received Best Actor nominations. It was the only time three actors in a single film were all contestants for the same Oscar.

A multi-million-dollar remake of *Mutiny*, in 1962, with Marlon Brando as Fletcher Christian had little appeal, while the original couldn't rake in the money fast enough.

OTHER NOMINEES:
ALICE ADAMS, RKO Radio
BROADWAY MELODY OF 1936, M-G-M
CAPTAIN BLOOD, Warner Bros.
DAVID COPPERFIELD, M-G-M
THE INFORMER, RKO Radio
LES MISERABLES, 20th Century-UA
LIVES OF A BENGAL LANCER, Paramount
A MIDSUMMER NIGHT'S DREAM, Warner Bros.
NAUGHTY MARIETTA, M-G-M
RUGGLES OF RED GAP, Paramount
TOP HAT, RKO Radio

Clark Gable is restrained from attacking Charles Laughton.

1935
best actor

Victor McLaglen
THE INFORMER

An unrelievedly grim tale of the Irish rebellion, *The Informer* is still considered one of the best movies ever made.

In it, as a brawling, drunken Irishman betraying his best friend to the hated British for a mere 20 pounds, Victor McLaglen gave one of the screen's most unforgettable performances.

McLaglen, a giant of a man, with a splashed nose as a souvenir of his pugilistic days, was born in Turnbridge Wells, Kent, England, in 1886. He was a professional boxer and wrestler, a circus barker, had

prospected for gold and tried a dozen other adventurous occupations before becoming one of movieland's classic bad men.

Over a 40-year career, he played opposite almost every female star of the day, from Mae West to Shirley Temple.

His first big hit was in 1927, in the first, and silent, version of *What Price Glory?* in which he was Captain Flagg, Edmund Lowe, Sgt. Quirk.

The public loved the way they scrapped their way through the picture so much, they teamed up as the badgering, battling pair several times more down through the years, from *The Cock-eyed World* in 1929 to a "cameo" spot in *Around the World in 80 Days* in 1956.

Another long-lasting association was McLaglen's connection with John Ford, *The Informer's* director. In the 1950s, when the big fellow's waning popularity no longer rated star parts, Ford always could find a spot for an old friend.

One such spot, in *The Quiet Man,* brought him an Oscar nomination as Best Supporting Actor. It was the first time an actor who already held an Oscar in the top category was subsequently nominated in the supporting one.

McLaglen was still active in the movies, and the last of his more than 150 films, *The Abductors,* directed by his son, Andrew, was showing on the nation's screens at the time of his death, in 1959 at the age of 74.

Some popular McLaglen films: *Dishonored, The Last Patrol, Klondike Anne, Under Two Flags, Wee Willie Winkle, Tampico, She Wore a Yellow Ribbon.*

OTHER NOMINEES:
CLARK GABLE, Mutiny On The Bounty
CHARLES LAUGHTON, Mutiny On the Bounty
FRANCHOT TONE, Mutiny On The Bounty

1935
best actress

Bette Davis
DANGEROUS

THE ACKNOWLEDGED First Lady of Hollywood, Bette Davis has been in movies close to 40 years, made some 90 pictures and given dozens of great performances, none more so in the eyes of many than in *Of Human Bondage*.

When it failed to bring her an Academy nomination, she became a heavy write-in candidate (a practice now barred by rule).

The following year she did come up as the winner, for her willful, self-centered, ex-Broadway luminary in *Dangerous*.

Fame didn't come easily to the saucer-eyed blonde from Massachusetts, who is the only actress ever to become president of the Academy of Motion Picture Arts and Sciences.

Called to Hollywood in 1931, two years after her stage debut, she made two bad pictures and was about to make a less-than-glorious return to New York, when George Arliss gave her her big chance in his *The Man Who Played God*.

She has been flashing her own brand of scheming, female witchery across the screen ever since, and has played with practically every top male star, from Errol Flynn to Humphrey Bogart.

For some 18 years she was under contract to Warner Bros. It was a stormy relationship, but during it, she won her two Oscars and the majority of her other eight nominations.

Never a beauty by Hollywood standards, Davis had, instead, a vivid personality, a mammoth talent, and a total dedication to her profession. "Work, when you love it and fulfill yourself is life at its best," she wrote in her amazingly frank autobiography, *The Lonely Life*.

This concentration on work brought Davis the fulfillment of holding the record number of Oscar nominations for many years. In 1967, Katharine Hepburn tied the score at two Oscars and ten nominations apiece, then pulled into the lead in 1968, with her third win.

Davis's eight non-Oscar-winning nominations were: *Dark Victory, The Letter, The Little Foxes, Now, Voyager, Mr. Skeffington, All About Eve, The Star, Whatever Happened to Baby Jane?*

OTHER NOMINEES:
ELISABETH BERGNER, Escape Me Never
CLAUDETTE COLBERT, Private Worlds
KATHARINE HEPBURN, Alice Adams
MIRIAM HOPKINS, Becky Sharp
MERLE OBERON, The Dark Angel

1936
best picture
The Great Ziegfeld
M-G-M

CAST: William Powell, Myrna Loy, Luise Rainer, Frank Morgan, Virginia Bruce, Fannie Brice, Leon Errol, Gilda Gray, Ray Bolger, Nat Pendleton, Reginald Owen
CREDITS: Producer, Hunt Stromberg; Director, Robert Z. Leonard; Screenplay, William Anthony McGuire; Costumes, Adrian; Cinematographer, Oliver Marsh

IMPRESARIO FLORENZ ZIEGFELD lived in the grand manner, and the movie that told his story for an Oscar win was a big, plush musical, as flamboyant as the man himself.

In *The Great Ziegfeld,* the audience followed his career from its lowly show-business start to the days of his glory when his glamourous, girly extravaganzas, known as *The Ziegfeld Follies,* were an eagerly awaited yearly event in New York. It also related the details of his two marriages, to actresses of great beauty—the first stormy, the second quietly happy.

That polished lady's man, William Powell, made a dashing Ziegfeld. Myrna Loy (his co-star in *The Thin man* series) was *Billie Burke,* the wife with whom he found happiness after his marital problems with Anna Held (played by a lovely importation from Vienna, Luise Rainer). As Anna, the Austrian actress made somewhat of a sensation, and the Academy's voters saw to it that she got an Oscar.

Many of those who were carried to fame by *The Ziegfeld Follies* were on hand. Fannie Brice poured her aching heart into her great torch song, *My Man;* rubbery Ray Bolger danced in his inimitable style, and Harriet Hoctor headlined a flashy ballet. Among the many fine performers present was vocalist Stanley Morner, later to rise to film-star status as Dennis Morgan.

William Powell played Ziegfeld; Luise Rainer, his first wife, Anna Held.

1936
best actor

Paul Muni
THE STORY OF LOUIS PASTEUR

PAUL MUNI's roles ranged from the seven faces in *Seven Faces,* to the dirt-poor Chinese peasant of *The Good Earth.* But Muni was best known for his biographical roles.

He made a frightening Al Capone in *Scarface,* and played Mexico's great hero, Benito Juarez in *Juarez.* He won his Oscar for his portrayal of the great French chemist Louis Pasteur, the discoverer of pasteurization, in *The Story of Louis Pasteur.*

He received five Academy nominations in all, an impressive number at any time, and the more so in Muni's case as he made just 23 films in his entire movie career. The other nominations were for: *The Valiant, I am a Fugitive from a Chain Gang, The Life of Emile Zola, The Last Angry Man.*

He was born Muni Weisenfreund in Lemberg, Austria, in 1895, and grew up in New York City. After some years with its noted Yiddish Art Theatre, he scored a solid success on Broadway in *Counselor-at-Law.* That was in 1931, when Hollywood SOS's were out for actors with stage experience for the new sound films. Muni answered Warner's call and remained under contract to that studio until 1939, when, after a long line of box-office successes, he had two flops in a row. He asked for his release and obtained it.

He'd been away from Broadway for eight years, now on his return, in Maxwell Anderson's *Key Largo,* he had one of the biggest hits of the season.

From that point on, he shuttled between Hollywood and Broadway. His last play, *Inherit the Wind,* in 1955, was perhaps his greatest stage triumph, and his film swan song, *The Last Angry Man,* brought him his final Oscar nomination in 1959.

Muni died in 1967, in Santa Barbara, California, after being in ill health for several years.

Other Muni films include: *Bordertown, Black Fury, Hudson's Bay, The Commandos Strike at Dawn, A Song to Remember.*

OTHER NOMINEES:
GARY COOPER, Mr. Deeds Goes To Town
WALTER HUSTON, Dodsworth
WILLIAM POWELL, My Man Godfrey
SPENCER TRACY, San Francisco

1936
best actress
Luise Rainer
THE GREAT ZIEGFELD

DARK-EYED, dark-haired, with a pixyish face and a charming accent, Luise Rainer was the first two-time Oscar winner in the two major acting categories.

The petite Viennese beauty got her start in that great European training ground of the 1920s and '30s, Max Reinhardt's famed Berlin theatrical ensemble, and she had considerable experience on the stages of Germany and Austria before making a sensationally successful movie debut opposite the popular William Powell in *Escapade* in 1935.

A year later, with her second picture, *The Great Ziegfeld*, she won her first Oscar. As Anna Held, Florenz Ziegfeld's first wife who is said to have gone on loving him until the day she died, she had the shortest role ever to win a Best Actress citation. Today, the picture is remembered best for its "telephone" scene in which Anna Held congratulates Ziegfeld on his coming union with Billie Burke. Rainer gave to it an almost unbearable poignancy, and it is still considered one of the most perfect bits of acting ever to be caught by the camera—a veritable lesson in what a great artist can make of a single scene.

When the starry-eyed Viennese said, "I am very happy to get it," when she accepted her Oscar, no actress in pictures seemed destined for a brighter future.

Yet Luise Rainer, who at the time was married to playwright Clifford Odets, was to do one of the fastest, most complete, fadeouts in cinema history.

OTHER NOMINEES:
IRENE DUNNE, Theodora Goes Wild
GLADYS GEORGE, Valiant Is the Word for Carrie
CAROLE LOMBARD, My Man Godfrey
NORMA SHEARER, Romeo and Juliet

1936
best supporting actor

Walter Brennan
COME AND GET IT

WITH *Come and Get It*, based on Edna Ferber's big novel of lumbering and the men who engage in it, Walter Brennan became the first Oscar winner in the newly established Best Supporting Actor category. Now 74, and still active in pictures, Brennan and an unknown cowboy from Montana named Gary Cooper, used to make the rounds together at one time, looking for odd bit parts and stunt work.

OTHER NOMINEES:
MISCHA AUER, My Man Godfrey
STUART ERWIN, Pigskin Parade
BASIL RATHBONE, Romeo and Juliet
AKIM TAMIROFF, The General Diet At Dawn

best supporting actress

Gale Sondergaard
ANTHONY ADVERSE

GALE SONDERGAARD was not only the first actress to win an Oscar in the newly established Best Supporting Actress category, but she won it for her first movie role, Faith in *Anthony Adverse*. The exotic brunette, born in Wisconsin, earned a second nomination in the same category, in 1946, as Lady Thiang, the king's neglected first wife, in *Anna and the King of Siam*. She has been out of films since 1950.

OTHER NOMINEES:
BEULAH BONDI, The Gorgeous Hussy
ALICE BRADY, My Man Godfrey
BONITA GRANVILLE, These Three
MARIA OUSPENSKAYA, Dodsworth

41

1937
best picture

The Life Of Emile Zola
WARNER BROS.

CAST: Paul Muni, Gale Sondergaard, Joseph Schild-kraut, Gloria Holden, Donald Crisp, Henry O'Neill, Louis Calhern, Erin O'Brien-Moore, Robert Warrick
CREDITS: Producer, Jack L. Warner; Director, William Dieterle; Screenplay, Norman Reilly Raine, Heinz Herald, Geza Herczeg; Cinematographer, Tony Gaudio

Paul Muni as Emile Zola

Emile Zola was not only France's most honored author, but one of her greatest liberals and wholly dedicated to fighting injustice wherever it occurred.

The film, ostensibly a biography of Zola, gave his earlier life a somewhat once-over-lightly look, then concentrated on his impassioned defense of Captain Albert Dreyfus, a Jew unjustly convicted of treason and sentenced to live out his life on France's infamous penal colony, Devil's Island.

The movie walked lightly around the issue of religious prejudice; pictures hadn't moved that far ahead in social consciousness as yet. Instead, it leveled its sights on the incompetence and chicanery within the French government and its military hierarchy.

As Captain Dreyfus, Joseph Schildkraut was right up in the Muni league when it came to the acting, and he received a "supporting" Oscar on presentation night. Muni himself received only a nomination, but he had been the winner the year before. This year, the competition between him and Spencer Tracy was brisk, and it was Tracy who bagged the prize.

THE DREYFUS CASE, one of history's classic examples of anti-Semitism in high places, was the background for *The Life of Emile Zola*. It was made as a prestige film and was not expected to be a money-maker, but found surprisingly wide general acceptance for so serious a film.

OTHER NOMINEES:
THE AWFUL TRUTH, Columbia
CAPTAINS COURAGEOUS, M-G-M
DEAD END, UA
THE GOOD EARTH, M-G-M
IN OLD CHICAGO, 20th Century-Fox
LOST HORIZON, Columbia
ONE HUNDRED MEN AND A GIRL, Universal
STAGE DOOR, RKO Radio
A STAR IS BORN, Selznick-UA

1937
best actor

Spencer Tracy
CAPTAINS COURAGEOUS

In 1930, a young stage actor named Spencer Tracy, who started his career as a robot in the Theatre Guild's *R.U.R.,* reached Broadway stardom as Killer Mears in a tough prison melodrama, *The Last Mile.* His performance brought Hollywood on the run.

He spent the next five years grinding out a raft of thoroughly forgettable films for the old Fox company, most often cast as a criminal, before moving to M-G-M.

The studio with the lion symbol pulled him out of the rut and into ever-increasing public attention with

Spencer Tracy and Freddie Bartholomew

such top films as *Fury, San Francisco* (which earned him his first Oscar nomination) and *Libeled Lady.*

In 1937, he tightened his hold on stardom with an Oscar, as the fisherman hero of Kipling's *Captains Courageous.* Freddie Bartholomew, a top juvenile star at the time, played the spoiled English kid taken in hand by Tracy and received top billing over Tracy.

It was quite a moment for the Academy when Tracy lovingly examined his Oscar—to find the inscription read "Dick Tracy"!

Tracy was born in Milwaukee in 1900 and grew up in a prosperous home. His boyhood pal was Bill O'Brien, who later changed his first name to Pat, became a movie star, too, and remained a lifelong friend.

Tracy cut out of Marquette University to join the Navy with O'Brien in World War I, and returned to his studies, this time at Wisconsin's Ripon College, with the coming of peace. The rugged-looking lad with the wavy dark hair had his sights set on hanging out a doctor's shingle, until he tried out for a school play.

A short time later, he quit college to attend New York's American Academy of Dramatic Arts. In the big town, he and old buddy Pat O'Brien, also a drama student, shared a room, expenses, a meager diet and unlimited dreams.

The year after Tracy won his first, mis-inscribed Oscar, he was to get another, for *Boys Town.*

Some pre-1937 Tracy films: *20,000 Years in Sing Sing, Bottoms Up, Riffraff, They Gave Him a Gun.*

OTHER NOMINEES:
CHARLES BOYER, Conquest
FREDRIC MARCH, A Star Is Born
ROBERT MONTGOMERY, Night Must Fall
PAUL MUNI, The Life of Emile Zola

1937
best actress

Luise Rainer
THE GOOD EARTH

WITH HER THIRD FILM, Luise Rainer was to prove the depth and scope of her talent. Only a truly gifted actress could have made such a convincing leap from the beautiful Anna Held, the toast of two continents, to Olan, the peasant heroine of Pearl Buck's great saga of Chinese farm life, *The Good Earth*.

The undertaking itself was one of monumental proportions. In those days, Hollywood had not yet learned the conveniences of "runaway" production. Hollywood made pictures in Hollywood then. So millions of feet of film were photographed by M-G-M personnel sent to China for the purpose, including the famous scene of swarms of locusts literally eating up the landscape. Chinese farmhouses were uprooted and reassembled on farmland near Hollywood.

Against this background, as authentic as it could be without having the entire picture shot in China, Luise Rainer not only played Olan —she *was* Olan.

Every trace of the sophisticated, meticulously groomed beauty that had stood her in such good stead as Anna Held was submerged in the strong, silent Chinese peasant working so stoically beside her husband (Paul Muni), uncomplainingly raising a family and holding it together with steel-like strength against adversity almost too great to be borne.

It was a virtuoso performance, and the Academy acknowledged it with another Oscar.

Usually, one Oscar means a tremendous boost to a player's popularity and price. Rainer, with two, was an exception. She was to say later that winning them was the worst thing that could have happened to her.

But it was poor scripts, not the Oscars that did her in. She was rushed into five pictures in two years, in a misguided attempt to cash in on her Oscars. All were bad, except *The Great Waltz* in 1938, a delightful musical based on the life of Johann Strauss. Five years were to elapse before she made another film, *The Hostages*. An undistinguished war picture based on the Lidice atrocities, it rang down the curtain on Rainer's movie career. It had burned brightly through only three pictures, and after being divorced from playwright Clifford Odets, she returned home to Austria.

Rainer's other films were: *The Emperor's Candlesticks, The Toy Wife, Dramatic School, The Big City*.

OTHER NOMINEES:
IRENE DUNNE, The Awful Truth
GRETA GARBO, Camille
JANET GAYNOR, A Star Is Born
BARBARA STANWYCK, Stella Dallas

1937
best supporting actor

Joseph Schildkraut
THE LIFE OF EMILE ZOLA

IT WAS as Captain Dreyfus, the victim of French anti-Semitism in *The Life of Emile Zola,* that Vienna-born Joseph Schildkraut won movieland's top accolade. What the tall, dark and handsome son of the great European tragedian, Rudolph Schildkraut, considered the supreme highlight of his distinguished 50-year career was his Otto Frank in the stage and screen versions of *The Diary of Anne Frank.* He died in 1964, at 68.

OTHER NOMINEES:
RALPH BELLAMY, The Awful Truth
THOMAS MITCHELL, Hurricane
H. B. WARNER, Lost Horizon
ROLAND YOUNG, Topper

best supporting actress

Alice Brady
IN OLD CHICAGO

TO BROADWAY, Alice Brady was a dramatic star *(Mourning Becomes Electra,* etc.). On the screen, she was known chiefly as a light comedienne. With her Oscar-winning mother in this tale of the O'Leary family whose cow, legend has it, started the great Chicago conflagration, she returned to drama. The daughter of a famed theatrical producer, she was, at one time, the highest paid star in the silents. She died in 1939, at 46.

OTHER NOMINEES:
ANDREA LEEDS, Stage Door
ANNE SHIRLEY, Stella Dallas
CLAIRE TREVOR, Dead End
DAME MAY WHITTY, Night Must Fall

1927/28-37
oscar winners
in other categories

DIRECTOR
FRANK BORZAGE, Seventh Heaven
LEWIS MILESTONE, Two Arabian
Knights (Comedy Direction)

WRITING
SEVENTH HEAVEN, Benjamin Glazer
(Adaptation)
UNDERWORLD, Ben Hecht
(Original Story)
THE FAIR CO-ED, Joseph Farnham
(Title Writing)*
LAUGH, CLOWN, LAUGH, Joseph
Farnham (Title Writing)*
TELLING THE WORLD, Joseph
Farnham (Title Writing)*

CINEMATOGRAPHY
SUNRISE, Charles Rosher,
Karl Struss

INTERIOR DECORATION
THE DOVE, William Cameron Menzies
THE TEMPEST,
William Cameron Menzies

HONORARY AND OTHER AWARDS
WARNER BROS. for producing
"The Jazz Singer," the pioneer
outstanding talking picture, which
has revolutionized the industry.
(statuette)
CHARLES CHAPLIN for versatility and
genius in writing, acting, directing
and producing "The Circus."
(statuette)

ARTISTIC QUALITY OF PRODUCTION*
SUNRISE, Fox

ENGINEERING EFFECTS*
WINGS, Paramount, Roy Pomeroy

1928/29

DIRECTOR
FRANK LLOYD, The Divine Lady

WRITING
THE PATRIOT, Hans Kraly
(Achievement)

CINEMATOGRAPHY
WHITE SHADOWS IN THE
SOUTH SEAS, Clyde De Vinna

INTERIOR DECORATION
THE BRIDGE OF SAN LUIS REY,
Cedric Gibbons

1929/30

DIRECTOR
LEWIS MILESTONE,
All Quiet On The Western Front

WRITING
THE BIG HOUSE, Frances Marion
(Achievement)

CINEMATOGRAPHY
WITH BYRD AT THE SOUTH POLE,
Joseph T. Rucker,
Willard Van Der Veer

INTERIOR DECORATION
KING OF JAZZ, Herman Rosse

SOUND RECORDING
THE BIG HOUSE, Douglas Shearer

*Not given after this year.

1930/31

DIRECTOR
NORMAN TAUROG, Skippy

WRITING
CIMARRON, Howard Estabrook
(Adaptation)
THE DAWN PATROL, John Monk
Saunders (Original Story)

CINEMATOGRAPHY
TABU, Floyd Crosby

INTERIOR DECORATION
CIMARRON, Max Ree

SOUND RECORDING
PARAMOUNT STUDIO SOUND DEPT.

SCIENTIFIC OR TECHNICAL
Class I
ELECTRICAL RESEARCH PRODUCTS,
INC., RCA-PHOTOPHONE, INC.,
and RKO RADIO PICTURES, Inc.,
DuPONT FILM MANUFACTURING
CORP. and EASTMAN KODAK CO.
Class II
FOX FILM CORP.
Class III
ELECTRICAL RESEARCH
PRODUCTS, INC.
RKO RADIO PICTURES, INC.
RCA-PHOTOPHONE, INC.

1931/32

DIRECTOR
FRANK BORZAGE, Bad Girl

WRITING
BAD GIRL, Edwin Burke
(Adaptation)
THE CHAMP, Frances Marion
(Original Story)

CINEMATOGRAPHY
SHANGHAI EXPRESS, Lee Garmes

INTERIOR DECORATION
TRANSATLANTIC, Gordon Wiles

SOUND RECORDING
PARAMOUNT STUDIO SOUND DEPT.

SHORT SUBJECTS
FLOWERS AND TREES, Walt Disney,
UA (Cartoons)
THE MUSIC BOX, Hal Roach, M-G-M
(Comedy)
WRESTLING SWORDFISH,
Mack Sennett, Educational (Novelty)

HONORARY AND OTHER AWARDS
WALT DISNEY for the creation of
Mickey Mouse. (statuette)

SCIENTIFIC OR TECHNICAL
Class II
TECHNICOLOR MOTION PICTURE
CORP.
Class III
EASTMAN KODAK CO.

1932/33

DIRECTOR
FRANK LLOYD, Cavalcade

ASSISTANT DIRECTOR
CHARLES BARTON, Paramount
SCOTT BEAL, Universal
CHARLES DORIAN, M-G-M
FRED FOX, Universal
GORDON HOLLINGSHEAD,
Warner Bros.
DEWEY STARKEY, RKO Radio
WILLIAM TUMMEL, Fox

WRITING
LITTLE WOMEN, Victor Heerman,
Sarah Y. Mason (Adaptation)
ONE WAY PASSAGE, Robert Lord
(Original story)

CINEMATOGRAPHY
A FAREWELL TO ARMS,
Charles Bryant Lang, Jr.

INTERIOR DECORATION
CAVALCADE, William S. Darling

SOUND RECORDING
A FAREWELL TO ARMS,
Harold C. Lewis

SHORT SUBJECTS
THE THREE LITTLE PIGS,
Walt Disney, UA (Cartoons)
SO THIS IS HARRIS,
RKO Radio (Comedy)
KRAKATOA, Educational (Novelty)

SCIENTIFIC OR TECHNICAL
Class II
ELECTRICAL RESEARCH
PRODUCTS, INC.
RCA-VICTOR CO., INC.
Class III
FOX FILM CORP., FRED JACKMAN
and WARNER BROS. PICTURES,
INC., and SIDNEY SANDERS of
RKO Studios, Inc.

1934

DIRECTOR
FRANK CAPRA, It Happened
One Night

ASSISTANT DIRECTOR
JOHN WATERS, Viva Villa

WRITING
IT HAPPENED ONE NIGHT,
Robert Riskin (Adaptation)
MANHATTAN MELODRAMA,
Arthur Caesar (Original Story)

CINEMATOGRAPHY
CLEOPATRA, Victor Milner

INTERIOR DECORATION
THE MERRY WIDOW, Cedric Gibbons,
Frederic Hope

SOUND RECORDING
ONE NIGHT OF LOVE, Paul Neal

SHORT SUBJECTS
THE TORTOISE AND THE HARE,
Walt Disney (Cartoons)
LA CUCARACHA, RKO Radio (Comedy)
CITY OF WAX, Educational (Novelty)

MUSIC
THE CONTINENTAL (The Gay
Divorcee), Con Conrad,
Herb Magidson (Song)
ONE NIGHT OF LOVE,
Louis Silvers (Score)

FILM EDITING
ESKIMO, Conrad Nervig

HONORARY AND OTHER AWARDS
SHIRLEY TEMPLE, in grateful
recognition of her outstanding
contribution to screen entertainment during the year 1934.
(miniature statuette)

SCIENTIFIC OR TECHNICAL

Class II
ELECTRICAL RESEARCH
PRODUCTS, INC.

Class III
COLUMBIA PICTURES CORP.
BELL AND HOWELL CO.

1935

DIRECTOR
JOHN FORD, The Informer

ASSISTANT DIRECTOR
CLEM BEAUCHAMP, Lives of a
Bengal Lancer
PAUL WING, Lives of a Bengal Lancer

WRITING
THE SCOUNDREL, Ben Hecht,
Charles MacArthur (Original Story)
THE INFORMER, Dudley Nichols
(Screenplay)

CINEMATOGRAPHY
A MIDSUMMER NIGHT'S DREAM,
Hal Mohr

INTERIOR DECORATION
THE DARK ANGEL, Richard Day

SOUND RECORDING
NAUGHTY MARIETTA, Douglas Shearer

SHORT SUBJECTS
THREE ORPHAN KITTENS,
Walt Disney, UA (Cartoons)
HOW TO SLEEP, M-G-M (Comedy)
WINGS OVER MT. EVEREST,
Educational (Novelty)

MUSIC
LULLABY OF BROADWAY
(Gold Diggers of 1935), Harry
Warren, Al Dubin (Song)
THE INFORMER, Max Steiner (Score)

FILM EDITING
A MIDSUMMER NIGHT'S DREAM,
Ralph Dawson

DANCE DIRECTION
DAVE GOULD, "I've Got a Feeling
You're Fooling" number (Broadway
Melody of 1936), "Straw Hat"
number (Folies Bergere)

HONORARY AND OTHER AWARDS
DAVID WARK GRIFFITH, for his
distinguished creative achievements
as director and producer and his
invaluable initiative and lasting
contributions to the progress of
the motion picture arts. (statuette)

SCIENTIFIC OR TECHNICAL
Class II
AGFA ANSCO CORP.
EASTMAN KODAK CO.

Class III
M-G-M
WILLIAM A. MUELLER
MOLE-RICHARDSON CO.
DOUGLAS SHEARER and
M-G-M STUDIO SOUND DEPT.
ELECTRICAL RESEARCH
PRODUCTS, INC.
PARAMOUNT PRODUCTIONS, INC.
NATHAN LEVINSON

1936

DIRECTOR
FRANK CAPRA, Mr. Deeds Goes
To Town

ASSISTANT DIRECTOR
JACK SULLIVAN, The Charge of
the Light Brigade

WRITING
THE STORY OF LOUIS PASTEUR,
Pierre Collings, Sheridan Gibney
(Original Story and Screenplay)

CINEMATOGRAPHY
ANTHONY ADVERSE, Gaetano Gaudio

INTERIOR DECORATION
DODSWORTH, Richard Day

SOUND RECORDING
SAN FRANCISCO, Douglas Shearer

SHORT SUBJECTS
COUNTRY COUSIN, Walt Disney, UA
(Cartoons)
BORED OF EDUCATION, Hal Roach,
M-G-M (One-reel)
THE PUBLIC PAYS, M-G-M (Two-reel)
GIVE ME LIBERTY, Warner Bros.
(Color)

MUSIC
THE WAY YOU LOOK TONIGHT
(Swing Time) (Song)
Jerome Kern, Dorothy Fields
ANTHONY ADVERSE, Leo Forbstein
(Score)

FILM EDITING
ANTHONY ADVERSE, Ralph Dawson

DANCE DIRECTION
SEYMOUR FELIX, "A Pretty Girl
Is Like a Melody" number
(The Great Ziegfeld)

HONORARY AND OTHER AWARDS
MARCH OF TIME for its significance
to motion pictures and for having
revolutionized one of the most
important branches of the
industry—the newsreel. (statuette)
W. HOWARD GREENE and HAROLD
ROSSON for the color cinematography of the Selznick
International Production, "The
Garden of Allah." (plaques)

SCIENTIFIC OR TECHNICAL
Class I
DOUGLAS SHEARER and
M-G-M STUDIO SOUND DEPT.
Class II
E. C. WENTE and
BELL TELEPHONE LABORATORIES
RCA MANUFACTURING CO., INC.
Class III
RCA MANUFACTURING CO., INC.
ELECTRICAL RESEARCH
PRODUCTS, INC.
RCA MANUFACTURING CO., INC.
UNITED ARTISTS STUDIO CORP.

1937

DIRECTOR
LEO McCAREY, The Awful Truth

ASSISTANT DIRECTOR
ROBERT WEBB, In Old Chicago

WRITING
A STAR IS BORN, William A.
Wellman, Robert Carson
(Original Story)
THE LIFE OF EMILE ZOLA, Heinz
Herald, Geza Herczeg, Norman
Reilly Raine (Screenplay)

CINEMATOGRAPHY
THE GOOD EARTH, Karl Freund

INTERIOR DECORATION
LOST HORIZON, Stephen Goosson

SOUND RECORDING
THE HURRICANE, Thomas Moulton

SHORT SUBJECTS
THE OLD MILL, Walt Disney,
RKO Radio (Cartoons)
PRIVATE LIFE OF THE GANNETS,
Educational (One-reel)
TORTURE MONEY, M-G-M (Two-reel)
PENNY WISDOM, Pete Smith,
M-G-M (Color)

MUSIC
SWEET LEILANI (Waikiki Wedding)
Harry Owens (Song)
ONE HUNDRED MEN AND A GIRL,
Charles Previn (Score)

FILM EDITING
LOST HORIZON, Gene Havlick,
Gene Milford

DANCE DIRECTION
HERMES PAN "Fun House" number
(Damsel In Distress)

**IRVING G. THALBERG
MEMORIAL AWARD**
Darryl F. Zanuck

HONORARY AND OTHER AWARDS
MACK SENNETT, for his lasting
contribution to the comedy
technique of the screen, the basic
principles of which are as
important today as when they
were first put into practice, the
Academy presents a Special Award
to that master of fun, discoverer
of stars, sympathetic, kindly,
understanding comedy genius—
Mack Sennett. (statuette)
EDGAR BERGEN for his outstanding
comedy creation, Charlie
McCarthy. (wooden statuette)
THE MUSEUM OF MODERN ART
FILM LIBRARY for its significant
work in collecting films dating
from 1895 to the present and
for the first time making available
to the public the means of
studying the historical and
aesthetic development of the
motion picture as one of the
major arts. (scroll certificate)
W. HOWARD GREENE for the color
photography of "A Star Is Born."
(This Award was recommended by
a committee of leading cinematographers after viewing all the
color pictures made during the
year.) (plaque)

SCIENTIFIC OR TECHNICAL
Class I
AGFA ANSCO CORP.

Class II
WALT DISNEY PRODS., LTD.
EASTMAN KODAK CO.
FARCIOT EDOUART and
PARAMOUNT PICTURES, INC.
DOUGLAS SHEARER and M-G-M
STUDIO SOUND DEPT.

Class III
JOHN ARNOLD and M-G-M
STUDIO CAMERA DEPT.
JOHN LIVADARY, Director of Sound
Recording for Columbia Pictures
Corp.
THOMAS T. MOULTON and
UA STUDIO SOUND DEPT.
RCA MANUFACTURING CO., INC.
JOSEPH E. ROBBINS and
PARAMOUNT PICTURES, INC.
DOUGLAS SHEARER and M-G-M
STUDIO SOUND DEPT.

1938-47
introduction to the second decade

THE FIRST YEAR of Oscar's second decade was one of repeats, with Bette Davis *(Jezebel)*, Spencer Tracy *(Boys Town)*, and Walter Brennan *(Kentucky)* all recipients of a second statuette. *You Can't Take It with You* was the winning film.

For some time prior to 1940, the results were given in advance to the press, with the understanding they were not to be released before 11:00 p.m. Oscar Night.

But in 1940, one Los Angeles paper jumped the gun. With the names appearing in its 8:45 p.m. edition, many of the guests arrived knowing the winners were *Gone with the Wind*, two of its players—Vivien Leigh, Hattie McDaniel—its director, Victor Fleming, and Robert Donat *(Goodbye, Mr. Chips)*.

A record crowd arrived early on Oscar Night in 1941, to make certain of hearing a special radio message from President Franklin Delano Roosevelt.

The sealed-envelope system came

Spencer Tracy and Bette Davis congratulate each other on their 1938 awards.

into use that year, after the newspaper leak of the year before.

James Stewart collected his *The Philadelphia Story* Oscar a few days before going into uniform—the first of Hollywood's big stars to enlist as the war clouds blackened.

Rebecca was the film of the year and Ginger Rogers, known before for her spectacular dancing, was acclaimed as a dramatic actress for *Kitty Foyle*.

By the time the 1942 affair rolled around, we were at war, and James Stewart returned in uniform to present Gary Cooper with an Oscar for playing a World War I hero

Vivien Leigh won the Best Actress Award in 1939 for "Gone with the Wind." Producer David O. Selznick is at her left, and Claudette Colbert, who won in 1934, is at right.

Speaker Wendell Wilkie is surrounded by 1941's winning foursome—Gary Cooper, Joan Fontaine, Mary Astor and Donald Crisp. Astor and Crisp hold the Oscar plaques given to supporting players in the earlier years.

Sergeant York, in the picture of that name. Donald Crisp was also in uniform as he came up for his supporting Oscar for *How Green Was My Valley,* which was also the best film. But the big story that year was sister against sister. Joan Fontaine

and Olivia De Havilland were both nominees for Best Actress. When Fontaine came up the winner for *Suspicion,* it created a family crisis.

The recipients of Oscars in 1943 found the trophy much lighter in weight. With metals essential war materials, Oscar went plaster for the duration. After the war, all plaster statuettes were exchanged for metal ones.

Winners that year for 1942 were *Mrs. Miniver,* two of its female players—Greer Garson and Teresa Wright—and James Cagney with *Yankee Doodle Dandy.*

On March 2, 1944, the Oscar presentations moved to a theatre for the first time, and Oscars honoring accomplishments for 1943 were handed out at Grauman's Chinese Theatre in Hollywood. They went to *Casablanca,* Paul Lukas *(Watch on the Rhine)* and Jennifer Jones *(The Song of Bernadette).*

In 1945, the entire awards program was broadcast over network radio for the first time. *Going My*

James Cagney accepts his 1942 award for "Yankee Doodle Dandy."

49

second decade-cont'd.

Way, its two "priests" (Bing Crosby, Barry Fitzgerald), Ingrid Bergman (*Gaslight*) and Ethel Barrymore (*None but the Lonely Heart*) were the Oscared for 1944.

With her win in the supporting category, Ethel Barrymore and her brother Lionel became Oscar's only sister-brother team.

By the time the 1945 Oscars were handed out, the war was over, and evening gowns and tails, which had been put aside for the duration, made their festive appearance again in paying honor to the movie greats of the year. Ray Milland, director Billy Wilder and their picture, *The Lost Weekend,* received Oscars, as did Joan Crawford (*Mildred Pierce*) who was ill and not present.

The Best Years of Our Lives was the top movie of 1946, and it brought second Oscars to Fredric March and director William Wyler, with the Best Supporting Actor accolade going to another of its cast, Harold Russell, a war amputee. Olivia De Havilland carried off the top feminine trophy, for *To Each His Own.*

Ingrid Bergman and Bing Crosby backstage after they picked up their 1944 Oscars

In the final year of the Academy Awards' second decade, the little golden men were claimed by *Gentleman's Agreement,* Ronald Colman (*A Double Life*) and Loretta Young (*The Farmer's Daughter*). Edmund Gwenn, on being named Best Supporting Actor for his Santa Claus in *Miracle on 34 Street* accepted his Oscar, saying, "Now I know there is a Santa Claus."

This was the year that the Academy first took note of foreign language films, giving a special Oscar to Italy's *Shoe-Shine.* (In 1956, the Best Foreign Language Film became a regular Oscar category.)

In its first year, the Academy had awarded 15 Oscars; in its second year, the number had dropped to seven. With its 20th year, the score stood at 29 regular Oscars awarded and more than a score more given out in various honorary and scientific categories. Oscar's third decade would see more regular awards categories established and new special honors added.

Ronald Colman and Loretta Young are honored as 1947's top thespians.

1938
best picture

You Can't Take It With You

COLUMBIA

CAST: Jean Arthur, Lionel Barrymore, James Stewart, Edward Arnold, Mischa Auer, Spring Byington, Halliwell Hobbes, Ann Miller, Donald Meek, H. B. Warner, Eddie Anderson, Harry Davenport

CREDITS: Producer-Director, Frank Capra; Screenplay, Robert Riskin, from the play by George S. Kaufman, Moss Hart; Cinematographer, Joseph Walker

THE Moss Hart-George S. Kaufman Pulitzer Prize-winning play, *You Can't Take It with You*, was one of the brightest comedies on Broadway in the 1930s. Filmed with a top cast, its fey quality and wild situations came over with laughter-filled impact.

The way of life of the unconventional Vanderhofs is as far out from most people's as can be imagined. Grandpa, the patriarch of the family, refuses to pay taxes because he does not believe in the theory of taxation. Others in the odd lot include a woman who became a writer because someone left them a typewriter, a ballet dancer who can't dance, and a musician whose sideline is making his own money.

The comedy gets hilarious when the daughter of the house invites her beau's ultra-conventional parents to meet her kooky folks.

James Stewart and Jean Arthur were the young lovers; Lionel Barrymore, the head of the clan; and the cast included Spring Byington, Mischa Auer, Edward Arnold and others prominent at the time. Of them, only Spring Byington was nominated for Oscar consideration, but few pictures have been blessed with such a perfect mix of acting talents.

With *You Can't Take It with You*, director Frank Capra, Oscared in 1934 for *It Happened One Night*, and in 1936 for *Mr. Deeds Goes to Town*, won his third Academy trophy in five years.

OTHER NOMINEES:
THE ADVENTURES OF ROBIN HOOD, Warner Bros.
ALEXANDER'S RAGTIME BAND, 20th Century-Fox
BOYS TOWN, M-G-M
THE CITADEL, M-G-M
FOUR DAUGHTERS, Warner Bros.-First National
GRAND ILLUSION, R.A.C., World Pictures
JEZEBEL, Warner Bros.
PYGMALION, M-G-M
TEST PILOT, M-G-M

Spring Byington, Ann Miller, James Stewart, and Jean Arthur

1938
best actor
Spencer Tracy
BOYS TOWN

Spencer Tracy and Mickey Rooney

WHEN SPENCER TRACY played a priest in the motion picture *San Francisco,* it brought him a nomination. His second essay as a man of the cloth meant an Oscar. With it, he duplicated Luise Rainer's twice-in-a-row win. It took 30 years for Katharine Hepburn to match them.

Based on fact, *Boys Town* was the story of Father Edward J. Flanagan and the refuge for homeless boys which he founded in Nebraska some three decades ago, and which still carries on under a successor.

As Father Flanagan, Tracy caught the personality and warmth of the priest who staunchly maintained there are no bad boys, only boys who need a chance.

Mickey Rooney, who was also in the cast of *Captains Courageous,* Tracy's first Oscar film, was a standout in *Boys Town.* Three years later, Tracy and Rooney made a sequel, *Men of Boys Town,* not as good as the original, but not bad on its own.

Tracy was to earn six more nominations, three in the 1950s (*Father of the Bride, Bad Day at Black Rock, The Old Man and the Sea*). Three more came his way in the '60s (*Inherit the Wind, Judgment at Nuremberg, Guess Who's Coming to Dinner*). That made nine, more than any other actor has won and only one under the distaff side record-holders, Bette Davis and Katharine Hepburn.

In 1942, he and Hepburn teamed up in *Woman of the Year.* The combination proved so much to the fans liking that they were teamed together eight times more: *Keeper of the Flame, Without Love, Sea of Grass, State of the Union, Adam's Rib, Pat and Mike, Desk Set, Guess Who's Coming to Dinner.*

For the last-named, Tracy came out of a four-year retirement, dictated largely by ill health. During its making, he kept saying it would be his last film, but as it came close to completion, old trouper Tracy began to hedge. When pressed for a fuller declaration, he grinned and said, "I always announce my retirement—until the next picture comes along."

But there was to be no next picture for Tracy. Shortly after *Guess* was finished he died of a massive heart attack in June of 1967, and his last nomination came posthumously.

Some other post-1938 Tracy films: *Dr. Jekyll and Mr. Hyde, Tortilla Flat, The Seventh Cross, The Actress, Broken Lance, The Last Hurrah, It's a Mad, Mad, Mad, Mad World.*

CHARLES BOYER, Algiers
JAMES CAGNEY, Angels with Dirty Faces
ROBERT DONAT, The Citadel
LESLIE HOWARD, Pygmalion

1938
best actress

Bette Davis
JEZEBEL

ONE THING the forthright descendant of sturdy New England pioneer stock was sure of, was her acting ability. She also knew the kind of gutsy part she felt would best display it.

When the studio failed to come up with such parts, Ruth Elizabeth Davis, as she was christened, took off for England and waged a long, costly court battle with Warner Bros. Technically, she lost, but she gained her objective — parts with bite and vitality such as *Jezebel*.

Davis had been one of the many aspirants, famous and unknown, who lost out in their bid to play Scarlett O'Hara. As *Jezebel's* headstrong, viciously spoiled Southern belle bedeviling the likes of Henry Fonda and George Brent in pre-Civil War New Orleans, she not only had her first costume part, but one that in some ways out-flashed Scarlett O'Hara.

It accounted for her second Oscar, and she followed it up with a nomination in each of the four following years. She was the number one female star, at home and abroad, as much admired by the critics as the public that kept movie cash registers busy around the world when a Davis film was the program.

She bought out her contract in 1949 and picked up another Oscar bid in 20th Century-Fox's Oscar-winning, all-star film, *All About Eve*.

With *Eve*, the Davis luck ran out. A string of run-of-the-mill films followed. She returned to Broadway, to score a tremendous success in Tennessee Williams' *Night of the Iguana*, as the crude owner of the decaying hotel in the Mexican hinterlands (played by Ava Gardner in the movie).

Never one to mince words, when Hollywood showed little interest in her return, Davis startled the film capital by taking out an ad in the motion-picture trade journals announcing her availability.

Then *Whatever Happened to Baby Jane*, a little "horror" film she made with the equally durable Joan Crawford, proved an unexpected hit in 1962. It brought her her tenth Academy nod, and renewed her career. Some recent Davis films: *Dead Ringer, Where Love Has Gone, Hush...Hush, Sweet Charlotte, The Nanny, The Anniversary*.

OTHER NOMINEES:
FAY BAINTER, White Banners
WENDY HILLER, Pygmalion
NORMA SHEARER, Marie Antoinette
MARGARET SULLAVAN, Three Comrades

1938
best supporting actor

Walter Brennan
KENTUCKY

THE LUMBER BUSINESS gave gravel-voiced Walter Brennan his first Oscar, in 1936. In *Kentucky,* horse-racing was to account for his second. Massachusetts-born Brennan himself had had every intention of becoming an engineer. But after a tour of duty in World War I, he headed west with his brand-new bride (they've now been married 47 years), because he heard that was where the action was, and movies have provided him with lots of it.

OTHER NOMINEES:
JOHN GARFIELD, Four Daughters
GENE LOCKHART, Algiers
ROBERT MORLEY, Marie Antoinette
BASIL RATHBONE, If I Were King

best supporting actress

Fay Bainter
JEZEBEL

WHEN FAY BAINTER got a Best-Supporting-Actress Oscar for her *Jezebel* role, she was also up for a Best Actress Award for *White Banners.* The first thespian to be nominated in two categories in one year, she was about to retire, after two decades as one of Broadway's brightest stars, when lured home to her native city for *Jezebel* and a whole new career in films. She died in 1968 at the age of 74.

OTHER NOMINEES:
BEULAH BONDI, Of Human Hearts
BILLIE BURKE, Merrily We Live
SPRING BYINGTON, You Can't Take It With You
MILIZA KORJUS, The Great Waltz

1939
best picture
Gone With The Wind
SELZNICK - M-G-M

CAST: Clark Gable, Vivien Leigh, Leslie Howard, Olivia De Havilland, Thomas Mitchell, Barbara O'Neil, Hattie McDaniel, Laura Hope Crews, Ona Munson, Butterfly McQueen, Evelyn Keyes, Ann Rutherford, Caroll Nye, Rand Brooks
CREDITS: Producer, David O. Selznick; Director, Victor Fleming; Screenplay, Sidney Howard, from the novel by Margaret Mitchell; Costumes, Walter Plunkett; Cinematographers, Ernest Haller and Ray Rennahan. Technicolor.

AFTER ALMOST three decades, *Gone with the Wind* has yielded its position as No. 1 box-office grosser to *The Sound of Music*. But it must be remembered that the Civil War classic earned much of its money when the box-office charge was approximately six times less than now.

The Civil War epic was eagerly awaited, for the story of the closely knit, plantation-owning O'Hara and Wilkes families, and what the war did to their lives, was known to millions through the original Margaret Mitchell best seller.

Moreover, there was much controversy over the signing of an unknown British actress, Vivien Leigh, as Scarlett O'Hara, after a well-publicized search of many months. No such problems surrounded the choice of Clark Gable as Rhett Butler—the public had demanded him.

The end result was a blockbuster of a movie, and few who saw it will ever forget such moments as the hundreds of wounded lying unattended on the ground in front of the railroad station; Atlanta going up in flames, the explosive love scenes between Scarlett and Rhett, or the gentle strength of Olivia de Havilland as Melanie.

Made in the Depression, the picture was brought in at a cost of less than $4 million, a figure that couldn't begin to pay its cost if it were made today. It earned ten Oscars—a record until Ben-Hur topped it by one in 1959. Recently transferred to 70mm film and equipped with a new stereophonic sound track, *Gone with the Wind* has now been reissued for the sixth time.

OTHER NOMINEES:
DARK VICTORY, Warner Bros.
GOODBYE, MR. CHIPS, M-G-M
LOVE AFFAIR, RKO Radio
MR. SMITH GOES TO WASHINGTON, Columbia
NINOTCHKA, M-G-M
OF MICE AND MEN, UA
STAGECOACH, UA
THE WIZARD OF OZ, M-G-M
WUTHERING HEIGHTS, UA

Clark Gable and Vivien Leigh at the ball

1939
best actor
Robert Donat
GOODBYE, MR. CHIPS

MADE FROM James Hilton's touching portrait of a British schoolmaster, from his early teaching days and problems to his old age as a beloved school institution, *Goodbye, Mr. Chips* had two superlative performances.

Robert Donat's schoolmaster meant an Oscar for the frail actor, and a nomination went to the glowingly lovely, young British actress who played his wife. It was her screen debut, and she would have an Oscar of her own three years later. Her name was Greer Garson.

Donat was one of that dedicated band of topnotch British thespians who prefer to make less money in the theatre, and turn only occasionally to film. In Donat's case, his movies numbered less than a score, and with *Mr. Chips*, he became a screen immortal.

The asthma-plagued actor was born in 1905 and made his stage debut at 16. He never set foot in Hollywood, but he became an American favorite with his first starring role in the British-made *The Count of Monte Cristo*. He added to his growing list of U.S. fans in the popular Alfred Hitchcock classic, *39 Steps*.

He first came to the attention of the people who go to the movies as Thomas Culpepper in Charles Laughton's *Henry VIII*. A year before he won a niche in the heart of the public with his touching *Mr. Chips*, he had been Academy-nominated for *The Citadel*.

Over the years, the world-famous Old Vic Company engaged much of his professional attention, and movies were allotted a relatively minor part of his limited physical resources. His greatest Old Vic success came as Becket in T. S. Eliot's *Murder in the Cathedral.*

Many of his post-Oscar films were of the art-house variety and either were seen by limited audiences, or not seen in the States at all. But what turned out to be his last film, Ingrid Bergman's *The Inn of the Sixth Happiness,* was widely shown, but not until Donat was gone. He died shortly after completing his role as the Chinese Mandarin. The year was 1958, and he was only 53.

Donat's films include: *The Ghost Goes West, Knight without Armor, Vacation from Marriage, The Winslow Boy, Lease of Life.*

OTHER NOMINEES:
CLARK GABLE, Gone With the Wind
LAURENCE OLIVIER, Wuthering Heights
MICKEY ROONEY, Babes in Arms
JAMES STEWART, Mr. Smith Goes To Washington

1939
best actress
Vivien Leigh
GONE WITH THE WIND

WHEN, after two years of searching for a Scarlett O'Hara for *Gone with the Wind,* Vivien Leigh was chosen, there were many complaints from almost every part of the nation.

Vivien Leigh was not only a practically unknown who had beaten out such leading contenders as Norma Shearer, Bette Davis and Katharine Hepburn, to say nothing of the hundred of young hopefuls who were interviewed and sometimes tested, but she was—of all things!—British. How *could* she be Margaret Mitchell's willful Southern belle?

With the picture's first showing in Atlanta, all protests died. The vivacious brunette with the large,

flashing dark eyes was Scarlett with every flirtatious toss of her pretty head, with every angry tap of her foot. She was Scarlett in all her glory as the belle of the ball, and Scarlett in her unshakable determination that nothing, not even something as catastrophic as the Civil War, would defeat her.

Vivien Leigh was 24 when she played Scarlett, and when David O. Selznick met her, she was in Hollywood, not to make a film, but to be near her fiancé, Laurence Olivier, who was making *Wuthering Heights* there.

A small, slender woman who was to battle tuberculosis and other ills most of her life with Scarlett-like determination, Vivien Leigh was born in Darjeeling, India, of British parents, in 1913. She studied at London's Royal Academy of Dramatic Arts and made her stage debut in 1936.

Shortly after, she joined the proud Old Vic Company, where one of her early assignments was to play Ophelia to Olivier's Hamlet. They were married in 1940, after playing *Romeo and Juliet* on Broadway to lukewarm notices.

Before *Gone with the Wind,* she made several minor British films. Only one, *A Yank at Oxford* (with Robert Taylor as the Yank), was widely distributed in the States.

After her Scarlett O'Hara, the pick of movie roles was hers, but she made only eight more films in her lifetime. One of them, *A Streetcar Named Desire,* brought her a second Oscar in 1951.

Some of her pre-1939 British films: *Fire Over England, Storm in a Teacup, The Sidewalks of London.*

OTHER NOMINEES:
BETTE DAVIS, Dark Victory
IRENE DUNNE, Love Affair
GRETA GARBO, Ninotchka
GREER GARSON, Goodbye, Mr. Chips

1939
best supporting actor

Thomas Mitchell
STAGECOACH

HIS WHISKEY-SOAKED Doc Boone in the first, unforgettable, *Stagecoach* brought Thomas Mitchell his Oscar and as Gerald O'Hara, father of Scarlett, in *Gone with the Wind,* he was equally memorable. Born in New Jersey of Irish parentage, Mitchell was one of the few character actors to become a star in his own right. He died in 1962, at the age of 70.

OTHER NOMINEES:
BRIAN AHERNE, Juarez
HARRY CAREY, Mr. Smith Goes To Washington
BRIAN DONLEVY, Beau Geste
CLAUDE RAINS, Mr. Smith Goes To Washington

best supporting actress

Hattie McDaniel
GONE WITH THE WIND

THE FIRST of her race to be honored by the Academy, Hattie McDaniel burst into happy tears on receiving an Oscar for her sly, devoted Mammy in *Gone with the Wind.* A vaudeville singer before turning to films, she was the Beulah ordered by May West to "peel me a grape" in *I'm No Angel.* Born in Wichita, Kansas, the 13th child of a Baptist minister, she was 57 when she died in 1952.

OTHER NOMINEES:
OLIVIA DE HAVILLAND, Gone With the Wind
GERALDINE FITZGERALD, Wuthering Heights
EDNA MAY OLIVER, Drums Along the Mohawk
MARIA OUSPENSKAYA, Love Affair

1940
best picture

Rebecca
SELZNICK-UNITED ARTISTS

CAST: Laurence Olivier, Joan Fontaine, Judith Anderson, George Sanders, Gladys Cooper, Leo G. Carroll, Nigel Bruce, C. Aubrey Smith, Reginald Denny
CREDITS: Producer, David O. Selznick; Director, Alfred Hitchcock; Screenplay, Robert E. Sherwood, Joan Harrison, from the novel by Daphne du Maurier; Cinematographer, George Barnes

THE 1940 Oscar-winning film was the second in a row for David O. Selznick, and his first production since *Gone with the Wind*. It was also the first American film directed by that British master of suspense, Alfred Hitchcock, and the only mystery to be Oscared in the Academy's 40 years.

Rebecca was based on Daphne DuMaurier's suspense novel, whose setting is Manderley, a somber estate over which the shadow of Rebecca, its owner's dead wife, hangs like an ominous cloud. When he brings his shrinking young second wife there, its eerie atmosphere envelopes her, and a crazed housekeeper keeps reminding her of the overpowering presence who preceded her.

By the time Manderley is consumed by flames and its young mistress free of the evil hanging over her, the audience has taken a chilling, spine-tingling excursion into the world of mystery and suspense.

Laurence Olivier was Manderley's enigmatic master, Joan Fontaine played his wife, and the role of the mad housekeeper was portrayed by that magnificent actress, Judith Anderson. All were Academy nominees. None got the Oscar this time, though the accolade went to both Olivier and Fontaine at a later date. Mystery-master Hitchcock has never been a winner.

OTHER NOMINEES:
ALL THIS, AND HEAVEN TOO, Warner Bros.
FOREIGN CORRESPONDENT, UA
THE GRAPES OF WRATH, 20th Century-Fox
THE GREAT DICTATOR, UA
KITTY FOYLE, RKO Radio
THE LETTER, Warner Bros.
THE LONG VOYAGE HOME, UA
OUR TOWN, UA
THE PHILADELPHIA STORY, M-G-M

Newlyweds Laurence Olivier and Joan Fontaine come home to Manderley.

1940
best actor
James Stewart
THE PHILADELPHIA STORY

AFTER MAKING some 24 films in the five years he had been in Hollywood, James Stewart won his first Oscar bid in 1939, as *Mr. Smith Goes To Washington's* neophyte Senator who tackles power politics.

He had to wait another year for the Oscar, which came to him for *Philadelphia Story,* where he was the young reporter assigned to cover the wedding of a socialite (Katharine Hepburn) and is first repelled, then fascinated, by her.

Stewart's Oscar was on proud display at his father's hardware store in Indiana, Pennsylvania, until his father's death.

Always the "good guy" in his more than 30 years on the screen, "Jimmy" Stewart has parlayed a long, lean frame, an engaging grin, shy embarrassment and an impressive talent into a career that has kept him a box-office draw that few actors become.

After time out to pile up an outstanding record in the Air Force during the war, the popular star, who became interested in acting in his Princeton days, picked up another Academy nomination with his first post-war film, Frank Capra's *It's a Wonderful Life,* and was Oscar-nominated twice more *(Harvey,* 1950; *Anatomy of a Murder,* 1959). His performance in *Anatomy* also drew the New York Film Critics Best Actor designation, and was one of the biggest triumphs in his long career.

While not basically a Western star, he starred in some of the biggest of them: *The Man from Lara-mie, How the West Was Won, Cheyenne Autumn, Two Rode Together, The Cheyenne Social Club.*

Brigadier General James Stewart U.S.A.F. Reserve, is retired, but actor Jimmy Stewart, now in his 60s, made a triumphant return to Broadway in 1970 in the *Harvey* revival.

Some recent Stewart films: *Dear Brigitte, Shenandoah, The Rare Breed, The Flight of the Phoenix, Firecreek, Bandolero!, Fools' Parade.*

OTHER NOMINEES:
CHARLES CHAPLIN, The Great Dictator
HENRY FONDA, The Grapes of Wrath
RAYMOND MASSEY, Abe Lincoln in Illinois
LAURENCE OLIVIER, Rebecca

Katharine Hepburn and James Stewart

1940
best actress
Ginger Rogers
KITTY FOYLE

With Kitty Foyle, the career gamble taken by Ginger Rogers paid off. She had bowed out of her phenomenally successful dancing partnership with Fred Astaire because she wanted to be an actress, not primarily a dancer.

Years before, when she met Lynn Fontanne and Alfred Lunt on the train coming west she confided her ambition "to be a fine actress like you" to Fontanne. It was the famed actress herself who presented Ginger Rogers with her Oscar, with a smiling, "I told you you'd make good."

Ginger Rogers started out by winning Charleston contests in the 1920s. She was on Broadway in *Girl Crazy* when Hollywood beckoned, and her first film was *Manhattan Mary*.

With *Flying Down to Rio* in 1933, the girl with the breezy personality and twinkling feet became Fred Astaire's best dancing partner since his sister Adele bowed off the stage for a titled Briton. Before their partnership ended a half-dozen years later, with *The Story of Vernon and Irene Castle*, they made ten enormously successful musicals to help take people's minds off the Depression. They joined forces once more, ten years later, for *The Barkleys of Broadway*.

When Ginger Rogers hung up her dancing shoes, she proved herself an actress of more than average ability, as the heroine of Christopher Morley's popular *Kitty Foyle*, who starts out as an innocent fifteen-year-old and winds up as a businesswoman

knowing all the answers.

After her Oscared performance, she went on to further prove her competence in everything from comedy (*The Major and The Minor, Roxie Hart, Dream Boat*) to drama and melodrama (*I'll Be Seeing You, Black Widow*).

In 1957, she pulled out of the movies altogether for TV and the stage, where she made her biggest hit as Carol Channing's replacement in Broadway's *Hello, Dolly!*

In 1965, the five-times-married star, born Virginia McMath in Independence, Missouri 54 years before, returned to filmland for two pictures. One was a thriller, *The Confession;* the other, Electronovision's *Harlow*, in which she played "Mama Jean."

Some other Rogers' successes: *The Gay Divorcee, Top Hat, Roberta* (all with Astaire), *Having Wonderful Time, Vivacious Lady, Lady in the Dark, Monkey Business, Oh Men, Oh Women.*

OTHER NOMINEES:
BETTE DAVIS, The Letter
JOAN FONTAINE, Rebecca
KATHARINE HEPBURN, The Philadelphia Story
MARTHA SCOTT, Our Town

1940
best supporting actor

Walter Brennan
THE WESTERNER

WITH *The Westerner,* Walter Brennan became the Academy's first three-time Oscar winner and was the only one until Katharine Heburn's win in 1968. "Acting isn't just my job, it's my hobby," says the spry septuagenarian. "I've been at it for 46 years, and there's nothing I like better. Besides, it beats sitting around waiting for the undertaker." In 1967, he played a character much older than he—the 900-year-old gnome in *The Gnome-Mobile.*

OTHER NOMINEES:
ALBERT BASSERMAN, Foreign Correspondent
WILLIAM GARGAN, They Knew What They Wanted
JACK OAKIE, The Great Dictator
JAMES STEPHENSON, The Letter

best supporting actress

Jane Darwell
THE GRAPES OF WRATH

THE FILMIZATION of *The Grapes of Wrath,* John Steinbeck's great saga of migratory farm workers in the depression era, provided Jane Darwell with the outstanding role in her 60-year stage and screen career. Her strong, understanding Ma Joad also earned her a well-deserved Oscar. The Missouri-born actress, last seen as the Cockney birdwoman in *Mary Poppins,* was making another movie when she died in 1967, at the age of 87.

OTHER NOMINEES:
JUDITH ANDERSON, Rebecca
RUTH HUSSEY, The Philadelphia Story
BARBARA O'NEIL, All This, and Heaven Too
MARJORIE RAMBEAU, Primrose Path

1941
best picture

How Green Was My Valley
20TH CENTURY-FOX

CAST: Walter Pidgeon, Maureen O'Hara, Donald Crisp, Roddy McDowall, Anna Lee, Sara Allgood, Barry Fitzgerald, Patric Knowles, Arthur Shields, John Loder

CREDITS: Producer, Darryl F. Zanuck; Director, John Ford; Screenplay, Philip Dunne, from a novel by Richard Llewellyn; Cinematographer, Arthur Miller

THE 1941 Oscar-movie was a mood piece rather than a story in the conventional sense. Instead of a true novel, the Richard Llewellyn best seller from which it was made, was a loving remembrance of his Welch childhood in a simple mining village where the life was poor and hard, but warm family relationships made it rich in love.

The action centers around the day-to-day life, the crises and joys, of the closely-knit coal-mining Morgan family, as seen through the eyes of its young son, Huw. The off-screen voice of Huw as a man ties together the episodic happenings he remembers out of the past.

Roddy McDowell, then a juvenile actor, was the young Huw, while the voice of Huw, grown up, was that of Irving Pichel. Donald Crisp received an Oscar as Huw's father. Others in the excellent cast included Maureen O'Hara as his sister, and Walter Pidgeon as the man she loved but didn't marry.

How Green was a difficult work to film in a way that would hold audience-attention, and the Academy acknowledged Director John Ford's achievement in doing so with one of their prized little golden men. It made his third, and when Ford won a fourth time, in 1952, with *The Quiet Man,* he became the most-Oscared director in the business.

OTHER NOMINEES:
BLOSSOMS IN THE DUST, M-G-M
CITIZEN KANE, RKO Radio
HERE COMES MR. JORDAN, Columbia
HOLD BACK THE DAWN, Paramount
THE LITTLE FOXES, RKO Radio
THE MALTESE FALCON, Warner Bros.
ONE FOOT IN HEAVEN, Warner Bros.
SERGEANT YORK, Warner Bros.
SUSPICION, RKO Radio

The village and its miners

1941
best actor
Gary Cooper
SERGEANT YORK

AMERICA again stood at the brink of war when *Sergeant York* was released, and the picture was a tremendous morale booster. It also meant an Oscar for long, lean, laconic Gary Cooper, as the deeply religious young farmer from the Tennessee mountains who became the outstanding American hero of

World War I.

At that time, "Coop" was already one of the best established male stars on the screen and had received one previous Oscar nomination, for that delightful comedy of 1936, *Mr. Deeds Goes to Town*.

His long list of screen credits included *The Spoilers, A Farewell to Arms,* and *The General Died at Dawn.* He had been Wild Bill Hickock in Cecil B. DeMille's *The Plainsman* and the romantic hero opposite Marlene Dietrich in *Desire*.

Though Gary Cooper didn't confine himself to Westerns, they were close to his heart. The good-looking young actor with the shy smile first titillated feminine hearts in a silent, *The Winning of Barbara Worth,* in 1926, and his first talkie was *The Virginian.* It set him firmly on the stellar throne that was to be his until the day he died.

Cooper was a Westerner himself, from Helena, Montana, where he was born in 1901. But he was hardly a typical Westerner. He had gone to school in England, and to college in Iowa, before coming to California with the intention of studying art.

He thought he wanted to be a cartoonist, but once he struck Hollywood, in 1924, he found himself fascinated by movies and started haunting the studios instead, picking up bit parts where he could.

In 1952, he was to become one of the three male stars (with Fredric March and Spencer Tracy) ever to be voted two Best Actor Oscars.

Some pre-1941 Cooper films: *Lives of a Bengal Lancer, Souls at Sea, Beau Geste, Northwest Mounted Police, The Westerner.*

OTHER NOMINEES:
CARY GRANT, Penny Serenade
WALTER HUSTON, All That Money Can Buy
ROBERT MONTGOMERY, Here Comes Mr. Jordan
ORSON WELLES, Citizen Kane

1941
best actress

Joan Fontaine
SUSPICION

JOAN FONTAINE received her first Oscar bid in 1940, in the title role of the chiller Alfred Hitchcock fashioned from Daphne DuMaurier's *Rebecca.*

Up to that time, her chief claim to distinction in the five years she had been in Hollywood consisted of being Olivia de Havilland's sister and the wife of the dashing Brian Aherne (whom she later divorced).

The following year, in another Hitchcock mystery, *Suspicion,* she picked up another nomination, as the timid young bride plagued by increasing doubts that the intentions of her husband (Cary Grant) were lethal, rather than loving.

This time, Olivia De Havilland was also a nominee *(Hold Back the Dawn).* When Fontaine's claim to the Oscar won out, it caused a sisterly rift that was years in the mending.

Joan Fontaine and Cary Grant

The De Havilland family had been American since Colonial days, but both the De Havilland girls were born in Tokyo, where their father was a distinguished international patent attorney.

They grew up in the tiny, but culturally rich, Northern California town of Saratoga, and Joan Fontaine, as a girl, studied to be an artist.

She switched her ambitions to acting, and appeared on Broadway in *Tea and Sympathy* after following her sister into the movies. (The name "Fontaine" is her mother's maiden name.)

Like her sister, she spent her early movie years in films that made little demand of her—*Quality Street, Damsel in Distress, Gunga Din,* to mention some.

Better roles in films such as *Jane Eyre, Frenchman's Creek* and *The Constant Nymph* (which earned her a third Oscar bid) followed, but it was not until 1945 that she had the kind of role-with-bite that she wanted. The picture was *Affairs of Susan,* in which she was an actress who changed her personality to suit her current beau. From then on she played the scheming, sophisticated woman.

The 1950s saw Joan Fontaine in too many mediocre-to-bad pictures, bringing the career of the four-times-married star to a virtual halt. In *Tender Is the Night,* made in 1962, her billing was secondary to Jennifer Jones. Her only film since was *The Devil's Own* (1967).

Some other Fontaine films: *Ivy, September Affair, Ivanhoe, Island in the Sun, Voyage to the Bottom of the Sea.*

OTHER NOMINEES:
BETTE DAVIS, The Little Foxes
OLIVIA DE HAVILLAND, Hold Back the Dawn
GREER GARSON, Blossoms in the Dust
BARBARA STANWYCK, Ball of Fire

1941
best supporting actor

Donald Crisp
HOW GREEN WAS MY VALLEY

HONORED by the Academy with an Oscar for his moving performance in *How Green Was My Valley*, Donald Crisp was a director in the days of silent films, who acted occasionally. When pictures began to talk, Crisp, who still has the burr of his native Scotland in his speech, switched to acting completely. Now 86 and after appearing in some 400 films, he lives in quiet retirement in Southern California.

OTHER NOMINEES:
WALTER BRENNAN, Sergeant York
CHARLES COBURN, The Devil and Miss Jones
JAMES GLEASON, Here Comes Mr. Jordan
SYDNEY GREENSTREET, The Maltese Falcon

best supporting actress

Mary Astor
THE GREAT LIE

THOUGH she won an Oscar as the girl who had a baby by Bette Davis's husband in *The Great Lie*, Mary Astor was more noted for her beauty than her acting. She started in the silents at the young age of 14, and her talkies include *Dodsworth, Meet Me in St. Louis*, and *Little Women*. Now about 60, she has written five novels since her startlingly frank autobiography, *My Story*, about her four marriages. Her last film was *Hush . . . Hush, Sweet Charlotte*.

OTHER NOMINEES:
SARA ALLGOOD, How Green Was My Valley
PATRICIA COLLINGE, The Little Foxes
TERESA WRIGHT, The Little Foxes
MARGARET WYCHERLY, Sergeant York

1942
best picture

Mrs. Miniver
M-G-M

CAST: Greer Garson, Walter Pidgeon, Teresa Wright, Dame May Witty, Richard Ney, Reginald Owen, Henry Travers, Henry Wilcoxon, Helmut Dantine
CREDITS: Producer, Sidney Franklin; Director, William Wyler; Screenplay, Arthur Wimperis, George Froeschel, James Hilton, Claudine West, from a novel by Jan Struther; Cinematographer, Joseph Ruttenberg

THAT *Mrs. Miniver* was propaganda is undeniable. It is also undeniable that *Mrs. Miniver* was what most propaganda films are not—a skillfully wrought movie able to stand on its own feet as entertainment.

Based on a series of articles by writer Jan Struther, the picture was actually conceived and started the year before, when the sympathies of the American people were on the side of the Allies, but the U.S. was not yet involved in the conflict.

By the time *Mrs. Miniver* was released, however, we were deep in the war.

What made *Mrs. Miniver* so appealing was that it presented the war, not in terms of massive battle scenes, but in terms of one family's experiences as they try to carry on both their normal activities and respond to the exigencies of war. Mr. Miniver answers the call for every small boat owner to join in the rescue of the British forces stranded on the beach at Dunkirk. The Minivers huddle in bomb shelters and their beloved daughter-in-law, the two-week bride of their aviator son, an RAF officer, is killed in an air raid. Throughout the focus is on Mrs. Miniver.

Greer Garson and Walter Pidgeon were the Minivers, a handsome, dedicated couple, and the rest of the cast gave them excellent support.

The picture rated six Oscars, with Garson and Teresa Wright winning the feminine honors.

OTHER NOMINEES:
THE INVADERS, Columbia
KING'S ROW, Warner Bros.
THE MAGNIFICENT AMBERSONS, RKO Radio
THE PIED PIPER, 20th Century-Fox
THE PRIDE OF THE YANKEES, RKO Radio
RANDOM HARVEST, M-G-M
THE TALK OF THE TOWN, Columbia
WAKE ISLAND, Paramount
YANKEE DOODLE DANDY, Warner Bros.

Walter Pidgeon, Greer Garson, Richard Ney, little Christopher Severn and Claire Sandars were the Miniver family.

1942
best actor
James Cagney
YANKEE DOODLE DANDY

BORN ON NEW YORK'S tough Lower East Side in 1904, James Cagney learned how to use his fists early and established his right to stardom in a series of gangster roles in which he was as rough on the girls who loved him as on his other victims.

He was first seen as a hood in 1930, in *Doorway to Hell,* and by the following year had star billing in *Public Enemy.* His first Academy nomination came for a gangster role, in *Angels with Dirty Faces,* made in 1938.

His Oscar, however, was earned in Yankee Doodle Dandy, a musical based on the career of George M. Cohan, and Cohan himself had chosen Cagney to play him.

This isn't as surprising as it

sounds. Before hitting Hollywood, Cagney was a vaudeville song-and-dance-man and a Broadway chorus boy, all of which provided invaluable background for the character of America's most beloved song writer and song-and-dance-man.

In accepting his Oscar, Cagney observed, "An actor is only as good, or as bad, as people think he is. I am glad so many people think I was good."

With his third Academy nomination, Cagney was back in the gangster groove, but in a musical, *Love Me Or Leave Me,* based on the life of singer Ruth Etting, who was portrayed by Doris Day.

The feisty, bantam-sized Cagney and another actor whose forebears came from the Emerald Isle—Pat O'Brien—made a great box-office twosome in a series of films which included *Here Comes the Navy, The Irish in Us, Ceiling Zero,* and *Boy Meets Girl.*

In 1955, he assumed the George M. Cohan mantle again, for a cameo bit in Bob Hope's biographical film about more stage Irish, *The Seven Little Foys.* The same year, he was the savagely embittered captain in *Mr. Roberts.*

After completing *One, Two, Three,* this enormously versatile performer retired in 1962 and has cold-shouldered all Hollywood's attempts to lure him back.

Some other Cagney films: *Each Day I Die, City for Conquest, The Strawberry Blonde, Blood on the Sun, White Heat, West Point Story, Come Fill the Cup, Man of a Thousand Faces,* (a biography of Lon Chaney), *The Gallant Hours.*

OTHER NOMINEES:
RONALD COLMAN, Random Harvest
GARY COOPER, The Pride of the Yankees
WALTER PIDGEON, Mrs. Miniver
MONTY WOOLLEY, The Pied Piper

1942
best actress

Greer Garson
MRS. MINIVER

AFTER Greer Garson's acceptance speech, the Academy had a new request to make of its honorees—to keep their thank you's short, please.

The beautiful redhead, who had made such a wonderful Mrs. Miniver, let her nimble Irish tongue run on for more than half an hour—the longest acceptance in the Academy's history.

The actress from County Down, Northern Island, a graduate of France's Grenoble University, made other news stemming back to *Mrs. Miniver* when she married Richard Ney, her handsome aviator "son" in the picture. Ney was younger than she, it is true, but Garson herself was only 33 when she essayed the role of a woman with a son old enough to marry.

Greer Garson began her career on the London stage. Her first movie was *Goodbye, Mr. Chips,* and it brought her a nomination. She got a second in 1941, for *Blossoms in the Dust*.

After her Oscar win, she collected three more nominations in as many years (*Madam Curie, Mrs. Parkington, Valley of Decision*). Walter Pidgeon, her *Mrs. Miniver* co-star, was with her in the first two.

She was the darling of the box office when, in 1946, movie ads coast to coast screamed the news, "Gable's back and Garson's got him!" Nevertheless, "the King's" first post-war film, *Adventure,* was a disappointment.

A sequel to *Mrs. Miniver,* called *The Miniver Story,* was made in 1950. It was not only a disappointment, but a disaster from which the Garson career never really recovered.

After a Western, *Strange Lady in Town,* which she made in 1955, Garson did not make another film until 1960, when she played Eleanor Roosevelt in *Sunrise at Campobello*. With it, she was back in the groove with another Academy bid, her seventh. But warm and strong and wonderful as her Eleanor Roosevelt was, the picture did not herald a rebirth of Greer Garson's career.

Divorced from Ney and married now to a wealthy Texan, she is a frequent visitor to movieland, but strictly for social purposes.

Other Greer Garson films include: *Random Harvest, Julia Misbehaves, Her Twelve Men, The Singing Nun, The Happiest Millionaire.*

OTHER NOMINEES:
BETTE DAVIS, Now, Voyager
KATHARINE HEPBURN, Woman of the Year
ROSALIND RUSSELL, My Sister Eileen
TERESA WRIGHT, The Pride of the Yankees

1942
best supporting actor

Van Heflin
JOHNNY EAGER

After graduating from the University of Oklahoma and picking up a Master's at Yale's famed theatrical training ground, the Baker Workshop, Van Heflin made his film debut in 1941 in *The Feminine Touch*. His second picture, *Johnny Eager*, landed him among the Oscared. For some years Heflin had alternated between movies and Broadway, where he made a sensation in *A Case of Libel*. Van Heflin died July 23, 1971 after suffering a heart attack in a swimming pool in Hollywood. He was 60. His films include: *Possessed, Patterns, The Greatest Story Ever Told, Stagecoach, Once a Thief, Airport*.

OTHER NOMINEES:
WILLAM BENDIX, Wake Island
WALTER HUSTON, Yankee Doodle Dandy
FRANK MORGAN, Tortilla Flat
HENRY TRAVERS, Mrs. Miniver

best supporting actress

Teresa Wright
MRS. MINIVER

WHEN New Yorker Teresa Wright won her Oscar in the "supporting" category, she was also up for Best Actress for *The Pride of the Yankees*. The tiny brunette had received a supporting-player bid the year before *(The Little Foxes)*, and except for a very occasional TV appearance, she has been inactive professionally for several years. Married to playwright Robert Anderson, she lives on a farm in Brewster, New York.

OTHER NOMINEES:
GLADYS COOPER, Now, Voyager
AGNES MOOREHEAD, The Magnificent Ambersons
SUSAN PETERS, Random Harvest
DAME MAY WHITTY, Mrs. Miniver

1943
best picture

Casablanca
WARNER BROS.

CAST: Humphrey Bogart, Ingrid Bergman, Paul Henreid, Claude Rains, Sydney Greenstreet, Peter Lorre, Conrad Veidt, S. Z. Sakall, Dooley Wilson
CREDITS: Producer, Hal Wallis; Director, Michael Curtiz; Screenplay, Julius J. Epstein, Philip G. Epstein, Howard Koch, from a play by Murray Burnett and Joan Alison; Cinematographer, Arthur Edeson

HUMPHREY BOGART was at the peak of his popularity, and Ingrid Bergman was well on her way to becoming the movies' newest superstar, when they were paired in *Casablanca*.

The picture itself could have been just an ordinary little melodrama. Instead, with an inspired cast and director, it became one of the screen's most haunting romances, and the Academy dubbed it the year's finest film.

Casablanca had an unexpected publicity break in that wartime year. As it was about to be released, the North African port city was much in the news. President Franklin D. Roosevelt, Winston Churchill and Stalin were holding a summit conference there.

The picture's plot was old-line melodrama. Bogart, the American owner of a plush cocktail bar, keeps aloof from the local and international intrigue swirling about him until he comes to the rescue of his old girlfriend (Bergman). She is still the love of his life, and she and her husband (Paul Henreid), a Czech refugee, must leave within three days or he will be turned over to Axis authorities.

Bogart has a pair of visas—insurance for himself—and as Bergman maneuvers to get them, the old spark is re-ignited for a brief, bittersweet replay of their romance.

The strains of *As Time Goes By* —"their" song in happier days—is used as a theme throughout, and singer-pianist Dooley Wilson's tender treatment of it has much to do with creating the right mood.

In a fortuitous blending of many talents, *Casablanca* emerged as a superior picture within a most ordinary framework.

Humphrey Bogart, Claude Rains, Paul Henreid and Ingrid Bergman

OTHER NOMINEES:
FOR WHOM THE BELL TOLLS, Paramount
HEAVEN CAN WAIT, 20th Century-Fox
THE HUMAN COMEDY, M-G-M
IN WHICH WE SERVE, UA
MADAME CURIE, M-G-M
THE MORE, THE MERRIER, Columbia
THE OX-BOW INCIDENT, 20th Century-Fox
THE SONG OF BERNADETTE, 20th Century-Fox
WATCH ON THE RHINE, Warner Bros.

1943
best actor
Paul Lukas
WATCH ON THE RHINE

Bette Davis and Paul Lukas

A SUAVE, hand-kissing Continental from Budapest, Paul Lukas was an established stage star in Hungary before he made his first American film, *Loves of an Actress,* in 1928. When the talkies arrived, his charm and smooth technique triumphed over a somewhat heavy accent and Lukas continued to screen-romance the likes of Nancy Carroll, Jean Arthur, Ruth Chatterton, Hedy La-Marr, and Carole Lombard, usually with no good in mind.

Though he did appear in such meaningful films of the 1930s as *Dodsworth, Little Women,* Alfred Hitchcock's *The Lady Vanishes* and *Confessions of a Nazi Spy,* most of his movies were much less consequential, hardly the stuff which enhances an actor's reputation.

By 1941, Lukas shook himself loose from Hollywood for Broadway, where he found the vehicle just tailored to his dramatic abilities. It was Lillian Hellman's timely, hard-hitting *Watch on the Rhine,* and as the German underground leader who flees the Nazis to continue his anti-Nazi activities in the U.S. until he is trapped, he was much acclaimed.

When Warner Bros. made *Watch* into a first-rate film, they kept Lukas in his original high-tension role. It earned him an Oscar. It also reactivated his Hollywood career, and he was seen the following year in another uncompromising expose of Nazi terrorist tactics, *Address Unknown.*

In 1951, Lukas joined Ethel Merman on Broadway in the rousing Irving Berlin-Howard Lindsey-Russell Crouse *Call Me Madam.* It ran a year, after which he went into another Gotham show, this time a drama, *Flight into Egypt,* before coming back to Hollywood in 1954.

Born in 1895, Lukas made his last movie appearance in 1965, with Peter O'Toole in the film version of Joseph Conrad's *Lord Jim.* Paul Lukas died August 16, 1971, aged 76, of a heart attack in Tangiers, Morocco where he was living.

Some other Lukas pictures: *Captain Fury, Strange Cargo, Experiment Perilous, Temptation, Berlin Express, Kim, 20,000 Leagues Under the Sea, The Roots of Heaven, 55 Days at Peking.*

OTHER NOMINEES:
HUMPHREY BOGART, Casablanca
GARY COOPER, For Whom the Bell Tolls
WALTER PIDGEON, Madame Curie
MICKEY ROONEY, The Human Comedy

1943
best actress

Jennifer Jones
THE SONG OF BERNADETTE

WHEN THE POPULAR Franz Werfel novel, *The Song of Bernadette,* was to be filmed, a search reminiscent of Scarlett O'Hara got underway.

What 20th Century-Fox was looking for was an actress with a fresh, virginal quality, so new to the screen she would have no other identity to moviegoers than the 19th century French peasant girl whose claim, that the Virgin Mary came to her in a vision, stirred up tremendous controversy.

The choice fell on 24-year-old Jennifer Jones. By coincidence, she was under contract to Scarlett-seeker David O. Selznick, who had changed her name from Phyllis Isley.

A wide-eyed, natural beauty, Oklahoma-born Jennifer Jones was

a child actress in her parents' touring stock company. Later, she studied at Northwestern University in Chicago and New York's American Academy of Dramatic Arts, where she met her first husband, actor Robert Walker. Her movie experience before *Bernadette* was limited to two low-budget films.

As the maid of Lourdes, Jennifer Jones carried the Bernadette story along as if she were living every step of her progression from the 14-year-old who saw a vision to the nunnery religiouse. It was almost inevitable that she merit an Oscar.

Selznick guided Jennifer Jones' career carefully, and she became his wife after she divorced Walker.

For three years straight after *Bernadette,* she was to appear on the Academy's roster of nominees. In 1944, she turned up in the secondary division for her role in *Since You Went Away.*

In 1945, she was again among the top-lined nominees, for *Love Letters,* and in 1946, for *Duel in the Sun.*

Nine years later, as the Eurasian heroine in *Love Is a Many-Splendored Thing,* she again rated a nomination. In 1957, after remaking two film classics—*A Farewell to Arms* and *The Barretts of Wimpole Street*—neither the equal of its original, she retired for five years.

She emerged in 1962, for F. Scott Fitzgerald's *Tender is the Night.* Since being widowed in 1965, she has made *The Idol* and *Angel, Angel, Down We Go.* She married industrialist Norton Simon on May 30, 1971.

Her other films include: *Portrait of Jennie, Madame Bovary, Ruby Gentry, Carrie, Man in the Gray Flannel Suit.*

OTHER NOMINEES:
JEAN ARTHUR, The More the Merrier
INGRID BERGMAN, For Whom the Bell Tolls
JOAN FONTAINE, The Constant Nymph
GREER GARSON, Madame Curie

1943
best supporting actor

Charles Coburn
THE MORE THE MERRIER

As THE rich philanthropist slyly taking advantage of wartime Washington's crowded housing to give young romance a boost, Coburn was a comedic delight in *The More the Merrier*. Savannah-born Coburn claimed his monocle was no affectation but to correct an eye deficiency. "No sense wearing two windowpanes where one will do," he said. Whatever its reason, it was his trademark on the stage and screen for some 60 years. Death took him in 1961, at the age of 84.

OTHER NOMINEES:
CHARLES BICKFORD, The Song of Bernadette
J. CARROL NAISH, Sahara
CLAUDE RAINS, Casablanca
AKIM TAMIROFF, For Whom the Bell Tolls

best supporting actress

Katina Paxinou
FOR WHOM THE BELL TOLLS

Katina Paxinou was Oscared for her role as the fiery Spanish gypsy revolutionary, Pilar, in *For Whom the Bell Tolls* — a part close to her heart, for she herself had worked for many liberal causes. After her win, Hollywood could find few parts for the star from Greece and she returned home to Athens and the Greek stage. She returned in 1958, for one film, *The Miracle*. She appeared in London with the Greek National Theater in 1966. She died of cancer on February 22, 1973 in her native Greece.

OTHER NOMINEES:
GLADYS COOPER, The Song of Bernadette
PAULETTE GODDARD, So Proudly We Hail
ANNE REVERE, The Song of Bernadette
LUCILE WATSON, Watch On the Rhine

1944
best picture
Going My Way
PARAMOUNT

CAST: Bing Crosby, Rise Stevens, Barry Fitzgerald, Frank McHugh, Gene Lockhart, James Brown, Jean Heather, Porter Hall
CREDITS: Producer-Director, Leo McCarey; Screenplay, Frank Butler, Frank Cavett, from a story by Leo McCarey; Cinematographer, Lionel Lindon

NOT SINCE Spencer Tracy's Father Flanagan in *Boys Town* had an actor been outstanding in priest's garb. *Going My Way* had not one, but two, who were—Bing Crosby and Barry Fitzgerald — and they walked off with two of the picture's seven Oscars. (Fitzgerald was also nominated for Best Actor.)

Going My Way itself was a cheerful, engaging film touching lightly on religious matters and placing its emphasis on the human side of the priestly fraternity. It also gave crooner Crosby the chance to show he was no slouch at acting, either.

Bing was Father Chuck O'Malley, young and progressive. Fitzgerald played crusty, conservative old Father Fitzgibbon.

From the moment Father O'Malley arrives at the fringe-area church that was the oldster's exclusive province for many years, the two clash. O'Malley has his work cut out for him; to bring Fitzgibbon around won't be easy.

But after the athletic, singing young priest makes choir singers instead of troublemakers out of the neighborhood toughs, pays off the worrisome mortgage via song, and straightens out a raft of other parish problems in his easy, amiable way, the oldster gives in.

The Crosby voice was still there to lend a lyric note (*Too-Ra-Loo-Ra-Loo-Ral; Swinging on a Star*), the performances in general were excellent (including opera star Rise Stevens), and *Going My Way* turned out to be one of Crosby's most popular films.

OTHER NOMINEES:
DOUBLE INDEMNITY, Paramount
GASLIGHT, M-G-M
SINCE YOU WENT AWAY, Selznick-UA
WILSON, 20th Century-Fox

As Father O'Malley, Bing Crosby straightens out another crisis.

75

1944
best actor

Bing Crosby
GOING MY WAY

FROM THE *Road* pictures (to Singapore in 1940, Zanzibar in '41, Morocco in '42) to the young priest of *Going My Way* was quite a leap. Harry Lillis Crosby, better known as Bing, made it with such ease the jump got him an Oscar.

The Tacoma-born crooner, who started his career with Paul Whiteman, went into the movies in 1930 and was soon a top box-office draw in such musicals as *She Loves Me Not, Here Is My Heart, Pennies from Heaven,* and *Anything Goes.* Then he started slipping in the late 1930s.

The Road to Singapore, which started Crosby and Bob Hope off on their traveling rivalry for the hand of sarong-girl Dorothy Lamour, put an effective end to the

slippage. The *Roads* themselves came to an end at Hong Kong, in 1962, after additional stops a Utopia, Rio, and Bali.

In 1940, Crosby and Fred Astaire made Irving Berlin's blockbuster, *Holiday Inn.* Its big number, *White Christmas,* has since become a Yuletide staple.

As the progressive young priest in *Going My Way,* Bing still sang. But the film took him so far out of the crooner class that he rated one of the film's seven Oscars as the actor of the year.

The following year Bing again wore a turned-around collar, in *The Bells of St. Mary's,* a worthy successor to the Oscar picture of the year before. It brought him a second nomination.

In 1954, in a complete change of pace, he played the has-been actor married to Grace Kelly in the somber *The Country Girl,* displaying unexpected dramatic depths. He and Kelly were both nominated for Oscars. She got one.

The same year saw the release of *White Christmas,* Bing's greatest success and one of the all-time top Hollywood grossers.

Now in his early 60s, Crosby still makes an occasional TV appearance, but hasn't made a picture since the 1965 remake of *Stagecoach,* in which he was the whisky-soaked Doc Boone. These days he can usually be found at home in Northern California, with his second family of small children and his young wife Kathy.

Some other Crosby hits: *Sing You Sinners, Birth of the Blues, Star Spangled Rhythm, Blue Skies, High Society.*

OTHER NOMINEES:
CHARLES BOYER, Gaslight
BARRY FITZGERALD, Going My Way
CARY GRANT, None But the Lonely Heart
ALEXANDER KNOX, Wilson

1944
best actress
Ingrid Bergman
GASLIGHT

Charles Boyer and Ingrid Bergman

AN AMERICA that had taken Garbo to its heart earlier eagerly welcomed another glamorously beautiful Swede with open arms in 1936. She was Ingrid Bergman, a spring-fresh blonde. Her first American film, *Intermezzo,* was as big a success here as the Swedish picture on which it was based had been in her homeland.

She received her first Academy nod in 1943, as Maria in Hemingway's *For Whom the Bell Tolls.* Her love scenes with Gary Cooper were highlights in that somber tale of the Spanish Civil War.

That same year, she and Humphrey Bogart made a super-romantic pair in the year's Best Picture, *Casablanca.* The following year, the Academy bestowed the first of her two Oscars upon her.

Her win came in *Gaslight,* an eerie psychological drama based on the Broadway thriller, *Angel Street.* In it, she was slowly being driven mad by her sinister husband (Charles Boyer).

Bergman was now definitely in the super-star class, and received two more nominations—in 1945, as an impetuous nun in *Bells of St. Mary's,* and as Joan in *Joan of Arc* in 1948. She'd played the Maxwell Anderson drama on Broadway two years before, to earn the stage's Tony Award for her Joan.

Her name was box-office magic, though *Arch of Triumph,* her eagerly awaited screen reunion with Boyer, was disappointing.

Ingrid Bergman had been trained at the Royal Dramatic Theatre in her native Stockholm, and was a top Swedish movie star before coming to the U.S.

A woman of transcendent beauty, she had both warmth and dignity. The public liked, too, her quiet home life, as the wife of a Los Angeles dentist and the mother of a little girl. Scandal never had touched her, nor seemed likely to.

Thus, when soon after she went to Italy in 1950 to make *Stromboli,* her romance with its married director, Roberto Rossellini, made headlines, her adoring public turned on her, outraged. Bergman, as a star, was dead in the United States.

But time cools down all passions and when the ban was finally lifted some six years later, Bergman was on her way to her second Oscar.

Some early Bergman hits: *Spellbound, Saratoga Trunk, Notorious.*

OTHER NOMINEES:
CLAUDETTE COLBERT, Since You Went Away
BETTE DAVIS, Mr. Skeffington
GREER GARSON, Mrs. Parkington
BARBARA STANWYCK, Double Indemnity

1944
best supporting actor

Barry Fitzgerald
GOING MY WAY

THE SMALL (5' 3") Irishman with the engaging brogue who proudly accepted Oscar for his wonderful Father Fitzgibbon in *Going My Way* had a late start as an actor. He was 41 when he gave up the civil service job he held for 20 years to become one of Dublin's famed Abbey Players. He imprinted his mark upon the screen in many fine films, including *The Long Voyage Home* and *How Green Was My Valley*. He made his last big movie, *The Catered Affair,* in 1956 and died in Dublin in 1961, at 71.

OTHER NOMINEES:
HUME CRONYN, The Seventh Cross
CLAUDE RAINS, Mr. Skeffington
CLIFTON WEBB, Laura
MONTY WOOLLEY, Since You Went Away

best supporting actress

Ethel Barrymore
NONE BUT THE LONELY HEART

ETHEL BARRYMORE was 65 when her *None but the Lonely Heart* performance added Oscar to her many distinctions. She, Lionel and John were the ninth generation of a distinguished theatrical family. She was Queen of Broadway for many years and lent her imposing talents to many films, including: *Rasputin and the Empress* (with her brothers); *The Paradine Case, Portrait of Jenny, Kind Lady, It's a Big Country, Young at Heart.* She died at 80 in 1959.

OTHER NOMINEES:
JENNIFER JONES, Since You Went Away
ANGELA LANSBURY, Gaslight
ALINE MacMAHON, Dragon Seed
AGNES MOOREHEAD, Mrs. Parkington

1945
best picture

The Lost Weekend
PARAMOUNT

CAST: Ray Milland, Jane Wyman, Philip Terry, Howard DaSilva, Doris Dowling, Frank Faylen, Mary Young

CREDITS: Producer, Charles Brackett; Director, Billy Wilder; Screenplay, Charles Brackett and Billy Wilder, from a novel by Charles Jackson; Cinematographer, John F. Seitz.

Ray Milland sneaks out a bottle of liquor.

ENTERTAINMENT is hardly the word for the film that came out of Charles Jackson's best-selling novel which takes an alcoholic on a five-day bender.

The Best Picture in the year that saw the end of World War II was as grim as any war picture could have been—a shaking experience that might have come right out of the files of Alcoholics Anonymous.

Weekend captured the viewer through the sheer, mounting horror of watching a man's deterioration, from the first drink through his desperate attempts to cadge more whisky by any means when his pockets are empty, to his bout with delirium tremens. That scene alone, the room acrawl with rats and all manner of loathsome creatures summoned into being by his liquor-logged brain, was enough to invoke nausea in all but the strongest stomach.

Ray Milland, hitherto a pleasant, light comedian with a way with women, came through with a stunning performance as a drink-driven protagonist, often holding the screen alone for long moments. He pulled the audience right along with him, and Oscar took due note of his achievement.

As his fiancee, Jane Wyman broke out of the comedy field, musical and otherwise, and two years later would turn up among the Oscar-winners herself *(Johnny Belinda)*.

The Lost Weekend meant Oscars for its director and screenplay writer also, but it was, primarily, a Ray Milland triumph.

OTHER NOMINEES:
ANCHORS AWEIGH, M-G-M
THE BELLS OF ST. MARY'S, RKO Radio
MILDRED PIERCE, Warner Bros.
SPELLBOUND, Selznick-UA

1945
best actor
Ray Milland
THE LOST WEEKEND

DEBONAIR RAY MILLAND labored in the Hollywood vineyards for some 13 years after he and Charles Laughton made a joint debut in *Payment Deferred,* before *The Lost Weekend* came his way.

A handsome, likable Welchman, Milland made his reputation as a deft, romantic comedian and earned star status in a good film of this genre, *Arise My Love,* with Claudette Colbert.

At one time or other, he was the heart throb of most of screenland's beauties, including Loretta Young *(The Doctor Takes a Wife)* and Ginger Rogers *(The Major and the Minor, Lady in the Dark),* and made three South Sea Island yarns with Dorothy Lamour.

Hollywood had no inkling Milland could ever rise to dramatic heights and power until his frightening picture of a dipsomaniac in the throws of delirium tremens came across the screen as a nightmare of stark realism, and the Academy bestowed its prized Oscar on him.

Milland was born in Wales in 1908, and had a go at a number of occupations, from architecture to soldiering before making his debut in London, then taking his charm, good looks and talents on to Hollywood.

Post-Oscar, box offices smiled on him in 1947 in *Golden Earrings,* as a British spy aided by a gypsy (Marlene Dietrich). Moviegoers also went for *The Big Clock,* a heart-in-your-mouth suspense film a year later. In 1954, he was the trick killer in Hitchcock's *Dial M for Mur-*der, with Grace Kelly.

But in the main, the 1950s were not a happy time for Ray Milland and other film luminaries whose reputations were based in the kind of romantic comedy that had become passé.

Milland has kept on making movies, usually in the low-budget, shocker class *(Premature Burial, X: The Man with the X-Ray Eyes).* He also tried his hand at directing himself *(A Man Alone, Lisbon)* and was seen in two TV series, *Meet Mr. McNulty* and *Markham.*

In 1966, he made a delayed Broadway debut, at the age of 58, in *The Hostile Witness.* In 1970 he had his first big break in years, as Ryan O'Neal's father in *Love Story.*

Some more recent Milland movies: *Three Brave Men, High Flight, The Girl in the Velvet Swing, Panic in the Year Zero, The Confession.*

OTHER NOMINEES:
BING CROSBY, The Bells of St. Mary's
GENE KELLY, Anchors Aweigh
GREGORY PECK, The Keys of the Kingdom
CORNEL WILDE, A Song to Remember

1945
best actress

Joan Crawford
MILDRED PIERCE

How TENSE Joan Crawford—bedded by an attack of influenza—was, as she listened to the radio Oscarcast announcing her entrance into the charmed circle of winners, can be judged by her later remark.

"I don't know how anybody can live through this suspense twice," the handsome, vibrant brunette, who won with *Mildred Pierce,* said.

She lived through it twice more, as a nominee, though not the winner, in 1947 *(Suspense)* and in 1952 *(Sudden Fear).*

The fabulous career of the girl from San Antonio, Texas, who was dancing in a Broadway chorus line at 16 and knocking on Hollywood's door at 17, spans some 40-odd years.

Her movie debut in 1926, in a silent, *Pretty Ladies,* marked the last use of her own name, Lucille LeSeur, professionally. Later that year, in *Sally, Irene and Mary,* she

emerged as Joan Crawford, and in 1928, she did her still-talked-about Charleston in *Our Dancing Daughters.*

One of filmdom's most durable luminaries, Joan Crawford has turned down dozens of stage offers. "Live audiences scare me," she claims, but she made the transition to sound without trouble. Her *Dance, Fools, Dance,* in 1931, was the first of eight films with Clark Gable (some others: *Chained, Dancing Lady, Strange Cargo*).

Soon after she and her longtime boss, M-G-M, parted company when a couple of her films lagged at the box office, she made *Mildred Pierce.* As the tough-minded waitress who grubs her way up to business success, but invites tragedy through her inability to handle her spoiled brat of a daughter, she was at her best in a pull-no-punches adaptation of James Cain's murder shocker.

In 1962, after a three-year screen absence, she joined forces with Bette Davis in the macabre *Whatever Happened to Baby Jane?,* which became a runaway box-office success. Since then, her Grand Gignol-genre movies have included *Straight Jacket* and *Berserk.*

Three of Joan Crawford's four marriages (to Douglas Fairbanks, Jr., Franchot Tone and Alfred Steele, president of Pepsi-Cola, Inc.) were much in the news. After Steele's death, she proved herself a capable businesswoman in the role of a Pepsi-Cola vice president.

Among her dozens of films are: *The Women, Humoresque, Goodbye, My Fancy, Johnny Guitar, Autumn Leaves, I Saw What You Did.*

OTHER NOMINEES:
INGRID BERGMAN, The Bells of St. Mary's
GREER GARSON, The Valley of Decision
JENNIFER JONES, Love Letters
GENE TIERNEY, Leave Her To Heaven

1945
best supporting actor

James Dunn
A TREE GROWS IN BROOKLYN

JAMES DUNN had been in pictures since 1931. He had a list of credits yards long, including playing opposite Shirley Temple in her first feature movie, *Stand Up and Cheer*, and in *Baby Take a Bow* and *Bright Eyes*. His career was in a slump when Oscar revitalized it as a result of his drunken waiter, Johnny Nolan, in *A Tree Grows in Brooklyn*. Dunn called it a "once in a lifetime break," but after five more years of movie-making, he left films for good, and became a TV regular in the *It's a Great Life* series. He was 61 when he died in 1967.

OTHER NOMINEES:
MICHAEL CHEKHOV, Spellbound
JOHN DALL, The Corn Is Green
ROBERT MITCHUM, G.I. Joe
J. CARROL NAISH, A Medal for Benny

best supporting actress

Anne Revere
NATIONAL VELVET

National Velvet brought a 12-year-old Elizabeth Taylor to national attention. It also brought Anne Revere an Oscar. A strong-faced woman who is a "remote" descendant of Paul Revere, she was acclaimed two years before as the mother in *The Song of Bernadette*. She became a top screen character actress (*Forever Amber*, *Body and Soul*, etc.) and alternated movie-making with Broadway (*Children's Hour*, *Toys in the Attic*). She made her last film, *The Great Missouri Raid*, in 1951.

OTHER NOMINEES:
EVE ARDEN, Mildred Pierce
ANN BLYTH, Mildred Pierce
ANGELA LANSBURY, The Picture of Dorian Gray
JOAN LORRING, The Corn Is Green

1946
best picture

The Best Years Of Our Lives
SAMUEL GOLDWYN-RKO RADIO

CAST: Fredric March, Myrna Loy, Dana Andrews, Teresa Wright, Virginia Mayo, Hoagy Carmichael, Cathy O'Donnell, Gladys George, Harold Russell, Steve Cochran

CREDITS: Producer, Samuel Goldwyn; Director, William Wyler; Screenplay, Robert E. Sherwood, from a novel by MacKinlay Kantor; Cinematographer, Gregg Toland

SOCIAL SIGNIFICANCE and entertainment proved the Oscar-winning combination for *The Best Years of Our Lives*, which examined the problems of three World War II servicemen trying to adjust to peace-time living.

The ex-sergeant has the easiest adjustment to make. His loving wife has remained faithful; his daughter is a girl to be proud of; his job at the bank, while dull, is waiting for him. His main difficulty is to get back into the groove after being lifted out of his comfortable niche into a world of violence.

The sailor's troubles are the most serious. But he is a man of courage and resource, determined not to let the prosthetic hooks that have replaced his hands stand in his way.

The Air Force officer is the most disoriented. A man who had soared on a wing of high excitement and authority, he now has to return to work that is menial and a faithless wife who flaunts her affairs in his face. He finds his out in alcohol.

In the excellent cast, Fredric March was the ex-sergeant; Myrna Loy, his wife; Teresa Wright, his daughter. World War II amputee Harold Russell played the sailor with professional perfection in the only picture he ever made. Dana Andrews was the hard-drinking former Air Force officer; Virginia Mayo, his strumpet-wife.

The movie was not only timely, but it told its story with dramatic power and warm understanding of human strengths and frailties. It gathered seven Oscars, including the picture, director, and both male acting categories.

OTHER NOMINEES:
HENRY V, UA
IT'S A WONDERFUL LIFE, RKO Radio
THE RAZOR'S EDGE, 20th Century-Fox
THE YEARLING, M-G-M

Teresa Wright, Myrna Loy and Fredric March

1946
best actor
Fredric March
THE BEST YEARS OF OUR LIVES

THE *Best Years of Our Lives* was to signal more than one milestone in the career of Fredric March. It earned him a second Oscar for his sensitive delineation of a disoriented war veteran returning to a civilian life and a family that seems strangely alien after years of combat duty. It also marked the demise of Fredric March, the matinee idol.

March was still one of the best looking men around, but he was also 49 and knowledgeable enough to know that the time had come to turn to the character type of role.

March made the transition with such good grace that he never lost his hold on his public. There are many who rate him as our best actor, and some of his finest films were made after *The Best Years*.

In 1948, came Lillian Hellman's *Another Part of the Forest*, in which Florence Eldridge made one of her rare movie appearances. It broke no box-office records, but offered a veritable feast of fine acting.

In 1951, in the film version of Arthur Miller's Pulitzer Prize Play, *Death of a Salesman*, his sharply etched salesman of the title brought out all the pathos of the man along with his cheapness. It accounted for his fifth Academy nomination. Several other actors hold five nominations, but the only males to win a greater number were Spencer Tracy who was nominated nine times, and Laurence Olivier, with six bids.

March also turned more and more to his beloved legitimate theatre in these years of his maturity. He and his wife, Florence Eldridge, starred in such prestige Broadway hits as Arthur Miller's revamp of the Ibsen classic, *Enemy of the People,* and Eugene O'Neill's *Long Day's Journey into Night*. In 1962, he made one of his few theatre appearances without his wife. The play was Paddy Chayefsky's Biblical allegory, *Gideon,* which became one of the season's most successful dramas.

March's post-1946 films include: *Executive Suite, The Desperate Hours, The Bridges at Toko-Ri, Middle of the Night, Seven Days in May, tick…tick…tick.*

OTHER NOMINEES:
LAURENCE OLIVIER, Henry V
LARRY PARKS, The Jolson Story
GREGORY PECK, The Yearling
JAMES STEWART, It's a Wonderful Life

1946
best actress
Olivia De Havilland
TO EACH HIS OWN

WHEN OLIVIA DE HAVILLAND had an Oscar to call her own at last, her resentment against losing out to her sister five years before came to the fore. The year-younger Joan Fontaine was on hand to congratulate big sister, but DeHavilland brusquely brushed her off.

The Oscar had not only eluded the beautiful Tokyo-born, California-raised actress in 1941, but in 1939 as well. Then she was up for a "supporting" award for her Melanie in *Gone with the Wind*.

The Civil War spectacle gave De Havilland her best opportunity since her movie debut in 1935, as Hermia in Max Reinhardt's production of *A Midsummer Night's Dream*. She made her first professional appearance anywhere earlier that year in the same role when Rheinhardt produced the Shakespearean fantasy for the Hollywood

Bowl, and the great German director specifically requested her for the movie.

She was an immediate film success, and Warner Bros. quickly signed her to a long-term contract. But the series of films, starting with *Captain Blood,* which she made with Errol Flynn, did little to enhance her status. Then came the break of being loaned to David O. Selznick for *Gone with the Wind*.

After her return to Warner, she was tapped again by the Academy for *Hold Back the Dawn* in 1941. Other than that, her pictures again did little for her. They included two more Flynn swashbucklers *(Santa Fe Trail, They Died with Their Boots On)* and such films as *Raffles, Strawberry Blonde,* and *The Male Animal.*

Like her friend, Bette Davis, she started feuding with the studio for better roles, was suspended several times, and fought a costly legal battle with them. Unlike Davis, she won her case.

She then went on to prove her right to the better roles she sought when she came up with an Oscar for her second free-lance venture, *To Each His Own.*

The picture was one of those soggy soap operas about the trials and tribulations of unmarried mothers. But the De Havilland performance of the single woman whose child grows up believing she is his aunt, was 14-carat gold. Three years later, she was to follow it up with another Oscar-win, for *The Heiress.*

Some other pre-1946 De Havilland films: *The Great Garrick, In This Our Life, Princess O'Rourke, Devotion.*

OTHER NOMINEES:
CELIA JOHNSON, Brief Encounter
JENNIFER JONES, Duel in the Sun
ROSALIND RUSSELL, Sister Kenny
JANE WYMAN, The Yearling

1946
best supporting
actor

Harold Russell
THE BEST YEARS OF OUR LIVES

IT WAS a poignant moment as ex-serviceman Harold Russell held his two Oscars proudly in his artificial hands as he stepped from the podium. One Oscar was for his gem of a performance as the sailor whose hands, but not his spirit, were a sacrifice to the God of War in *The Best Years of Our Lives*. The other was a special honorary Oscar, for bringing hope and courage to his fellow veterans.

OTHER NOMINEES:
CHARLES COBURN, The Green Years
WILLIAM DEMAREST, The Jolson Story
CLAUDE RAINS, Notorious
CLIFTON WEBB, The Razor's Edge

best supporting
actress

Anne Baxter
THE RAZOR'S EDGE

THIS BRIGHT, pretty granddaughter of Frank Lloyd Wright received her Oscar for her tragic Sophie in *The Razor's Edge* and was nominated again, four years later, in *All About Eve*. Anne Baxter made her movie debut *(Twenty Mule Team)* at 17, and her some 40-odd films include *Cimarron, The Ten Commandments, The Busy Body, Fools' Parade* and two Universal World Premiere Films, *Stranger on the Run* and *Midnight Patient* that were made to be shown directly on TV in the U.S. and in theatres in other countries.

OTHER NOMINEES:
ETHEL BARRYMORE, The Spiral Staircase
LILLIAN GISH, Duel in the Sun
FLORA ROBSON, Saratoga Trunk
GALE SONDERGAARD, Anna and the King of Siam

1947
best picture
Gentleman's Agreement
20TH CENTURY-FOX

CAST: Gregory Peck, Dorothy McGuire, John Garfield, Celeste Holm, Anne Revere, June Havoc, Albert Dekker, Jane Wyatt, Dean Stockwell, Sam Jaffe
CREDITS: Producer, Darryl F. Zanuck; Director, Elia Kazan; Screenplay, Moss Hart, from the novel by Laura Z. Hobson; Cinematographer, Arthur Miller

NOVELIST LAURA Z. HOBSON's best seller about anti-Semitism could not have been made into a film before the war. But in the sober climate of the coming about of peace after years of warfare, the screen began to look around for more mature subjects. It was time to tackle such social problems as racial and religious prejudice, and the Hobson novel was a perfect vehicle for the purpose and was carefully made into a first-rate film.

The story concerned a non-Jewish newspaperman who poses as a Jew to gather material for a series of articles on discrimination.

In the course of his investigation, he runs into the kind of situations he'd never been exposed to before. There are the hotels and clubs with a "no Jews allowed" rule; he finds out his secretary has changed her name to disguise her Jewish origin; his landlord turns out to be a bigot, and his fiancée is irked that she can't let people know he's not really Jewish.

In the course of his six-month exploration of the problem, he becomes aware that there is no area of his life that is untouched by the ugly tentacles of religious prejudice.

The picture, its director — Elia Kazan — and supporting actress Celeste Holm were all honored by Oscars. Gregory Peck, as the forthright hero, and Dorothy McGuire, in a supporting role, also won nominations.

An interesting sidelight was the appearance of John Garfield, who already had star status, in a relatively minor role, because he believed in the film so deeply.

OTHER NOMINEES:
THE BISHOP'S WIFE, RKO Radio
CROSSFIRE, RKO Radio
GREAT EXPECTATIONS, Universal-International
MIRACLE ON 34TH STREET, 20th Century-Fox

John Garfield, Gregory Peck, Dorothy McGuire, and Celeste Holm

1947
best actor
Ronald Colman
A DOUBLE LIFE

A MAJOR STAR for more than 30 years, Ronald Colman's career spanned from the silents to the talkies, and his fans — especially the feminine contingent of moviegoers— were legion.

In the second year of the Academy's existence, the romantic, moustached Englishman had been nominated in the best thespian category for two films, *Bulldog Drummond* and *Condemned*. He was tapped again in 1942 (*Random Harvest*), but didn't actually capture the top accolade until he was 56 years old and his career was on the wane.

The movie for which Colman was Oscared was hardly one of his best, but it gave him a chance to put on a dazzling histrionic display in a Jekyll-Hyde dual role, as an actor playing Othello who is going mad and begins to confuse his real life with his stage existence. His wife (Signe Hasso) is also his Desde-mona, and as his mental condition worsens, his unfounded suspicions about her and their agent, (Edmond O'Brien) increase to a tragic end. (The picture also introduced a promising newcomer to the screen— Shelley Winters.)

The good-looking star who had to wait so long for his Oscar was born in Richmond, Surrey, England, in 1891. He came to the U.S. with limited British stage and screen experience, and made his screen debut in 1921, as George Arliss's son in *Twenty Dollars a Week*.

His voice was rich and distinctive, and with the coming of sound he rode high in *Arrowsmith, Under Two Flags, Lost Horizon, A Tale of Two Cities.*

He made only three more films after his Oscar win: *Champagne for Caesar,* and "cameo" appearances in *Around the World in 80 Days* and *The Story of Mankind.* As so many movie stars have done, Colman then turned to radio and TV. His TV series, *The Halls of Ivy* (with his wife, Benita Hume), enjoyed a vogue for a time. He died in 1958.

Some other Colman hits: *The Prisoner of Zenda, If I Were King, The Light That Failed, The Late George Apley.*

OTHER NOMINEES:
JOHN GARFIELD,
 Body and Soul
GREGORY PECK,
 Gentleman's Agreement
WILLIAM POWELL,
 Life With Father
MICHAEL REDGRAVE,
 Mourning Becomes
 Electra

1947
best actress
Loretta Young
THE FARMER'S DAUGHTER

LORETTA YOUNG'S Oscar was the biggest upset in the Academy's history. It had been an almost foregone conclusion that the little golden man would go to Rosalind Russell for her Electra in Eugene O'Neill's *Mourning Becomes Electra.*

Loretta Young started off her acceptance speech by saying, "When I first came to Hollywood one hundred and fifty years ago, I wanted one of these . . ."

She was not around that long; it just seemed that way. The girl from Salt Lake City started her career at the young age of four, was a screen regular by 14, and was only 40 when she quit the movies for TV, in 1953.

Loretta Young was a professional to her finger tips. She studied every role carefully and painstakingly acquired an authentic Swedish accent for her Oscar-winning performance as the farm girl from Minnesota who starts out as a Congressman's maid and winds up as a Congresswoman.

The year after her Oscar win she gave—though it didn't bring her even a nomination—what was possibly the finest performance of her long movie tenure, as the sex-obsessed schoolteacher in the melodramatic *The Accused.* She did win a second Oscar bid for her motorcycling nun in *Come to the Stable.*

By the time the sophisticated beauty with the marvelous flair for clothes made her last film, *It Happens Every Thursday,* in 1953, she had been in close to 100 of them and had played with practically every top male star in the business, from James Cagney and Ronald Coleman, to Clark Gable and Cary Grant.

When she took off to carve a new career on TV, she was as successful on the small home screen as on its big brother. Her anthology series, *The Loretta Young Show,* on which she tackled a different role every week, ran for some six years, and in its course she collected several Emmys to put on display beside her Oscar.

Still in her early fifties and as stunningly lovely as ever, Loretta Young evidently has no plans to reactivate the career that started at an age when most children begin kindergarten.

Some other Loretta Young films: *Caravan, The Crusades, Clive of India, Ramona, Love Is News, Kentucky, The Doctor Takes a Wife, A Night to Remember, Along Came Jones, The Stranger, Key to the City, Cause for Alarm.*

OTHER NOMINEES:
JOAN CRAWFORD, Possessed
SUSAN HAYWARD, Smash Up
DOROTHY McGUIRE, Gentleman's Agreement
ROSALIND RUSSELL, Mourning Becomes Electra

1947
best supporting actor

Edmund Gwenn
MIRACLE ON 34TH STREET

EDMUND GWENN, who won his Oscar as Santa Claus in *The Miracle on 34th Street,* was a British actor who got his start when George Bernard Shaw selected him for the chauffeur in his *Man and Superman.* He played in five more Shavian opuses in London before coming to Broadway in 1922. He entered the movies in 1936 and was in such films as *Anthony Adverse, The Keys of the Kingdom, Random Harvest* and *Green Dolphin Street.* He died in 1959 at 82.

OTHER NOMINEES:
CHARLES BICKFORD, The Farmer's Daughter
THOMAS GOMEZ, Ride the Pink Horse
ROBERT RYAN, Crossfire
RICHARD WIDMARK, Kiss of Death

best supporting actress

Celeste Holm
GENTLEMAN'S AGREEMENT

CELESTE HOLM, the stage's original Ado Annie in *Oklahoma!,* made her second movie appearance in that searching probe of anti-Semitism, *Gentleman's Agreement,* and was Oscared for it. The blonde New Yorker has two other nominations to her credit, for *Come to the Stable* (1949) and *All About Eve* (1950). In addition to a busy acting schedule, she finds time to entertain the troops in Vietnam, tour for the State Department, and other social and civic activities.

OTHER NOMINEES:
ETHEL BARRYMORE, The Paradine Case
GLORIA GRAHAME, Crossfire
MARJORIE MAIN, The Egg and I
ANNE REVERE, Gentleman's Agreement

1938-47
oscar winners
in other categories

1938

DIRECTOR
FRANK CAPRA, You Can't Take It
With You

WRITING
PYGMALION, Ian Dalrymple, Cecil
Lewis, W. P. Lipscomb
(Adaptation)
BOYS TOWN, Eleanore Griffin,
Dore Schary (Original Story)
PYGMALION, George Bernard Shaw
(Screenplay)

CINEMATOGRAPHY
THE GREAT WALTZ,
Joseph Ruttenberg

INTERIOR DECORATION
ADVENTURES OF ROBIN HOOD,
Carl J. Weyl

SOUND RECORDING
THE COWBOY AND THE LADY,
Thomas Moulton

SHORT SUBJECTS
FERDINAND THE BULL, Walt
Disney, RKO Radio (Cartoons)
THAT MOTHERS MIGHT LIVE,
M-G-M (One-reel)
DECLARATION OF INDEPENDENCE,
Warner Bros. (Two-reel)

MUSIC
THANKS FOR THE MEMORY
(Big Broadcast Of 1938) Ralph
Rainger, Leo Robin (Song)
ALEXANDER'S RAGTIME BAND,
Alfred Newman (Score)
THE ADVENTURES OF ROBIN HOOD,
Erich Wolfgang Korngold
(Original Score)

FILM EDITING
THE ADVENTURES OF ROBIN HOOD,
Ralph Dawson

**IRVING G. THALBERG
MEMORIAL AWARD**
Hal B. Wallis

HONORARY AND OTHER AWARDS
DEANNA DURBIN and MICKEY
ROONEY for their significant
contribution in bringing to the
screen the spirit and
personification of youth, and as
juvenile players setting a high
standard of ability and
achievement. (miniature statuette
trophies)
HARRY M. WARNER in recognition
of patriotic service in the
production of historical short
subjects presenting significant
episodes in the early struggle
of the American people for
liberty. (scroll)
WALT DISNEY for "Snow White
And The Seven Dwarfs,"
recognized as a significant screen
innovation which has charmed
millions and pioneered a great
new entertainment field for the
motion picture cartoon. (one
statuette—seven miniature
statuettes)

OLIVER MARSH and ALLEN DAVEY
for the color cinematography of
the M-G-M production,
"Sweethearts." (plaques)
For outstanding achievement in
creating Special Photographic and
Sound Effects in the Paramount
production, "Spawn Of The
North." Special Effects by
GORDON JENNINGS, assisted by
JAN DOMELA, DEV JENNINGS,
IRMIN ROBERTS and ART SMITH.
Transparencies by FARCIOT
EDOUART, assisted by LOYAL
GRIGGS. Sound Effects by
LOREN RYDER, assisted by HARRY
MILLS, LOUIS H. MESENKOP and
WALTER OBERST. (plaques)
J. ARTHUR BALL for his outstanding
contributions to the advancement
of color in Motion Picture
Photography. (scroll)

**SCIENTIFIC OR TECHNICAL
CLASS III**
JOHN AALBERG and RKO RADIO
STUDIO SOUND DEPT.
BYRON HASKIN and the SPECIAL
EFFECTS DEPT. OF
WARNER BROS. STUDIO

1939

DIRECTOR
VICTOR FLEMING, Gone With
The Wind

WRITING
MR. SMITH GOES TO
WASHINGTON, Lewis R. Foster
(Original Story)
GONE WITH THE WIND,
Sidney Howard (Screenplay)

CINEMATOGRAPHY
WUTHERING HEIGHTS, Gregg
Toland (Black and White)
GONE WITH THE WIND, Ernest
Haller, Ray Rennahan (Color)

INTERIOR DECORATION
GONE WITH THE WIND,
Lyle Wheeler

SOUND RECORDING
WHEN TOMORROW COMES,
Bernard B. Brown

SHORT SUBJECTS
THE UGLY DUCKLING, Walt Disney,
RKO Radio (Cartoons)
BUSY LITTLE BEARS,
Paramount (One-reel)
SONS OF LIBERTY, Warner Bros.
(Two-reel)

MUSIC
OVER THE RAINBOW (The Wizard
Of Oz) Harold Arlen,
E. Y. Harburg (Song)
STAGECOACH, Richard Hageman,
Frank Harling, John Leipold,
Leo Shuken (Song)
THE WIZARD OF OZ, Herbert
Stothart (Original Score)

FILM EDITING
GONE WITH THE WIND,
Hal C. Kern, James E. Newcom

SPECIAL EFFECTS
THE RAINS CAME, E. H. Hansen,
Fred Sersen

**IRVING G. THALBERG
MEMORIAL AWARD**
David O. Selznick

HONORARY AND OTHER AWARDS
DOUGLAS FAIRBANKS
(Commemorative Award)—
recognizing the unique and
outstanding contribution of
Douglas Fairbanks, first President
of the Academy, to the
international development of the
motion picture. (statuette)
MOTION PICTURE RELIEF FUND—
acknowledging the outstanding
services to the industry during
the past year of the Motion
Picture Relief Fund and its
progressive leadership. Presented
to JEAN HERSHOLT, President;
RALPH MORGAN, Chairman of the
Executive Committee; RALPH
BLOCK, First Vice-President;
CONRAD NAGEL. (plaques)
JUDY GARLAND for her outstanding
performance as a screen juvenile
during the past year.
(miniature statuette)
WILLIAM CAMERON MENZIES for
outstanding achievement in the
use of color for the enhancement
of dramatic mood in the
production of "Gone With
The Wind." (plaque)
TECHNICOLOR COMPANY for its
contributions in successfully
bringing three-color feature
production to the screen.
(statuette)

**SCIENTIFIC OR TECHNICAL
CLASS III**
GEORGE ANDERSON, Warner Bros.
JOHN ARNOLD, M-G-M
THOMAS T. MOULTON, FRED ALBIN
and SOUND DEPT. of SAMUEL
GOLDWYN STUDIO
FARCIOT EDOUART, JOSEPH E.
ROBBINS, WILLIAM RUDOLPH
and PARAMOUNT PICTURES, INC.
EMERY HUSE, RALPH B. ATKINSON
HAROLD NYE
A. J. TONDREAU
F. R. ABBOTT, HALLER BELT,
ALAN COOK and BAUSCH &
LOMB OPTICAL CO.
MITCHELL CAMERA CO.
MOLE-RICHARDSON CO.
CHARLES HANDLEY, DAVID JOY
and NATIONAL CARBON CO.
WINTON HOCH and TECHNICOLOR
MOTION PICTURE CORP.
DON MUSGRAVE and SELZNICK
INTERNATIONAL PICTURES, INC.

1938-47 cont'd.

1940

DIRECTOR
JOHN FORD, The Grapes Of Wrath

WRITING
ARISE, MY LOVE, Benjamin Glazer,
John S. Toldy (Original Story)
THE GREAT McGINTY, Preston
Sturges (Original Screenplay)
THE PHILADELPHIA STORY, Donald
Ogden Stewart (Screenplay)

CINEMATOGRAPHY
REBECCA, George Barnes
(Black and White)
THIEF OF BAGDAD,
George Perinal (Color)

INTERIOR DECORATION
PRIDE AND PREJUDICE,
Cedric Gibbons, Paul Groesse
(Black and White)
THIEF OF BAGDAD,
Vincent Korda (Color)

SOUND RECORDING
STRIKE UP THE BAND,
Douglas Shearer

SHORT SUBJECTS
MILKY WAY, M-G-M (Cartoons)
QUICKER 'N A WINK, Pete Smith,
M-G-M (One-reel)
TEDDY, THE ROUGH RIDER,
Warner Bros. (Two-reel)

MUSIC
WHEN YOU WISH UPON A STAR
(Pinocchio) Leigh Harline,
Ned Washington (Song)
TIN PAN ALLEY,
Alfred Newman (Score)
PINOCCHIO, Leigh Harline,
Paul J. Smith, Ned Washington
(Original Score)

FILM EDITING
NORTH WEST MOUNTED POLICE,
Anne Bauchens

SPECIAL EFFECTS
THE THIEF OF BAGDAD, Lawrence
Butler, Jack Whitney

HONORARY AND OTHER AWARDS
BOB HOPE, in recognition of his
unselfish services to the Motion
Picture Industry. (special
silver plaque)
COLONEL NATHAN LEVINSON for
his outstanding service to the
industry and the Army during the
past nine years, which has made
possible the present efficient
mobilization of the motion
picture industry facilities for the
production of Army Training
Films. (statuette)

SCIENTIFIC OR TECHNICAL
CLASS I
20TH CENTURY-FOX FILM CORP.

CLASS III
WARNER BROS. STUDIO ART
DEPT. and ANTON GROT

1941

DIRECTOR
JOHN FORD, How Green Was
My Valley

WRITING
HERE COMES MR. JORDAN,
Harry Segall (Original Story)
CITIZEN KANE, Herman J.
Mankiewicz, Orson Welles
(Original Screenplay)
HERE COMES MR. JORDAN, Sidney
Buchman, Seton I. Miller
(Screenplay)

CINEMATOGRAPHY
HOW GREEN WAS MY VALLEY, Arthur
Miller (Black and White)
BLOOD AND SAND, Ernest Palmer,
Ray Rennahan (Color)

INTERIOR DECORATION*
HOW GREEN WAS MY VALLEY,
Richard Day, Nathan Juran;
Thomas Little (Black and White)
BLOSSOMS IN THE DUST, Cedric
Gibbons, Urie McCleary;
Edwin B. Willis (Color)

SOUND RECORDING
THAT HAMILTON WOMAN,
Jack Whitney

SHORT SUBJECTS
LEND A PAW, Walt Disney,
RKO Radio (Cartoons)
OF PUPS AND PUZZLES,
M-G-M (One-reel)
MAIN STREET ON THE MARCH,
M-G-M (Two-reel)

DOCUMENTARY
CHURCHILL'S ISLAND, UA

MUSIC
THE LAST TIME I SAW PARIS
(Lady Be Good) Jerome Kern,
Oscar Hammerstein II (Song)
ALL THAT MONEY CAN BUY,
Bernard Herrmann (Scoring of
a Dramatic Picture)
DUMBO, Frank Churchill, Oliver
Wallace (Scoring of a
Musical Picture)

FILM EDITING
SERGEANT YORK, William Holmes
SPECIAL EFFECTS
I WANTED WINGS, Farciot Edouart,
Gordon Jennings, Louis Mesenkop

IRVING G. THALBERG
MEMORIAL AWARD
Walt Disney

HONORARY AND OTHER AWARDS
REY SCOTT for his extraordinary
achievement in producing
"Kukan," the film record of
China's struggle, including its
photography with a 16mm camera
under the most difficult and
dangerous conditions. (certificate)

THE BRITISH MINISTRY OF
INFORMATION for its vivid and
dramatic presentation of the
heroism of the RAF in the
documentary film, "Target For
Tonight." (certificate)

LEOPOLD STOKOWSKI and his
associates for their unique
achievement in the creation of
a new form of visualized music
in Walt Disney's production
"Fantasia," thereby widening
the scope of the motion picture
as entertainment and as an art
form. (certificate)

WALT DISNEY, WILLIAM GARITY,
JOHN N. A. HAWKINS and the
RCA MANUFACTURING CO., for
their outstanding contribution to
the advancement of the use of
sound in motion pictures through
the production of "Fantasia."
(certificates)

*Set Decoration honored for first
time along with Art Direction.

SCIENTIFIC OR TECHNICAL
CLASS II
ELECTRICAL RESEARCH PRODUCTS
DIVISION OF WESTERN
ELECTRIC CO., INC.
RCA MANUFACTURING CO.
CLASS III
RAY WILKINSON and the
PARAMOUNT STUDIO
LABORATORY
CHARLES LOOTENS and the
REPUBLIC STUDIO SOUND DEPT.
WILBUR SILVERTOOTH and the
PARAMOUNT STUDIO
ENGINEERING DEPT.
PARAMOUNT PICTURES, INC., and
20TH CENTURY-FOX FILM CORP.
DOUGLAS SHEARER and the M-G-M
STUDIO SOUND DEPT., and
LOREN RYDER and the
PARAMOUNT STUDIO
SOUND DEPT.

1942

DIRECTOR
WILLIAM WYLER, Mrs. Miniver

WRITING
THE INVADERS, Emeric Pressburger
(Original Story)
WOMAN OF THE YEAR,
Michael Kanin, Ring Lardner, Jr.
(Original Screenplay)
MRS. MINIVER, George Froeschel,
James Hilton, Claudine West,
Arthur Wimperis (Screenplay)

CINEMATOGRAPHY
MRS. MINIVER, Joseph Ruttenberg
(Black and White)
THE BLACK SWAN, Leon Shamroy
(Color)

INTERIOR DECORATION
THIS ABOVE ALL, Richard Day
Joseph Wright; Thomas Little
(Black and White)
MY GAL SAL, Richard Day,
Joseph Wright; Thomas Little
(Color)

SOUND RECORDING
YANKEE DOODLE DANDY,
Nathan Levinson

SHORT SUBJECTS
DER FUEHRER'S FACE, Walt Disney,
RKO Radio (Cartoons)
SPEAKING OF ANIMALS AND THEIR
FAMILIES, Paramount (One-reel)
BEYOND THE LINE OF DUTY,
Warner Bros. (Two-reel)

DOCUMENTARY
BATTLE OF MIDWAY, U.S. Navy
KOKODA FRONT LINE, Australian
News Information Bureau
MOSCOW STRIKES BACK, Artkino
PRELUDE TO WAR, U.S. Army
Special Services

MUSIC
WHITE CHRISTMAS (Holiday Inn)
Irving Berlin (Song)
NOW, VOYAGER, Max Steiner
(Scoring of a Dramatic or
Comedy Picture)
YANKEE DOODLE DANDY, Ray
Heindorf, Heinz Roemheld
(Scoring of a Musical Picture)

FILM EDITING
THE PRIDE OF THE YANKEES,
Daniel Mandell

SPECIAL EFFECTS
REAP THE WILD WIND, Farciot
Edouart, Gordon Jennings,
William L. Pereira,
Louis Mesenkop

92

IRVING G. THALBERG MEMORIAL AWARD
Sidney Franklin

HONORARY AND OTHER AWARDS
CHARLES BOYER for his progressive cultural achievement in establishing the French Research Foundation in Los Angeles as a source of reference for the Hollywood Motion Picture Industry. (certificate)
NOEL COWARD for his outstanding production achievement in "In Which We Serve." (certificate)
M-G-M STUDIO for its achievement in representing the American Way of Life in the production of the "Andy Hardy" series of films. (certificate)

SCIENTIFIC OR TECHNICAL
CLASS II
CARROLL CLARK, F. THOMAS THOMPSON and RKO RADIO STUDIO ART and MINIATURE DEPTS.
DANIEL B. CLARK and 20TH CENTURY-FOX FILM CORP.

CLASS III
ROBERT HENDERSON and PARAMOUNT STUDIO ENGINEERING and TRANSPARENCY DEPTS.
DANIEL J. BLOOMBERG and REPUBLIC STUDIO SOUND DEPT.

1943
DIRECTOR
MICHAEL CURTIZ, Casablanca

WRITING
THE HUMAN COMEDY, William Saroyan (Original Story)
PRINCESS O'ROURKE, Norman Krasna (Original Screenplay)
CASABLANCA, Julius J. Epstein, Philip G. Epstein, Howard Koch (Screenplay)

CINEMATOGRAPHY
THE SONG OF BERNADETTE, Arthur Miller (Black and White)
PHANTOM OF THE OPERA, Hal Mohr, W. Howard Greene (Color)

INTERIOR DECORATION
THE SONG OF BERNADETTE, James Basevi, William Darling; Thomas Little (Black and White)
PHANTOM OF THE OPERA, Alexander Golitzen, John B. Goodman, Russell A. Gausman, Ira S. Webb (Color)

SOUND RECORDING
THIS LAND IS MINE, Stephen Dunn

SHORT SUBJECTS
YANKEE DOODLE MOUSE, M-G-M (Cartoons)
AMPHIBIOUS FIGHTERS, Paramount (One-reel)
HEAVENLY MUSIC, M-G-M (Two-reel)

DOCUMENTARY
DECEMBER 7TH, U.S. Navy (Short Subjects)
DESERT VICTORY, British Ministry of Information (Features)

MUSIC
YOU'LL NEVER KNOW (Hello, Frisco, Hello) Harry Warren, Mack Gordon (Song)
THE SONG OF BERNADETTE, Alfred Newman (Scoring of a Dramatic or Comedy Picture)
THIS IS THE ARMY, Ray Heindorf (Scoring of a Musical Picture)

FILM EDITING
AIR FORCE, George Amy

SPECIAL EFFECTS
CRASH DIVE, Fred Sersen, Roger Heman

IRVING G. THALBERG MEMORIAL AWARD
Hal B. Wallis

HONORARY AND OTHER AWARDS
GEORGE PAL for the development of novel methods and techniques in the production of short subjects known as Puppetoons. (plaque)

SCIENTIFIC OR TECHNICAL
CLASS II
FARCIOT EDOUART, EARLE MORGAN, BARTON THOMPSON and PARAMOUNT STUDIO ENGINEERING and TRANSPARENCY DEPTS.
PHOTO PRODUCTS DEPARTMENT, E. I. duPONT de NEMOURS AND CO., INC.

CLASS III
DANIEL J. BLOOMBERG and REPUBLIC STUDIO SOUND DEPT.
CHARLES GALLOWAY CLARKE and 20TH CENTURY-FOX STUDIO CAMERA DEPT.
FARCIOT EDOUART and PARAMOUNT STUDIO TRANSPARENCY DEPT.
WILLARD H. TURNER and RKO RADIO STUDIO SOUND DEPT.

1944
DIRECTOR
LEO McCAREY, Going My Way

WRITING
GOING MY WAY, Leo McCarey (Original Story)
WILSON, Lamar Trotti (Original Screenplay)
GOING MY WAY, Frank Butler, Frank Cavett (Screenplay)

CINEMATOGRAPHY
LAURA, Joseph LaShelle (Black and White)
WILSON, Leon Shamroy (Color)

INTERIOR DECORATION
GASLIGHT, Cedric Gibbons, William Ferrari; Edwin B. Willis, Paul Huldschinsky (Black and White)
WILSON, Wiard Ihnen; Thomas Little (Color)

SOUND RECORDING
WILSON, E. H. Hansen

SHORT SUBJECTS
MOUSE TROUBLE, M-G-M (Cartoons)
WHO'S WHO IN ANIMAL LAND, Paramount, (One-reel)
I WON'T PLAY, Warner Bros. Featurette (Two-reel)

DOCUMENTARY
WITH THE MARINES AT TARAWA, U.S. Marine Corps. (Short Subjects)
THE FIGHTING LADY, 20th Century-Fox & U.S. Navy (Features)

MUSIC
SWINGING ON A STAR (Going My Way) James Van Heusen, Johnny Burke (Song)
SINCE YOU WENT AWAY, Max Steiner (Scoring of a Dramatic or Comedy Picture)
COVER GIRL, Carmen Dragon, Morris Stoloff (Scoring of a Musical Picture)

FILM EDITING
WILSON, Barbara McLean

SPECIAL EFFECTS
THIRTY SECONDS OVER TOKYO, A. Arnold Gillespie, Donald Jahraus, Warren Newcombe, Douglas Shearer

IRVING G. THALBERG MEMORIAL AWARD
Darryl F. Zanuck

HONORARY AND OTHER AWARDS
MARGARET O'BRIEN, outstanding child actress of 1944. (miniature statuette)
BOB HOPE, for his many services to the Academy, a Life Membership in the Academy of Motion Picture Arts and Sciences.

SCIENTIFIC OR TECHNICAL
CLASS II
STEPHEN DUNN and RKO RADIO STUDIO SOUND DEPT. and RADIO CORPORATION OF AMERICA

CLASS III
LINWOOD DUNN, CECIL LOVE and ACME TOOL MANUFACTURING CO.
GROVER LAUBE and 20TH CENTURY-FOX STUDIO CAMERA DEPT.
WESTERN ELECTRIC CO.
RUSSELL BROWN, RAY HINSDALE, JOSEPH E. ROBBINS
GORDON JENNINGS
RADIO CORPORATION OF AMERICA and RKO RADIO STUDIO SOUND DEPT.
DANIEL J. BLOOMBERG and REPUBLIC STUDIO SOUND DEPT.
BERNARD B. BROWN, JOHN P. LIVADARY
PAUL ZEFF, S. J. TWINING, GEORGE SEID
PAUL LERPAE

93

1945

DIRECTOR
BILLY WILDER, The Lost Weekend

WRITING
THE HOUSE ON 92ND STREET,
Charles G. Booth (Original Story)
MARIE-LOUISE, Richard Schweizer
(Original Screenplay)
THE LOST WEEKEND, Charles
Brackett, Billy Wilder (Screenplay)

CINEMATOGRAPHY
THE PICTURE OF DORIAN GRAY,
Harry Stradling (Black and White)
LEAVE HER TO HEAVEN,
Leon Shamroy (Color)

INTERIOR DECORATION
BLOOD ON THE SUN, Wiard Ihnen;
A. Roland Fields
(Black and White)
FRENCHMAN'S CREEK, Hans Dreier,
Ernst Fegte; Sam Comer (Color)

SOUND RECORDING
THE BELLS OF ST. MARY'S,
Stephen Dunn

SHORT SUBJECTS
QUIET PLEASE, M-G-M (Cartoons)
STAIRWAY TO LIGHT,
M-G-M (One-reel)
STAR IN THE NIGHT,
Warner Bros. (Two-reel)

DOCUMENTARY
HITLER LIVES?, Warner Bros.
(Short Subjects)
THE TRUE GLORY, Govts. of
Great Britain and USA
(Features)

MUSIC
IT MIGHT AS WELL BE SPRING
(State Fair) Richard Rodgers,
Oscar Hammerstein II (Song)
SPELLBOUND, Miklos Rozsa
(Scoring of a Dramatic or
Comedy Picture)
ANCHORS AWEIGH, Georgie Stoll
(Scoring of a Musical Picture)

FILM EDITING
NATIONAL VELVET, Robert J. Kern

SPECIAL EFFECTS
WONDER MAN, John Fulton,
A. W. Johns

HONORARY AND OTHER AWARDS
WALTER WANGER for his six years
service as President of the
Academy of Motion Picture Arts
and Sciences. (special plaque)
PEGGY ANN GARNER, outstanding
child actress of 1945.
(miniature statuette)
THE HOUSE I LIVE IN, tolerance
short subject; produced by
Frank Ross and Mervyn LeRoy;
directed by Mervyn LeRoy;
screenplay by Albert Maltz; song
"The House I Live In" music
by Earl Robinson, lyrics by
Lewis Allen; starring Frank
Sinatra; released by RKO
Radio. (statuette)
REPUBLIC STUDIO, DANIEL J.
BLOOMBERG and REPUBLIC
SOUND DEPT. for the building
of an outstanding musical scoring
auditorium which provides
optimum recording conditions
and combines all elements of
acoustic and engineering design.
(certificates)

94

SCIENTIFIC OR TECHNICAL

CLASS III
LOREN L. RYDER, CHARLES R.
DAILY and PARAMOUNT STUDIO
SOUND DEPT.

MICHAEL S. LESHING, BENJAMIN
C. ROBINSON, ARTHUR B.
CHATELAIN, ROBERT C.
STEVENS, JOHN G. CAPSTAFF

1946

DIRECTOR
WILLIAM WYLER, The Best Years
Of Our Lives

WRITING
VACATION FROM MARRIAGE,
Clemence Dane (Original Story)
THE SEVENTH VEIL, Muriel Box,
Sydney Box (Original Screenplay)
THE BEST YEARS OF OUR LIVES,
Robert E. Sherwood (Screenplay)

CINEMATOGRAPHY
ANNA AND THE KING OF SIAM,
Arthur Miller (Black and White)
THE YEARLING, Charles Rosher,
Leonard Smith, Arthur Arling
(Color)

INTERIOR DECORATION
ANNA AND THE KING OF SIAM,
Lyle Wheeler, William Darling;
Thomas Little, Frank E. Hughes
(Black and White)
THE YEARLING, Cedric Gibbons,
Paul Groesse; Edwin B. Willis
(Color)

SOUND RECORDING
THE JOLSON STORY,
John Livadary

SHORT SUBJECTS
THE CAT CONCERTO,
M-G-M (Cartoons)
FACING YOUR DANGER,
Warner Bros. (One-reel)
A BOY AND HIS DOG, Warner Bros.
(Two-reel Featurettes)

DOCUMENTARY
SEEDS OF DESTINY, U.S. War
Dept. (Short Subjects)

MUSIC
ON THE ATCHISON, TOPEKA AND
SANTA FE (The Harvey Girls)
Harry Warren, Johnny Mercer
(Song)
THE BEST YEARS OF OUR LIVES,
Hugo Friedhofer (Scoring of a
Dramatic or Comedy Picture)
THE JOLSON STORY, Morris Stoloff
(Scoring of a Musical Picture)

FILM EDITING
THE BEST YEARS OF OUR LIVES,
Daniel Mandell

SPECIAL EFFECTS
BLITHE SPIRIT, Thomas Howard

**IRVING G. THALBERG
MEMORIAL AWARD**
Samuel Goldwyn

HONORARY AND OTHER AWARDS
LAURENCE OLIVIER for his
outstanding achievement as actor,
producer and director in bringing
"Henry V" to the screen.
(statuette)

HAROLD RUSSELL for bringing
hope and courage to his fellow
veterans through his appearance
in "The Best Years Of Our
Lives." (statuette)

ERNST LUBITSCH for his
distinguished contributions to the
art of the motion picture. (scroll)

CLAUDE JARMAN, JR., outstanding
child actor of 1946.
(miniature statuette)

SCIENTIFIC OR TECHNICAL

CLASS III
HARLAN L. BAUMBACH and
PARAMOUNT WEST COAST LAB.

HERBERT E. BRITT

BURTON F. MILLER and WARNER
BROS. STUDIO SOUND and
ELECTRICAL DEPTS.

CARL FAULKNER of 20th
Century-Fox Studio Sound Dept.

MOLE-RICHARDSON CO.
ARTHUR F. BLINN, ROBERT O.
COOK, C. O. SLYFIELD and
WALT DISNEY STUDIO
SOUND DEPT.

BURTON F. MILLER and WARNER
BROS. STUDIO SOUND DEPT.

MARTY MARTIN and HAL ADKINS
of RKO Radio Studio
Miniature Dept.

HAROLD NYE and WARNER BROS.
STUDIO ELECTRICAL DEPT.

1947

DIRECTOR
ELIA KAZAN,
Gentleman's Agreement

WRITING
MIRACLE ON 34TH STREET, 20th
Century-Fox, Valentine Davies
(Original Story)
THE BACHELOR AND THE
BOBBY-SOXER, Sidney Sheldon
(Original Screenplay)
MIRACLE ON 34TH STREET,
George Seaton (Screenplay)

CINEMATOGRAPHY
GREAT EXPECTATIONS, Guy Green
(Black and White)
BLACK NARCISSUS, Jack Cardiff
(Color)

ART DIRECTION-SET DECORATION
GREAT EXPECTATIONS,
John Bryan; Wilfred Shingleton
(Black and White)
BLACK NARCISSUS,
Alfred Junge (Color)

SOUND RECORDING
THE BISHOP'S WIFE,
Goldwyn Sound Dept.

SHORT SUBJECTS
TWEETIE PIE,
Warner Bros. (Cartoons)
GOODBYE MISS TURLOCK,
M-G-M (One-reel)
CLIMBING THE MATTERHORN,
Monogram (Two-reel, color)

DOCUMENTARY

FIRST STEPS, Division of Films and Visual Education (Short Subjects)

DESIGN FOR DEATH, RKO Radio (Features)

MUSIC

ZIP-A-DEE-DOO-DAH (Song Of The South) Music, Allie Wrubel; Lyrics, Ray Gilbert (Song)

A DOUBLE LIFE, Miklos Rozsa (Scoring of a Dramatic or Comedy Picture)

MOTHER WORE TIGHTS, Alfred Newman (Scoring of a Musical Picture)

FILM EDITING

BODY AND SOUL, Francis Lyon, Robert Parrish

SPECIAL EFFECTS

GREEN DOLPHIN STREET, A. Arnold Gillespie, Warren Newcombe, Douglas Shearer, Michael Steinore

HONORARY AND OTHER AWARDS

JAMES BASKETTE for his able and heart-warming characterization of Uncle Remus, friend and story teller to the children of the world. (statuette)

BILL AND COO, in which artistry and patience blended in a novel and entertaining use of the medium of motion pictures. (plaque)

SHOE-SHINE—the high quality of this motion picture, brought to eloquent life in a country scarred by war, is proof to the world that the creative spirit can triumph over adversity. (statuette)

COLONEL WILLIAM N. SELIG, ALBERT E. SMITH, THOMAS ARMAT and GEORGE K. SPOOR (one of) the small group of pioneers whose belief in a new medium, and whose contributions to its development, blazed the trail along which the motion picture has progressed, in their lifetime, from obscurity to world-wide acclaim. (statuettes)

SCIENTIFIC OR TECHNICAL

CLASS II

C. C. DAVIS and ELECTRICAL RESEARCH PRODUCTS, DIVISION OF WESTERN ELECTRIC CO.

C. R. DAILY and PARAMOUNT

STUDIO FILM LABORATORY, STILL and ENGINEERING DEPTS.

CLASS III

NATHAN LEVINSON and WARNER BROS. STUDIO SOUND DEPT.

FARCIOT EDOUART, C. R. DAILY, HAL CORL, H. G. CARTWRIGHT and PARAMOUNT STUDIO TRANSPARENCY and ENGINEERING DEPTS.

FRED PONEDEL

KURT SINGER and RCA-VICTOR DIVISION of the RADIO CORPORATION OF AMERICA

JAMES GIBBONS

1948-57
introduction to the third decade

Jose Ferrer accepts as Judy Holliday listens. They turned in the top performances of 1950.

IN ITS THIRD DECADE something new was added to Oscar Night, March 19, 1953, when the Academy Awards were televised for the first time. Home viewers by the millions saw the giving out of Oscars for 1952 to *The Greatest Show on Earth,* Gary Cooper (*High Noon*), Shirley Booth (*Come Back, Little Sheba*), and winners in the various other categories.

The first year (1948) of this new decade in Oscar's history was a year of firsts. *Hamlet* became the first British production to be chosen for an Oscar, and when its star, Laurence Olivier, got one also, he and Vivien Leigh became the first and only Academy Awards-winning couple.

At the same time, Walter Huston, who won in the supporting actor category, and his director son, John, became the only members of the same family ever to win Oscars on the same evening. Their wins came

for *Treasure of Sierra Madre.* Jane Wyman, a former song-and-dance-girl, was named the best of the fair sex, for the highly dramatic *Johnny Belinda.*

For the 22nd Annual Awards Presentation, on March 23, 1950, Oscar moved to the Pantages Theatre, located at Hollywood and Vine, and the little golden statuettes would be given out there for a number of years to come.

All the King's Men and two of its cast, Broderick Crawford and supporting-actress Mercedes McCam-

Broderick Crawford, Olivia de Havilland, Mercedes McCambridge and Dean Jagger make a proud winning foursome for 1949.

Frank Sinatra beams at being chosen Best Supporting Actor in 1953. His win gave his slumping career a boost.

Marlon Brando is congratulated on being dubbed Best Actor of 1954 by Bob Hope, longtime Oscar Night emcee.

bridge, were honorees that evening, for 1949 Oscars. So, too, was Olivia de Havilland, winning her second top-actress-of-the-year citation (*The Heiress*).

At the 1951 Oscar affair, 1950's *All About Eve* was the acclaimed movie. An oddity about *Eve* was that though it received a record 14 nominations, only one of its cast, supporting player George Sanders, picked up an Oscar. Jose Ferrer (*Cyrano de Bergerac*) and Judy Holliday (*Born Yesterday*) were rated the performers of the year.

Though the musical, *An American in Paris*, was the 1951 picture choice. three actors in another nominated film, *A Street Car Named Desire*, were recipients of the coveted golden statuette. They were Best Actress Vivien Leigh, and Karl Malden and Kim Hunter in the supporting area. Humphrey Bogart was tops in the men's field for his *The African Queen* performance.

With the 26th Annual Presentation, William Holden (*Stalag 17*) became the only actor unable to even say thank you. TV time ran out on him. The following year, when he presented Grace Kelly with her *The Country Girl* trophy, he managed to get in his own belated thank you for 1953.

The best production in that year was *From Here to Eternity,* and Audrey Hepburn picked up the main feminine award for *Roman Holiday*.

After being nominated the three preceding years, Marlon Brando hit the Oscar jackpot in *On the Waterfront,* which was also named the outstanding film of 1954.

Grace Kelly shows her delight in her 1954 Oscar.

97

Anthony Quinn, Dorothy Malone and Yul Brynner took home Oscars for 1956.

Jack Lemmon, Jo Van Fleet and Ernest Borgnine are the happy 1955 winners.

Songwriters James Van Heusen, left, and Sammy Cahn accepting Oscar from Maurice Chevalier for the Best Song of 1958, "All The Way."

On Oscar Night in 1956, a modest little film, *Marty,* Ernest Borgnine, who played the name role, and Anna Magnani (*The Rose Tattoo*) topped the 1955 contingent. Magnani was in Italy at the time, and the next year, when she presented Yul Brynner with his *The King and I* statuette, she said, "I feel like tonight I won."

Other honors for 1956 went to *Around the World in 80 Days* as the year's ace film, and to Ingrid Bergman (*Anastasia*).

The last year of its third decade saw the 1957 Oscars distributed on Oscar Night, March 26, 1958, to *The Bridge on the River Kwai,* and to Alec Guinness for his role in it. A comparative newcomer, Joanne Woodward, represented the fair sex, with a top win for *Three Faces of Eve.*

As Oscar stood at the threshold of his fortieth year, he was preeminent in filmdom—the undisputed king in the field of motion-picture awards.

1948
best picture

Hamlet
UNIVERSAL-INTERNATIONAL

CAST: Laurence Olivier, Jean Simmons, Eileen Herlie, Basil Sydney, Felix Aylmer, Norman Woodland, Terence Morgan, Stanley Holloway, Anthony Quayle, Peter Cushing
CREDITS: Producer-Director, Laurence Olivier; from the play by William Shakespeare; Cinematographer, Desmond Dickenson

THE SCREEN has seen many Hamlets, from J. Forbes-Robertson in a silent film to Maximilian Schell's German-language version in 1962. But Laurence Olivier's Melancholy Dane, and the movie he produced and directed is unique.

The Olivier *Hamlet* is an exquisitely wrought film. A veritable pageant in misty black and white, it holds the eye riveted upon the stage while the ear listens intently to the soaring beauty of the lines, as spoken by Olivier and his gifted cast.

The Academy had to take notice of this superb British production, and it became the first foreign-made picture to win an Oscar.

Olivier performed some expert surgery on Shakespeare's original. He cut out static moments, telescoped some speeches, and pruned the play's unwieldy four hours down to a more acceptable movie length of two-and-a-half hours. Predictably, the Bard-purists had some harsh words for this tampering, but Olivier wanted a picture that moved, that would appeal to people who never had any interest in Shakespeare before, as well as those who loved him. He achieved just what he set out to do.

Olivier chose his expert cast chiefly from his associates at London's famed Old Vic Theatre, and he entrusted the tragically driven-to-madness Ophelia to an 18-year-old actress named Jean Simmons, who came through like a veteran.

Actor Olivier earned an Oscar; so did the picture, the art direction and the costume design. But director Olivier had to make do with a nomination.

OTHER NOMINEES:
JOHNNY BELINDA, Warner Bros.
THE RED SHOES, Eagle-Lion
THE SNAKE PIT, 20th Century-Fox
TREASURE OF SIERRA MADRE, Warner Bros.

Hamlet (Laurence Olivier) seeks out his father's ghost.

1948
best actor
Laurence Olivier
HAMLET

THE ACTOR who was to become the greatest Hamlet of his time was born in an English parsonage in 1907, and went into the British theatre at an early age.

He made his Broadway debut in 1929, in *Murder on the Second Floor,* and was one of the stage actors frantically summoned to Hollywood during the sound upheaval. But Laurence Olivier's initial picture, *The Temporary Widow,* and the four that followed, were light romances that took little advantage of his talents.

In 1933, what seemed to be the big break came—a call to play opposite the Great Garbo in *Queen Christina.* But Garbo was adamant about wanting her longtime co-star in silents, John Gilbert, and Olivier received his walking papers.

Somewhat bitterly, he returned to Broadway for *The Green Bay Tree,* then went back to the English stage.

The role of Heathcliff in *Wuthering Heights* lured Olivier back to Hollywood in 1939 and gave him his first Oscar nomination. His second came with *Rebecca,* the 1940 best movie. The same year saw him and Vivien Leigh on the New York stage in *Romeo and Juliet,* an event that was less than enthusiastically received. It also was the year he and Vivien Leigh were married.

After a short stint in the British Navy in World War II, Olivier went on to become one of the Old Vic's brightest stars, and to produce, direct, and star in two superb Shakespearean films, both British-made.

The first was *Henry V,* which resulted in his third Oscar nomination. The second was *Hamlet,* which became the Academy's choice as 1948's top film, and made Olivier an Oscar-winner at last. He received three more nominations: in 1956 for *Richard III,* in 1960 for *The Entertainer* and *Othello,* 1965.

In 1947, Olivier, who spends most of his time in the theatre, was knighted by King George V, at the relatively young age of 41, and he is now Lord Olivier.

Divorced from Vivien Leigh in 1960, he is now married to actress Joan Plowright. Cancer sidelined him in 1967, but he has since made *The Shoes of the Fisherman, Oh! What a Lovely War,* and *The Battle of Britain.*

His films include: *The Prince and the Showgirl* (with Marilyn Monroe), *Spartacus, Term of Trial, Bunny Lake Is Missing.*

OTHER NOMINEES:
LEW AYRES, Johnny Belinda
MONTGOMERY CLIFT, The Search
DAN DAILEY, When My Baby Smiles At Me
CLIFTON WEBB, Sitting Pretty

1948
best actress

Jane Wyman
JOHNNY BELINDA

IN ONE of the shortest acceptance speeches on record, Jane Wyman brought a chuckle as she took her *Johnny Belinda* Oscar and said, "I accept this very gratefully for keeping my mouth shut. I think I'll do it again."

The deaf-mute heroine of *Johnny Belinda* was a role of extraordinary difficulty and complexity, and Jane Wyman went into intensive training for it. She worked with deaf mutes and became expert at sign language. When the actual shooting started, she used earplugs to cut out all sound. It is doubtful if even a bona-fide deaf mute could have given a more convincing or heart-wrenching portrayal of the farm girl known to the neighborhood as "the Dummy."

She bears an illegitimate child after being raped, and proves an utterly loving and competent mother, yet must fight to keep little Johnny Belinda because of her muteness. Only one person helps her in her fight, the town's new doctor (Lew Ayres) who is her one friend.

Jane Wyman is a Missouri girl, born in 1914, who got her start as a singer on radio. She made her movie debut at 22, then waited ten years to graduate from secondary parts—usually as the brassy blond comedy relief.

The Lost Weekend was her breakthrough. It gave her her first chance to show she could build a meaningful, three-dimensional character. The following year, as the mother in *The Yearling,* she won her first Oscar nomination, and she followed up her *Johnny Belinda* Oscar with two more nominations (*Blue Veil,* 1951; *Magnificent Obsession,* 1954).

The pertly pretty actress, who divorced Ronald Reagan the same year she acquired Oscar, enjoyed several years of popularity after her Oscar win, in films that ranged from the stark drama of *The Glass Menagerie* to two lighthearted musicals with Bing Crosby (*Here Comes the Groom,* 1951; *Just for You,* 1952).

Her popularity began to drop as her films went downhill in quality. After *Bon Voyage* (1962), she had a whirl at TV. In 1969 she was back in films as the feminine lead in *How to Commit Marriage,* with Bob Hope and Jackie Gleason.

Some Wyman films: *One More Tomorrow, Larceny, Inc., Stage Fright, Three Guys Named Mike, Lucy Gallant, All that Heaven Allows, Holiday for Lovers.*

OTHER NOMINEES:
INGRID BERGMAN, Joan of Arc
OLIVIA DE HAVILLAND, The Snake Pit
IRENE DUNNE, I Remember Mama
BARBARA STANWYCK, Sorry, Wrong Number

1948
best supporting actor

Walter Huston
TREASURE OF SIERRA MADRE

BORN IN TORONTO, Canada, in 1884, Oscar-winner Walter Huston spent 15 years in vaudeville as a song-and-dance-man before becoming a dramatic star. His many Broadway hits include *Desire Under the Elms* and *Knickerbocker Holiday*, in which his singing of Kurt Weill's *September Song* was a highlight. In movies since the days of silents, his biggest film success came with *Dodsworth*, in a repeat of the role he played on the stage. He died in 1949, just one day after his 66th birthday.

OTHER NOMINEES:
CHARLES BICKFORD, Johnny Belinda
JOSE FERRER, Joan of Arc
OSCAR HOMOLKA, I Remember Mama
CECIL KELLAWAY, The Luck of the Irish

best supporting actress

Claire Trevor
KEY LARGO

FILM AND STAGE STAR Claire Trevor is a New Yorker who got her training at the American Academy of Dramatic Arts and Columbia University, and goes back and forth between Broadway and Hollywood. To her *Key Largo* Oscar she added an Emmy for her distinguished performance in the TV version of *Dodsworth*. Her many films include: *Lucy Gallant*, *Marjorie Morningstar*, *How to Murder Your Wife*.

OTHER NOMINEES:
BARBARA BEL GEDDES, I Remember Mama
ELLEN CORBY, I Remember Mama
AGNES MOOREHEAD, Johnny Belinda
JEAN SIMMONS, Hamlet

1950
best picture

All About Eve
20TH CENTURY-FOX

CAST: Bette Davis, Anne Baxter, George Sanders, Celeste Holm, Gary Merrill, Thelma Ritter, Hugh Marlowe, Marilyn Monroe, Gregory Ratoff

CREDITS: Producer, Darryl F. Zanuck; Director, Joseph L. Mankiewicz; Screenplay, Joseph L. Mankiewicz, from a novel by Mary Orr; Cinematographer, Milton Krasner.

ALL ABOUT EVE is one of the best back-stage films ever made. A wry comedy, it had an expert, multi-star cast, and it sparkled with crisp, sophisticated dialogue.

The picture also put new life into the bogged-down career of Bette Davis, and it introduced her to the man who became her fourth husband — actor Gary Merrill, with whom she had some sizzling romantic scenes.

Davis portrayed an aging stage star fighting to retain her position against the next generation on the way up, as personified by bright, talented and ambitious Anne Baxter. Baxter, in turn, once she does displace Davis, finds another young aspirant hot on her heels.

In the role said to be based on Tallulah Bankhead (and hotly denied by all concerned), Davis was dominant, but she did not overshadow such fine performances as those of Celeste Holm, Thelma Ritter and George Sanders, whose cynical drama critic rated the year's "supporting" Oscar in the male division. Marilyn Monroe, a young unknown at the time, made an excellent impression as Sanders's untalented but well-stacked protege.

The picture earned an unprecedented number of nominations, 14, and wound up with six Oscars in all, but the Best Actress accolade was among the missing. Anne Baxter had insisted on being nominated in that category, along with Bette Davis, instead of in the "supporting" section. As a result, Academy votes were so split between the two that neither won.

OTHER NOMINEES:
BORN YESTERDAY, Columbia
FATHER OF THE BRIDE, M-G-M
KING SOLOMON'S MINES, M-G-M
SUNSET BOULEVARD, Paramount

Anne Baxter, Bette Davis, Marilyn Monroe, and George Sanders

1950
best actor

Jose Ferrer
CYRANO DE BERGERAC

OTHER ACTORS have played *Cyrano de Bergerac* before Jose Ferrer, and Jose Ferrer was a Broadway star before Cyrano. But Ferrer and Cyrano were made for each other.

As Rostand's swordsman with the over-sized nose and the eloquence of a poet, the actor with one of the stage's finest speaking voices first burst dazzlingly onto Broadway in 1946. When he brought his *Cyrano* to the screen, United Artists equipped him with a $5,000 nose, and the Academy put an Oscar in his hands.

The Puerto-Rican-born actor who, like James Stewart, did his first acting in student productions at Princeton, had won a previous Academy nomination two years earlier, in his movie debut as The Dauphin in *Joan of Arc,* and he was nominated for the third time, again in a biographical role, for *Moulin Rouge.* For his exquisitely played Toulouse-Lautrec, he suffered torturous hours of having his legs tied behind to simulate that tormented artist's dwarfed stature.

For a time after his Oscar win, he seemed to be all over at once. On the screen he was seen in *The Caine Mutiny, The Shrike, The Great Man,* etc. On the stage his name blazed on the marquees of theatres where successes like *Twentieth Century* and *The Shrike* were playing, and he directed another of the Big Town's smash hits, *Stalag 17.*

Then, for a time, the steam seemed to go out of his career and it was his stormy, oft-again, on-again marriage to singer Rosemary Clooney that was more apt to be in the newspaper, not his acting or directing exploits.

The lapse was temporary. His incipient Nazi in the 1965 *Ship of Fools* was a highlight of that somber film, as was his side-splitting, boozy thespian in last year's *Enter Laughing,* and he has recently been Cervantes in that wondrous stage musical, *Man of LaMancha.*

But Cyrano remains his masterpiece, and the movie has found a place in *Motion Picture Almanac's* list of the "Great Hundred" films of all time.

Some recent Ferrer films: *Nine Hours to Rama, The Greatest Story Ever Told, Lawrence of Arabia, Cervantes.*

OTHER NOMINEES:
LOUIS CALHERN, The Magnificent Yankee
WILLIAM HOLDEN, Sunset Boulevard
JAMES STEWART, Harvey
SPENCER TRACY, Father of the Bride

1950
best actress
Judy Holliday
BORN YESTERDAY

JUDY HOLLIDAY was a sparkling blonde, as bright as her Billie Dawn in *Born Yesterday* was dim-witted.

A New Yorker (real name Judith Tuvim), she started her career in *The Revuers,* the clever night-club act put together by the talented Adolph Green and Betty Compden. She was still practically unknown when she was rushed into *Born Yesterday,* a few days before its Broadway opening, to replace its ailing star, Jean Arthur.

Born Yesterday and Judy Holliday received ecstatic notices, and she was an overnight star.

As the dumb-blonde mistress of a millionaire junkman, who acquires culture-in-a-hurry under the tutelage of a young newspaperman, she kept full-house audiences in uproarious laughter. No one who heard her turn on her mouthy vulgar protector with such choice witticisms as "You're just not couth!" will ever forget her.

Yet when *Born Yesterday* was to be turned into a movie, Billie Dawn was offered to a number of other actresses with more screen name-value before landing back in Judy Holliday's capable hands. With her, were Broderick Crawford, as the man keeping her, and William Holden, as the supplier of culture.

She had been in three pictures before, only one of which—Katharine Hepburn-Spencer Tracy's *Adam's Rib*—offered her a part where she could show her comedic gifts. *Born Yesterday,* of course, gave her the scope she needed, and her

riotous repeat of her stage Billie Dawn was a critical and box-office triumph, besides gaining her an Oscar.

After five more comedies, which included the hilarious *The Solid Gold Cadillac,* with Paul Douglas, her co-star on Broadway in *Born Yesterday,* she returned to Gotham for another smash hit, *The Bells Are Ringing,* in 1956.

Four years later she made it into a film, with Dean Martin opposite her. But good as *The Bells* was, it did only so-so business at a time when musicals were not high on the list of what moviegoers wanted.

The Bells proved to be her last picture, and two years later, in 1962, she made her final stage appearance, in *Hot Spot,* which was only moderately successful.

Judy Holliday died in 1965, a victim of cancer at the age of 43.

Her other films after *Born Yesterday* were: *The Marrying Kind, It Should Happen to You, Phffft, Full of Life.*

OTHER NOMINEES:
ANNE BAXTER, All About Eve
BETTE DAVIS, All About Eve
ELEANOR PARKER, Caged
GLORIA SWANSON, Sunset Boulevard

1950
best supporting actor

George Sanders
ALL ABOUT EVE

Of the five *All About Eve* players in the Academy Awards race, only George Sanders, its cynical critic, came through with an Oscar. The Russian-born Sanders became an actor by accident. He was in the textile business in England when his rich singing voice, often raised at parties, brought him a stage offer. He accepted, became the most urbane of stage and screen English men, and wrote his autobiography, *Memoirs of a Professional Cad,* several years ago.

George Sanders committed suicide (an overdose of barbiturates) on April 25, 1972, in Spain, aged 65 (leaving a note – I am bored, I have lived enough).

OTHER NOMINEES:
JEFF CHANDLER, Broken Arrow
EDMUND GWENN, Mister 880
SAM JAFFE, The Asphalt Jungle
ERICH VON STROHEIM, Sunset Boulevard

best supporting actress

Josephine Hull
HARVEY

THOUGH she had been on the stage since the age of 19, Josephine Hull scored her two big Broadway hits— *Arsenic and Old Lace* and *Harvey*— late in life. When they were converted to film, she played her original role in each, and became an Oscar winner with *Harvey*. The daughter of Boston socialites, she was born in Newton, Massachusetts in 1884 and died in 1959.

OTHER NOMINEES:
HOPE EMERSON, Caged
CELESTE HOLM, All About Eve
NANCY OLSON, Sunset Boulevard
THELMA RITTER, All About Eve

1951
best picture
An American In Paris
M-G-M

CAST: Gene Kelly, Leslie Caron, Oscar Levant, Nina Foch, Georges Guetary
CREDITS: Producer, Arthur Freed; Director, Vincente Minnelli; Screenplay, Alan Jay Lerner; Choreography, Gene Kelly; Music by George Gershwin; Cinematographers, Alfred Kilks, John Alton. Technicolor

THE ACADEMY'S CHOICE of *An American in Paris* as the year's top film caused considerable dissatisfaction. The first musical to be named since *The Great Ziegfeld* in 1936, the picture was indeed short on plot, as charged. But it was just as long on entertainment.

It provided Gene Kelly with the chance to showcase his superb choreographic talents to the full, as well as to dance; Oscar Levant played Gershwin's *Concerto in F,* and Paris had never looked lovelier through the eyes of the Technicolor camera.

The slim story revolves around an ex-GI who doesn't go home with the rest of the boys, but lingers on in Paris to try his hand at painting. He falls for a young French girl while a wealthy American tries hard to take him under her wing.

Kelly was, of course, the happy-go-lucky ex-GI, and he hand-picked Leslie Caron, a 19-year-old pixie he saw two years before in the Ballet de Champs Elysee, to dance along with him. Their spectacular 20-minute ballet sequence to the George Gershwin suite that gave the picture its name was a movie mile-

Leslie Caron and Gene Kelly

stone—the longest dance number on film to that date.

An American was good for six Oscars; Arthur J. Freed, its producer, was honored with the Irving G. Thalberg Memorial Award and to Kelly himself went a special Oscar commemorating his multiple talents and "brilliant achievements" in the field of film choreography.

OTHER NOMINEES:
DECISION BEFORE DAWN, 20th Century-Fox
A PLACE IN THE SUN, Paramount
QUO VADIS, M-G-M
A STREETCAR NAMED DESIRE, Warner Bros.

1951
best actor
Humphrey Bogart
THE AFRICAN QUEEN

"BOGIE" died in 1957, but the Bogart legend has never stopped growing, and today's young people are as intrigued by his tough maleness with its leaven of tenderness as was the generation ahead of him.

Bogart was Oscar-honored for his free-wheeling, drunken skipper who, on a voyage down an African river, takes delight in shocking his only passenger, a disapproving woman missionary. He spruces up and starts minding his language as he falls for the lady and she for him.

Both Bogart and Katharine Hepburn, as the prim spinster who finds out what it means to be a woman in love, were quite wonderful, and *Queen* accounted for one of Hepburn's numerous Academy nominations.

Bogart came from wealthy, cultured surroundings, but had drifted aimlessly as a youth before hitting on the idea of becoming an actor. Making less than a sensation on Broadway, he came west, and caused no commotion in Hollywood, either. He made three minor films, then went back east in 1932.

Three years later, he was the talk of Broadway as the ruthless killer in *The Petrified Forest,* and when he repeated the role in the movie version a year later, it set the pattern for his future screen eminence.

His first Oscar nomination came with *Casablanca* in 1943, and 11 years later, in 1954, he received his third and final Oscar bid, for his psychotic Captain Queeg in *The Caine Mutiny.*

Bogart had four wives, and his last marriage to actress Lauren Bacall, many years his junior, was one of Hollywood's most publicized romances. It started with their first film together, Hemingway's *To Have and to Have Not.*

Bacall was a screen newcomer and her sexy, husky-voiced invitation, "If you want anything, just whistle," was the picture's most memorable moment. They also teamed up in *The Big Sleep* and *Key Largo.*

Their 12-year-marriage produced two children (his only offspring) and lasted until he died of cancer at the age of 57.

Other Bogart film classics: *The Maltese Falcon, Treasure of Sierra Madre, Knock on Any Door, Barefoot Contessa, The Desperate Hours.*

OTHER NOMINEES:
MARLON BRANDO, A Streetcar Named Desire
MONTGOMERY CLIFT, A Place in the Sun
ARTHUR KENNEDY, Bright Victory
FREDRIC MARCH, Death of a Salesman

1951
best actress
Vivien Leigh
A STREETCAR NAMED DESIRE

Vivien Leigh and Marlon Brando

IN HER FIRST Hollywood role since *Gone with the Wind,* Vivien Leigh was a Southern belle again. This time, there were no objections to her playing the tragic, aging heroine of Tennessee William's *A Streetcar Named Desire.* She had proved her right to Southern-bellehood more than a decade before, and she was in *Desire* on the London stage for many months.

As the fading Blanche du Bois of New Orleans, deliberately provoking the animal instincts of her lusty brother-in-law (Marlon Brando) to cover up her own sexual maladjustments, Vivien Leigh gave one of the great virtuoso performances of the screen.

Three years before, when Olivier brought home his *Hamlet* Oscar, they became the only Oscar-winning husband-wife team in Academy annals. Now it was a foregone conclusion that she would add still another Oscar to their household, and the predictions were right.

Vivien Leigh's bad health kept her inactive part of the time between her two Oscar-winning performances, and she made only four films in these 12 years. including the popular wartime tear-jerker, *Waterloo Bridge,* again with her *A Yank at Oxford* partner, Robert Taylor.

The same year she was Oscared for *Desire,* the Oliviers were seen on the New York stage in an interesting and successful pairing of Shakespeare's grim tragedy, *Antony and Cleopatra,* and George Bernard Shaw's comic *Caesar and*

Cleopatra, on alternating schedules.

In 1959, she appeared in Gotham without him, in *Duel of Angels,* and they were divorced in 1960. Three years later, New York saw her in her first musical, *Tovarich,* and loved her in it. She was 50 at the time.

She returned to Hollywood once more, this time for Stanley Kramer's all-star, 1965 production of *Ship of Fools,* based on Katherine Anne Porter's jumbo novel of a Germany-bound ship at the dawn of Nazism. One of its more memorable moments was Leigh's clobbering a drunken Lee Marvin, trying to paw her, with her shoe.

Two years later, Vivien Leigh passed away, at 54.

Her other post-1939 films were: *That Hamilton Woman, Caesar and Cleopatra, Anna Karinina, The Deep Blue Sea, The Roman Spring of Mrs. Stone.*

OTHER NOMINEES:
KATHARINE HEPBURN, The African Queen
ELEANOR PARKER, Detective Story
SHELLEY WINTERS, A Place in the Sun
JANE WYMAN, The Blue Veil

113

1951
best supporting actor

Karl Malden
A STREETCAR NAMED DESIRE

BIG, ROUGH-HEWN KARL MALDEN was first smitten with the dubious charms of *Streetcar Named Desire*'s tormented Blanche duBois in the Broadway production. He repeated the role on film, getting an Oscar for it. The Indiana-born actor, of Yugoslavian ancestry, was Oscar-nominated for a second time in 1954, for his waterfront priest in *On the Waterfront*.

OTHER NOMINEES:
LEO GENN, Quo Vadis
KEVIN McCARTHY, Death of a Salesman
PETER USTINOV, Quo Vadis
GIG YOUNG, Come Fill the Cup

best supporting actress

Kim Hunter
A STREETCAR NAMED DESIRE

As STELLA in the Broadway production of *A Streetcar Named Desire*, Kim Hunter won the stage's prestigeous Donaldson and New York Drama Critics awards. She followed them with an Oscar when she transferred Stella to the movies. The Detroit-born actress' many films include *Lilith* and *The Swimmer*. She had her most challenging role since *Streetcar* in *Planet of the Apes*, as the sympathetic chimpanzee-psychologist who comes to Charlton Heston's rescue.

OTHER NOMINEES:
JOAN BLONDELL, The Blue Veil
MILDRED DUNNOCK, Death of a Salesman
LEE GRANT, Detective Story
THELMA RITTER, The Mating Season

1952
best picture

The Greatest Show On Earth
CECIL B. DEMILLE-PARAMOUNT

CAST: Betty Hutton, Cornel Wilde, Charlton Heston, James Stewart, Dorothy Lamour, Gloria Grahame, Lyle Bettger, Henry Wilcoxon, Emmett Kelly
CREDITS: Producer-Director, Cecil B. DeMille; Screenplay, Fredric M. Frank, Theodore St. John, Barre Lydon, from a story by Fredric M. Frank, Theodore St. John, Frank Cavett; Cinematographers, George Barnes, J. Peverell Marlev W. Kelley. Technicolor

The Greatest Show on Earth had all the earmarks of a Cecil B. DeMille production. It was big, gaudy, flamboyant. It garnered no critical kudos, but it made beautiful music at the box office.

DeMille was 70 when the circus struck him as typical DeMille fare. With his usual thoroughness, he made a long and careful study of the Ringling Brothers-Barnum & Bailey Circus, at its home base, Sarasota, Florida, and on tour, before he was ready to let the cameras roll. Most of the picture was filmed either at Sarasota, or during actual circus performances in Philadelphia.

The story hardly mattered; the spectacular three-ring activities, complete with Ringling's most sensational acts, were what counted.

The story is triple-pronged. It concerns a financially troubled circus manager (Charlton Heston) whose top aerialist (Betty Hutton) is caught between her feelings for him and her sense of loyalty to another performer (Cornel Wilde) who was crippled in an accident. It is also the story of a clown (James Stewart) whose make-up disguises a man wanted by the police, and of a jealous elephant trainer (Lyle Bettger) and his flighty assistant (Gloria Grahame).

Ringling performers served as instructors for the Hollywood contingent. The great Emmett Kelly cued Stewart on the ways of the clown, and Betty Hutton spent months of painstaking practice on the high bar under the watchful eyes of Ringling's high-wire luminaries.

On Oscar night, Cecil B. DeMille's big circus pageant not only was crowned the year's top picture, but DeMille himself was the recipient of the coveted Irving G. Thalberg Memorial Award, honoring his long, distinguished career.

After the circus wreck, Charlton Heston is given first aid treatment.

OTHER NOMINEES:
HIGH NOON, UA
IVANHOE, M-G-M
MOULIN ROUGE, UA
THE QUIET MAN, Republic

115

1952
best actor

Gary Cooper
HIGH NOON

In 1952, Gary Cooper was able to place a second Oscar beside the one he already possessed for *Sergeant York.* The new win was for *High Noon,* which is one of the great Westerns of all time.

Cooper needed a hit at the moment. He was still in the superstar class, but he had not had a really smash success since *Saratoga Trunk* in 1946. In that, he was again paired with Ingrid Bergman, with whom he made the tremendously successful *For Whom the Bell Tolls.*

High Noon was short, as features go, a mere hour and a quarter, and its storyline was straight, simple and characteristically Western.

An ex-sheriff learns that a murderer he had sent up for life has been pardoned and is due in town at noon. Waiting are his three buddies. The four plan to kill the lawman, so he enlists the townspeople's help to eliminate them instead. As the time nears, one by one those who had pledged their help renege. He is alone as he goes to meet the killers and battle it out with blazing guns.

What emerged from that ordinary basic plot was a fascinating character study of a three-dimensional man who combined moral strength and physical courage with the fears and apprehensions common to all men.

Director Fred Zinnemann kept his story accelerating steadily in pace, and a single musical number with an insistent beat was repeated over and over to heighten the tension.

In her second screen appearance, as Cooper's young bride whose wedding day was so sorely troubled, was the 19-year-old beauty who later became Princess Grace of Monaco.

Cooper was to appear opposite much younger girls (Audrey Hepburn in *Love in the Afternoon;* Rita Hayworth in *They Came to Cordura*) as long as he lived. His last movie, *The Naked Edge,* with Deborah Kerr, was made shortly before he died.

On April 17, 1961, at the 1960 Academy Awards' presentation, James Stewart announced a special Oscar for Cooper, then revealed that "Coop" had less than a month to live.

Some other later Cooper films: *The Court-Marshal of Billy Mitchell, Friendly Persuasion, 10 North Frederick.*

OTHER NOMINEES:
MARLON BRANDO, Viva Zapata!
KIRK DOUGLAS, The Bad and the Beautiful
JOSE FERRER, Moulin Rouge
ALEC GUINNESS, The Lavender Hill Mob

1952
best actress
Shirley Booth
COME BACK, LITTLE SHEBA

SHIRLEY BOOTH was the recipient of a Tony Award, the New York Drama Critics' best actress citation and other stage honors as the heroine of Broadway's *Come Back, Little Sheba.* When she came out to Hollywood to transfer her poignant role to film, she added an Oscar to them.

Born in New York in 1907, Shirley Booth was on the stage at 18 and made her first big hit, in *Three Men on a Horse,* a decade later. She followed it up with *My Sister Eileen* and other top shows.

She was in her 40s when the lead in William Inge's stark anatomy of a bad marriage, *Come Back, Little Sheba,* came her way. She scored such an outstanding triumph that Hollywood beckoned her to repeat her blousy wife of a man seeking solace in the bottle because he had been forced to give up his ambitions and marry beneath him. The movie captured all the pathos of her stage performance, with Burt Lancaster opposite her as her frustrated spouse.

But Shirley Booth was neither young nor beautiful, and Hollywood could come up with few character parts to suit her talents. Her fifth and final movie was Thornton Wilder's *The Matchmaker,* which later became the basis for the musical, *Hello Dolly!*

As Dolly Levi, Booth was in her element, but the film failed at the box office, and she went back to New York, little dreaming that the turning point of her career was imminent.

Ignoring the pooh-poohing of friends and advisors who claimed the role was beneath her, she signed a five-year contract, in 1961, to play Hazel in the TV series of the same name. As a result, she added two Emmys to her collection of awards, her name became known in every hamlet in the nation, and *Hazel* is still plying her merry way via the profitable rerun circuit.

Shirley Booth's other films are: *About Mrs. Leslie, Main Street to Broadway* (guest spot), *Hot Spell.*

OTHER NOMINEES:
JOAN CRAWFORD, Sudden Fear
BETTE DAVIS, The Star
JULIE HARRIS, The Member of the Wedding
SUSAN HAYWARD, With a Song In My Heart

1952
best supporting actor

Anthony Quinn
VIVA ZAPATA!

WITH A TALENT as tall as his six-foot-three frame, Anthony Quinn has been everything from a North African sheik to a Filipino guerrilla and a bewildered Romanian peasant. It seems almost a happenstance, but most fitting, that the Mexican-born actor was to receive the first of his two Oscars as the brother of Mexico's great revolutionary hero in that magnificent biographical film, *Viva Zapata!*

OTHER NOMINEES:
RICHARD BURTON, My Cousin Rachel
ARTHUR HUNNICUTT, The Big Sky
VICTOR McLAGLEN, The Quiet Man
JACK PALANCE, Sudden Fear

best supporting actress

Gloria Grahame
THE BAD AND THE BEAUTIFUL

OSCARED for her Southern belle in *The Bad and the Beautiful*, Gloria Grahame was also in the Best Picture of 1952—*The Greatest Show on Earth*. She is a native of Southern California and was discovered in a student production at Hollywood High School. She made her movie debut in 1944, in *Blonde Fever*, has been on the Broadway stage and was in the *Sam Benedict* TV series. Her pictures include: *The Big Heat, Sudden Fear, Not as a Stranger, Oklahoma!*

OTHER NOMINEES:
JEAN HAGEN, Singin' in the Rain
COLETTE MARCHAND, Moulin Rouge
TERRY MOORE, Come Back, Little Sheba
THELMA RITTER, With a Song In My Heart

1953
best picture

From Here To Eternity
COLUMBIA

CAST: Burt Lancaster, Deborah Kerr, Montgomery Clift, Frank Sinatra, Donna Reed, Philip Ober, Ernest Borgnine, Jack Warden, Mickey Shaughnessy
CREDITS: Producer, Buddy Adler; Director, Fred Zinnemann; Screenplay, Daniel Taradash, from the novel by James Jones; Cinematographer, Burnett Guffey

HOLLYWOOD was aghast when Columbia's Harry Cohn announced he would make a movie of *From Here to Eternity*. James Jones's huge novel of military life in Hawaii just before the Japanese strike on Pearl Harbor was jam-packed with language and sex situations Hollywood usually didn't tackle.

Surprisingly, the picture turned out to be, not sensational junk, but sensationally good. It also had one of the most provocative casts in memory.

Here was that acme of ladylike behavior, Deborah Kerr, involved in some of the hottest scenes yet seen, as a captain's unhappy wife seeking solace in the arms of a tough sergeant (Burt Lancaster) with his own resentments against the Army. There was a non-singing Frank Sinatra dying a terrible, sadistic death in the stockade. Donna Reed, usually a namby-pamby good girl, turned in a sizzling performance as a bad one involved in an affair with Montgomery Clift, a young private clashing with the Army code in an endeavor to hang onto his own values.

The Japanese attack on Pearl Harbor ended the smaller, personal crises, but by the time it did, solid characterizations in a tough exposé of the tensions generated within ordinary human beings caught in the artificial, stultifying fraternity of a military barracks made fascinating viewing.

All five leads were Oscar nominees, and Sinatra and Donna Reed were Oscared. In all, the film accounted for eight of the coveted little statuettes given that year.

OTHER NOMINEES:
JULIUS CAESAR, M-G-M
THE ROBE, 20th Century-Fox
ROMAN HOLIDAY, Paramount
SHANE, Paramount

The beach scene with Deborah Kerr and Burt Lancaster

1953
best actor
William Holden
STALAG 17

WILLIAM HOLDEN won his Oscar for *Stalag 17,* an abrasive World War II comedy-drama in which he was a cynical sergeant not trusted by other internees planning a break.

But it is the concensus of opinion that his young gigolo-companion to Gloria Swanson's aging actress in *Sunset Boulevard* was much the finer performance. It brought him a nomination, but no Oscar.

Born in Illinois, big, good-looking Bill Holden grew up in Southern California and got into pictures with no sweat. A scout discovered him at the Pasadena Playhouse while he was still in college, and he became a star with his very first picture.

He was also quickly typed "nice boy," and he was just that in a flock of early films, made both before and after his three-year Army stretch.

It took *Sunset Boulevard* to break the pattern. From then on, from *Escape from Fort Bravo, The Moon Is Blue* and *The Bridge on the River Kwai* down to *Alvarez Kelly* and his very recent *The Devil's Brigade,* he has played meaty, instead of cardboard, characters.

A highly successful businessman, also, Holden's world-wide interests have been taking up more and more of his time in the last few years, keeping him on the go from the U.S. to Europe, Asia and Africa.

Now at the half-century mark in age and worth millions, Bill Holden can afford to be, and is, highly selective about the relatively few roles he does accept these days.

Some other Holden films: *Sabrina, The Bridges at Toko-Ri, Love Is a Many-Splendored Thing, The Proud and the Profane, The World of Suzie Wong, The Seventh Dawn, The Wild Bunch, The Wild Rovers.*

OTHER NOMINEES:
MARLON BRANDO, Julius Caesar
RICHARD BURTON, The Robe
MONTGOMERY CLIFT, From Here to Eternity
BURT LANCASTER, From Here to Eternity

1953
best actress
Audrey Hepburn
ROMAN HOLIDAY

AUDREY HEPBURN is one of a handful of deeply talented young actresses who were plucked out of nowhere to become overnight stars.

She had danced in the chorus of a few London musicals and been a bit player in a couple of English movies when she went on location to Monte Carlo for a minor film, at just the right moment. French writer Colette, whose novel, *Gigi,* was being turned into a play (non-musical), for Broadway, saw her. "There, I said to myself, is Gigi!" is the way Colette herself explained her reaction.

The inexperienced 22-year-old did so well in *Gigi* in Gotham that Hollywood sat up and took notice.

Gregory Peck and Audrey Hepburn.

The next thing she knew, she was being co-starred in *Roman Holiday* with one of the screen's top male stars, Gregory Peck.

As the runaway princess who goes on the town in the Italian capital with an American newspaperman, she captured an Oscar, and has been a major screen luminary from that moment on.

The biggest male stars have played opposite her—Henry Fonda, Burt Lancaster, Cary Grant, and Gary Cooper. She earned Oscar bids in 1954 for *Sabrina* (with Humphrey Bogart); in 1959 for *The Nun's Story,* and again in 1961 for *Breakfast at Tiffany's.* She lost out in 1964, for *My Fair Lady,* as gossip has it, because of the controversy that evolved over the part not being given to Julie Andrews, who had played it on the stage. Hepburn was back in the lineup of Oscar nominees in 1967, as the young, blind wife terrorized by hoods in *Wait Until Dark.*

The tall boyishly slim star, who repeatedly appears on the lists of the world's best-dressed women, was born in Brussels in 1929. She and her Dutch mother lived through the World War II Nazi occupation of Holland, and ballet-student Hepburn gave underground concerts to help raise money for the Dutch Resistance movement.

In 1968, she divorced actor-director Mel Ferrer, whom she married when they were both on Broadway in *Ondine.* She is now married to Dr. Andrea Dotti, a psychiatrist.

Other Hepburn films include: *Love in the Afternoon, The Children's Hour, Charade, Two for the Road.*

OTHER NOMINEES:
LESLIE CARON, Lili
AVA GARDNER, Mogambo
DEBORAH KERR, From Here to Eternity
MAGGIE McNAMARA, The Moon Is Blue

1953
best supporting actor

Frank Sinatra
FROM HERE TO ETERNITY

FEW WOULD have made book the night before Frank Sinatra won his Oscar that he'd be a national institution some 16 years later, at the age of 51. Sinatra's career seemingly peaked during the war years of the '40s, when his crooning sent the bobby-sox crowd into squealing frenzy. It was definitely on the skids when *From Here to Eternity* gave it an Oscar-boost. In recent years, Sinatra has specialized in tough lawmen in films such as *Tony Rome, Lady in Cement* and *The Detective*.

OTHER NOMINEES:
EDDIE ALBERT, Roman Holiday
BRANDON DE WILDE, Shane
JACK PALANCE, Shane
ROBERT STRAUSS, Stalag 17

best supporting actress

Donna Reed
FROM HERE TO ETERNITY

IOWA-BORN DONNA REED attended Los Angeles City College, prudently studying stenography as well as drama. In 1941, at 20, she made her first movie *(The Getaway)* and has never needed the stenography. Her Oscar came to her as Montgomery Clift's girlfriend in *From Here to Eternity.* Her popular TV series, *The Donna Reed Show,* went on in 1957 and lasted some ten years. Her pictures include: *Three Hours to Kill, The Last Time I Saw Paris, The Benny Goodman Story, Ransom!, Beyond Mombasa.*

OTHER NOMINEES:
GRACE KELLY, Mogambo
GERALDINE PAGE, Hondo
MARJORIE RAMBEAU, Torch Song
THELMA RITTER, Pickup on South Street

1954
best picture
On The Waterfront
COLUMBIA

CAST: Marlon Brando, Eva Marie Saint, Karl Malden, Lee J. Cobb, Rod Steiger, Pat Henning, Leif Erickson, Martin Balsam, James Westerfield, John Hamilton

CREDITS: Producer, Sam Spiegel; Director, Elia Kazan; Screenplay, Budd Schulberg; Cinematographer, Boris Kaufman

A LOW-BUDGET FILM, heavy with social significance, packed a tremendous wallop, cleaned up at the box office and was the 1954 Best Picture winner.

On the Waterfront was a rough, tough melodrama of corruption on the New York waterfront, and its semi-documentary form increased its savage impact.

Longshoreman Ted Malloy goes along unquestioningly with the shakedown and intimidation tactics of the waterfront boss until he realizes he was a tool in the murder of a fellow dock worker. Then, after much agonized soul-searching, he gets up the courage to take his story to the Crime Commission. From that point on, he is a marked pigeon.

His brother is killed in retaliation, his co-workers turn against him, and he himself is the victim of violence before he becomes the catalyst that finally frees the union from the corruption that holds its men in bondage.

If Marlon Brando had never done another thing worthwhile in films, his Ted Malloy would be enough to secure his place in the annals of Hollywood greats. He had received Oscar bids the three previous years; now the Oscar was his.

Eva Marie Saint, in her first film, accounted for another of the picture's eight Oscars. Rod Steiger, another new-to-films thespian, was nominated; so, too, were Lee J. Cobb and Karl Malden. Composer-conductor Leonard Bernstein also received a nomination, for his first movie score.

Karl Malden and Eva Marie Saint aid a badly beaten Marlon Brando.

OTHER NOMINEES:
THE CAINE MUTINY, Columbia
THE COUNTRY GIRL, Paramount
SEVEN BRIDES FOR SEVEN
   BROTHERS, M-G-M
THREE COINS IN THE FOUNTAIN,
   20th Century-Fox

123

1954
best actor

Marlon Brando
ON THE WATERFRONT

TO SOME, Marlon Brando is the screen's finest actor. Others feel he has not lived up to his potential. Still others complain he sounds as if he has marbles in his mouth.

The gray-eyed, heavy-set actor who evokes such a divergence of opinion got to tote an Oscar home on his fourth consecutive nomination—as the longshoreman in *On the Waterfront* who first goes along with the labor racketeers who infest the waterfront, then turns witness against them.

Brando's three previous Academy nods had been for *Streetcar Named Desire* (1951), *Viva Zapata!* (1952) and *Julius Caesar* (1953).

The Omaha-born young thespian, who'd taken a delight in shocking Hollywood with his sloppy dress and rude manners when he first came to town, is a born rebel. He was expelled from the military academy where his folks had sent him to be toned down, then drifted to New York. One of his two sisters was go-ing to dramatic school there, so he decided to acquire some dramatic training, too. He went on the stage at 19, as one of the sons in *I Remember Mama*. Four years later, as the brutal Stanley Kowalski in *Streetcar Named Desire,* Brando was the sensation of Broadway.

His movie Kowalski was just as electrifying, but the acting honors for *Desire* went, not to Brando, but to Vivien Leigh, Karl Malden, and Kim Hunter. He received a fifth Academy nod in 1957, for *Sayonara*.

The actor who once quipped that he didn't care for Hollywood but "didn't have the moral fiber to turn down all that money," won the much-sought-after title role in the film version of *The Godfather*. Between pictures, Brando retreats to his home on the South Seas island where he made *Mutiny on the Bounty*.

Brando's films include: *Teahouse of the August Moon, The Ugly American, The Chase, Morituri, The Appaloosa, The Countess from Hong Kong, Reflections in a Golden Eye, The Night of the Following Day.*

OTHER NOMINEES:
HUMPHREY BOGART, The Caine Mutiny
BING CROSBY, The Country Girl
JAMES MASON, A Star Is Born
DAN O'HERLIHY, Adventures of Robinson Crusoe

1954
best actress

Grace Kelly
THE COUNTRY GIRL

SHE IS A COOL BEAUTY who was born into great wealth and had the air of a princess long before she acquired the title.

Grace Kelly's father was a multi-millionaire industrialist and politician, but the theatre was also part of her background. The eminent playwright, George Kelly (*Craig's Wife*, *The Show-Off*) was her uncle.

Instead of taking the society route, Grace Kelly went to New York, attended the American Academy of Dramatic Arts, became a top model for a while, and made her Hollywood debut at the age of 22, in 1951. The picture was a forgettable little something named *14 Hours*. Her next film was one of the unforgettable greats of filmdom —*High Noon*—but its focus was entirely on Gary Cooper.

With her third picture, *Mogambo,* the Academy took notice of her adulterous wife with a nomination, and the Oscar itself came her way with her next film, Clifford Odets' *The Country Girl*. As its bitter, aging wife of a slipping actor, she hid her beauty behind big horn-rimmed glasses and a shapeless, well-worn sweater. She also achieved a depth of characterization she had never shown before.

Her association with Alfred Hitchcock was to prove the most significant factor in her life. She had already made two Hitchcock thrillers—*Dial M for Murder* and *Rear Window*—when she went on location to Monaco for still another Hitchcock suspense film, *To Catch a Thief,* with Cary Grant. While there, she met Monaco's handsome Prince Rainier. Two years later, on a spring day in 1956, they were married amid all the trappings of royal splendor, and they now have three children.

In 1962, there was talk of her doing another film for Hitchcock, but the citizens of her tiny principality took umbrage at the idea. They had no objection, however, to her being the narrator on TV's *A Tour of Monaco* the same year.

Grace Kelly's entire career encompassed just 11 pictures, the others being: *The Bridges of Toko-Ri, Green Fire, The Swan, High Society.*

OTHER NOMINEES:
DOROTHY DANDRIDGE, Carmen Jones
JUDY GARLAND, A Star Is Born
AUDREY HEPBURN, Sabrina
JANE WYMAN, The Magnificent Obsession

1954
best supporting actor

Edmond O'Brien
THE BAREFOOT CONTESSA

THE PRIZED OSCAR came Edmond O'Brien's way for his loud-mouthed press agent in *The Barefoot Contessa*. Born in New York in 1915, O'Brien started in summer stock, became a Broadway actor and made his movie debut in the original *Hunchback of Notre Dame*, in 1939. His most recent pictures are *Birdman of Alcatraz, Rio Conchos, Seven Days in May, The Fantastic Voyage, The Wild Bunch*.

OTHER NOMINEES:
LEE J. COBB, On the Waterfront
KARL MALDEN, On the Waterfront
ROD STEIGER, On the Waterfront
TOM TULLY, The Caine Mutiny

best supporting actress

Eva Marie Saint
ON THE WATERFRONT

A VERY pregnant Eva Marie Saint came up for the Oscar she was awarded for her first film, *On the Waterfront*, and she brought a wave of laughter as she gasped, "I may have the baby right here!" In the 13 years since that night, she has added another baby to her household and less than a dozen more films. Some recent ones: *The Stalking Moon, Loving*.

OTHER NOMINEES:
NINA FOCH, Executive Suite
KATY JURADO, Broken Lance
JAN STERLING, The High and The Mighty
CLAIRE TREVOR, The High and The Mighty

1955
best picture

Marty
UNITED ARTISTS

CAST: Ernest Borgnine, Betsy Blair, Esther Minciotti, Augusta Ciolli, Karen Steele, Joe Mantell, Jerry Paris, Frank Sutton
CREDITS: Producer, Harold Hecht; Director, Delbert Mann; Screenplay, Paddy Chayefsky, from his television play; Cinematographer, Joseph LaShelle

WITH *Marty*, Oscar proved his eyes aren't so focused on big-budget films with name stars that he can't recognize excellence in a "small" film minus a single star name.

Marty was somewhat of a screen phenomenon even before the Academy tagged it the year's best. It was made from a television play that had already been seen by millions. It cost less than $350,000 to make. It was about ordinary people such as you rub elbows with every day, and its two toplined players had absolutely no marquee value.

The actor chosen was Ernest Borgnine, who had been a reliable film villain, usually in B pictures, for years; the other was Betsy Blair, whom Hollywood knew better as Mrs. Gene Kelly.

Marty first walked off with the Cannes film Festival best picture designation, and garnered numerous other honors, including the New York Film Critics citation as the best of the year, before winning the top accolade of them all—the Oscar.

Marty was the story of two sensitive, physically unattractive people: a 35-year-old butcher whose Italian family keeps nagging him to get married, and the plain-looking, little schoolteacher he runs into by chance when her date fails to show. After they meet the picture proceeds to reveal how these two lonely, frustrated people diffidently grope their way to love.

Marty not only cleaned up at the box office and brought Borgnine to the fore, but it is still the "smallest" picture ever to win an Oscar.

OTHER NOMINEES:
LOVE IS A MANY-SPLENDORED THING,
   20th Century-Fox
MISTER ROBERTS, Warner Bros.
PICNIC, Columbia
THE ROSE TATTOO, Paramount

Ernest Borgnine and "mother" Esther Minciotti

1955
best actor
Ernest Borgnine
MARTY

ERNEST BORGNINE had been a far-out-from-left-field choice to play Marty, his entry into Oscar's exclusive circle.

Born in Connecticut of Italian parentage, Borgnine was a skinny, 134-pound truck driver when he decided to enlist in the Navy in 1935. He was unhitched ten years later, after serving through World War II, a hefty 215-pounder without a trade.

At his mother's suggestion, he decided to study acting under the G.I. Bill, and after some slim experience on the stage that included a part in Helen Hayes' *Mrs. McThing,* and some TV appearances, the young actor decided to go west.

Hollywood kept him fairly busy, but the parts were small, the pictures inconsequential, and he was, without exception, the villain. As the sadistic Fatso in *From Here to Eternity,* he received his first real notice.

But Fatso and Marty were moons apart and Borgnine only got the chance to read for the part because Rod Steiger who played it on TV originally, was not available. By the time the reading was over, author Paddy Chayefsky and director Delbert Mann had found their man.

Borgnine's Marty was a study in inarticulate sensitivity, as the lonely bachelor and his feminine counterpart (Betsy Blair) fumbled their way into romance.

His performance took Borgnine out of the deep-dyed villain class, his paycheck fattened, but the pic-tures he got did little to help build a following.

Then, in 1962, the TV series *McHale's Navy* came along, and ex-star Borgnine, promoted to Commander Quinton McHale, took off on a long, very successful voyage, with stopovers for such fine films as *The Dirty Dozen.*

Other recent Borgnine films: *McHale's Navy* (movie version), *Flight of the Phoenix, Ice Station Zebra, The Wild Bunch, The Adventurers.*

OTHER NOMINEES:
JAMES CAGNEY, Love Me or Leave Me
JAMES DEAN, East of Eden
FRANK SINATRA, The Man With the Golden Arm
SPENCER TRACY, Bad Day at Black Rock

1955
best actress

Anna Magnani
THE ROSE TATTOO

IN 1946, art house patrons in the U.S. were electrified by a picture called *Open City* and an actress in it. The actress, Anna Magnani, the picture—a rawly powerful story of wartime Rome—and the director, Rossellini, were all Italian and previously unknown to Americans.

The picture became one of the biggest hits on the art-house circuit, and its earthy heroine exploded into instant stardom. She tore across a screen with a fire and a fury unknown on the American screen.

Among her many admirers was Tennessee Williams, and he wrote a stage play for her, *The Rose Tattoo*. Magnani was a stage veteran in Italy

and had appeared in Italian versions of such popular American plays as *The Petrified Forest* and *Anna Christie*. But she was hesitant to try Broadway, fearing her English wasn't up to the task.

In 1955, she did agree to do the movie. Her English proved adequate and, as the Sicilian-born seamstress who shuts herself up in her own neurotic, grieving world when her husband dies, then emerges with a vengeance when she becomes enamored of a simple-minded truck-driver (Burt Lancaster), her portrayal was frenzied, yet believable. She was a screaming, object-throwing virago one moment, a deeply loving woman, the next, and she won both the Oscar and the New York Film Critics "best actress" citation for it.

When her name was called out as the Oscar winner, Magnani herself was asleep in Rome. The reporter who awakened her with the news had a hard time convincing her that he wasn't joking.

But the actress who was born in the slums of Rome in 1908 and got her start as a singer in some of its rougher cafes, was among those the Oscar did not prove the Open Sesame it normally does.

Wild Is The Wind, made in 1957, proved only fair at the box office, and 1960's *The Fugitive Kind* was a failure, despite its cast of three Oscar winners—Magnani, Joanne Woodward, and Marlon Brando.

Magnani felt it was time to pack up and go home to Italy. *The Secret of Santa Vittoria* is her first film in English in years.

Some Magnani Italian-language films: *Ways of Love, Bellissima, Awakening.*

Anna Magnani died September 27, 1973 in her native Italy.

OTHER NOMINEES:
SUSAN HAYWARD, I'll Cry Tomorrow
KATHARINE HEPBURN, Summertime
JENNIFER JONES, Love is a Many-Splendored Thing
ELEANOR PARKER, Interrupted Melody

129

1955
best supporting actor

Jack Lemmon
MISTER ROBERTS

SINCE JACK LEMMON won his Oscar in the "supporting" category, as a young officer in *Mr. Roberts,* he has become a major star. He has also earned three Academy nominations in the Best Actor division for *Some Like It Hot, The Apartment, Days of Wine and Roses.* In the last few years, Lemmon has concentrated on comedies: *The Fortune Cookie, The Great Race, The Odd Couple, The Out-of-Towners.*

OTHER NOMINEES:
ARTHUR KENNEDY, Trial
JOE MANTELL, Marty
SAL MINEO, Rebel Without a Cause
ARTHUR O'CONNELL, Picnic

best supporting actress

Jo Van Fleet
EAST OF EDEN

JO VAN FLEET was a movie neophyte when she caught the Academy's eye. But behind her expert handling of a difficult role in *East of Eden*—a madam who comes back into the lives of the family she deserted, with tragic consequences—was years of stage training and success. Now chiefly a housewife, she still accepts an occasional part, such as Paul Newman's mother in *Cool Hand Luke,* if it attracts her enough.

OTHER NOMINEES:
BETSY BLAIR, Marty
PEGGY LEE, Pete Kelly's Blues
MARISA PAVAN, The Rose Tattoo
NATALIE WOOD, Rebel Without a Cause

1956
best picture
Around the World In 80 Days
TODD-UNITED ARTISTS

CAST: David Niven, Cantinflas, Robert Newton, Shirley MacLaine, "Cameo" stars: Charles Boyer, Joe E. Brown, Ronald Colman, Noel Coward, Marlene Dietrich, Hermione Gingold, Jose Greco, Cedric Hardwicke, Trevor Howard, Glynis Johns, Beatrice Lillie, Victor McLaglen, John Mills, Robert Morley, Cesar Romero, Frank Sinatra, Red Skelton
CREDITS: Producer, Michael Todd; Director, Michael Anderson; Screenplay, James Poe, John Farrow, S. J. Perelman, from the novel by Jules Verne; Cinematographer, Lionel Lindon. Technicolor

Cantinflas and his boss, David Niven, enjoy the good life aloft.

WITH *Around the World in 80 Days,* showman Mike Todd made a splashy entrance into movie-making, but died in a plane crash before he could follow it up.

The Jules Verne classic was made in Todd-AO, a new, simplified wide-screen process, and was shot simultaneously in Cinemascope, for theatres unable to handle Todd-AO.

David Niven was Phileas Fogg, the very proper 19th century Britisher who bets he can circle the globe within 80 days precisely—an unheard of feat in those pre-aviation days. He makes his mad dash by balloon, train, boat, stagecoach, rickshaw, even elephant and ostrich.

Accompanying him is his nimble-witted valet, Passepartout (Mexican comic Cantinflas made his American film debut in the role). Somewhere along the line, an Indian princess (Shirley MacLaine) gets into the act, and hot on their trail is a detective (Robert Newton) suffering from the delusion that Fogg-Niven is a bank robber in flight.

The fast-talking Todd inveigled an astounding number of big-name stars into doing walk-on bits. Charles Boyer, Ronald Colman, Marlene Dietrich, Hermione Gingold, Beatrice Lillie, John Mills and Frank Sinatra are just some of the personalities who put in fleeting appearances.

An eye-boggling Technicolor travelogue as well as tremendous fun, *Around the World's* spectacular photography accounted for one of the film's five Oscars.

The picture came out when Hollywood was in a state of acute TV jitters, and it proved people will flock to movie houses instead of hug the small screen, if the theatrical film-fare is enough to their liking. Box-office business was so brisk, the film is now being reissued.

OTHER NOMINEES:
FRIENDLY PERSUASION, Allied Artists
GIANT, Warner Bros.
THE KING AND I, 20th Century-Fox
THE TEN COMMANDMENTS, Paramount

1956
best actor
Yul Brynner
THE KING AND I

As THE Siamese ruler who wanted to be a modern monarch yet retain his ancient privileges, Yul Brynner —bald-pated, bare-chested, exuding magnetic sex appeal and arrogance —came on screen with dynamic impact in *The King and I*.

It was inevitable that the Academy should dub him Best Actor for that virtuoso performance. The picture itself, and Deborah Kerr, as its English governness to the King's children, also won nominations.

Brynner had been seen in two other fine performances that year, in

Anastasia and *The Ten Commandments*. Before then, his only other movie had been a minor gangster film some seven years earlier, in which he had hair.

The star who found self-imposed baldness such an asset has told more than one story about his origins, the most frequent being that he was born on Sakhalin Island, off the coast of Siberia, in July, 1920, of a mixed marriage.

A circus acrobat before going on the stage in Paris after a fall from the high trapeze ended his circus days at the age of 19, the exotic-looking Brynner came to the U.S. in 1941 with a small Parisian repertory theatre.

During the war years, he put his fluent French and Russian to work for the Office of War Information's Voice of America.

After a post-war appearance in 1945 on Broadway, with Mary Martin in *Lute Song,* Brynner went into TV, as an actor at first, then a director.

He was happily helming CBS's *Danger* and *Studio One,* when he was lured back to Broadway to co-star with the late, great Gertrude Lawrence in the Rodgers-Hammerstein musical, *The King and I,* for a three-year run.

Much concerned about the welfare of his fellow man, Brynner devotes much of his time to the U.N. World Organization in his capacity as a Special Consultant, a volunteer job that takes him all over the world.

His screen credits include: *The Sound and the Fury, The Magnificent Seven, Morituri, Cast a Giant Shadow, The Double Man, Triple Cross, The Madwoman of Chaillot.*

OTHER NOMINEES:
JAMES DEAN, Giant
KIRK DOUGLAS, Lust For Life
ROCK HUDSON, Giant
SIR LAURENCE OLIVIER, Richard III

1956
best actress
Ingrid Bergman
ANASTASIA

By 1956, the headline-making scandal between *Stromboli*'s star and its married director that had toppled her off her pedestal was eight years in the past. She was Rossellini's wife and there were three little Rossellinis.

It was time to test whether the American public was ready to forgive and forget. It was. It hailed Ingrid Bergman in the made-abroad *Anastasia* with open arms, and was pleased that she was Oscared for her role as the girl who claimed to be the daughter of the last Czar of Russia.

Bergman herself was delighted, but she didn't venture to put in an appearance at the Academy Awards ceremony. She had intended to listen to the Oscarcast over the radio in Paris, but was so nervous she had to take sedatives. They put her to sleep so she missed all the excitement of her winning.

Bergman—divorced from Rossellini by now and married to Swedish theatrical producer Lars Schmidt—didn't set foot on American soil again until 1967. When she came, it was not for a picture, but to play in an unproduced Eugene O'Neill drama, *More Stately Mansions*. She scored a hit in it, both in Los Angeles and then in New York. Finally, after making a number of pictures abroad for U.S. companies, she was in Hollywood's *Cactus Flower* and *A Walk in the Spring Rain*.

How much that meant to the actress, still a great beauty in her 50s, can be gauged by her statement, "I'd like to act until I am a hundred, and I'd like my tombstone to read: 'She acted until the last day of her life. Here lies a good actress'."

Some post-1956 Bergman films: *The Inn of the Sixth Happiness, Indiscreet, The Visit, The Yellow Rolls Royce.*

OTHER NOMINEES:
CARROLL BAKER, Baby Doll
KATHARINE HEPBURN, The Rainmaker
NANCY KELLY, The Bad Seed
DEBORAH KERR, The King and I

1956
best supporting actor

Anthony Quinn
LUST FOR LIFE

'TONY QUINN never judges a role by its size, only by its challenge. He found that challenge in the relatively small part of Van Gogh's friend, the famed painter Gaughin. Quinn was in just one segment of *Lust for Life*, but no one who saw him will ever forget his vitality and overflowing love of life. Nominated twice since for Best Actor—*Wild Is the Wind, Zorba the Greek* — Quinn, now in his 50s, is still one of the screen's most virile actors and vivid personalities.

OTHER NOMINEES:
DON MURRAY, Bus Stop
ANTHONY PERKINS, Friendly Persuasion
MICKEY ROONEY, The Bold and the Brave
ROBERT STACK, Written on the Wind

best supporting actress

Dorothy Malone
WRITTEN ON THE WIND

DOROTHY MALONE, who collected an Oscar as the spoiled rich girl in *Written on the Wind,* began her career in 1946, in *The Big Sleep,* after a talent scout spotted her in a college production. Except for time out to stage a dramatic battle with a near-fatal illness, the beautiful, willowy blonde from Texas was Constance on TV's *Peyton Place* from the start of the series until the role was dropped after the 1967-1968 season. Some of her pictures are: *Too Much, Too Soon; The Last Voyage, Tarnished Angels.*

OTHER NOMINEES:
MILDRED DUNNOCK, Baby Doll
EILEEN HECKART, The Bad Seed
MERCEDES McCAMBRIDGE, Giant
PATTY McCORMACK, The Bad Seed

1957
best picture

The Bridge On The River Kwai
COLUMBIA

CAST: William Holden, Alec Guinness, Jack Hawkins, Sessue Hayakawa, James Donald, Andre Morrel, Geoffrey Horne
CREDITS: Producer, Sam Spiegel; Director, David Lean; Screenplay, Pierre Boulle, from his novel; Cinematographer, Jack Hildyard. Technicolor

Geoffrey Horne, Jack Hawkins and William Holden find the jungle rough going.

SOME EIGHT OSCARS went to *Bridge on the River Kwai,* including the Best Picture, Best Actor and Best Director Awards. It has grossed more than $20,000,000, and ABC-TV paid a record-breaking $2,000,000 for a two-time network showing.

The picture that garnered these honors and proved a box-office blockbuster was one of the grimmest indictments of war ever filmed. Set in a Japanese prisoner-of-war camp deep in an Asian jungle, *Kwai*'s conflict was between two men who represent the military mind at its most rigid—Colonel Nicholson (Alec Guinness), the stiff-necked, strictly-by-the-book commander of a troop of captured British soldiers,

Though enemies, Sessue Hayakawa and Alec Guinness are curiously alike.

and his Japanese counterpart (Sessue Hayakawa), commandant of the POW camp.

The struggle between them comes to a climax when Nicholson agrees to build a railroad to prove his men's superiority over their captors. He puts so much of himself into the construction, he finally loses sight of the fact that his bridge will benefit the enemy, and when he spots a troop of British saboteurs, his half-mad effort to prevent the bridge's destruction precipitates pure carnage. By the time the bridge has been destroyed, every one of the film's principals has also been annihilated.

One by-product of the picture—which was made in the steaming Ceylon jungle—was to make William Holden a millionaire. Though the picture focuses on Guinness, Holden's name value was such that he could demand top billing. But for it, he took a relatively small salary plus a percentage of the profits.

OTHER NOMINEES:
PEYTON PLACE, 20th Century-Fox
SAYONARA, Warner Bros.
TWELVE ANGRY MEN, UA
WITNESS FOR THE PROSECUTION, UA

1957
best actor

Alec Guinness
THE BRIDGE ON THE RIVER KWAI

UNTIL *Bridge on the River Kwai,* Alec Guinness's American following was limited to patrons of the small art houses. They became an appreciative cult of his wonderful sense of comedy in such chucklesome British films as *Kind Hearts and Coronets, The Lavender Hill Mob, The Man in the White Suit* and *Captain's Paradise.*

With his Colonel Nicholson, in which he peeled away, layer by layer, the mind and makeup of the complete military man, Guinness not only won an Oscar, but became an international screen favorite.

Before *Kwai,* he made one just moderately successful Hollywood picture, *The Swan,* with Grace Kelly. Now the tall, reserved Londoner was eagerly wooed for such blockbusters as *Lawrence of Arabia* and *Dr. Zhivago. Lawrence* won an Oscar, *Zhivago* an Oscar nomination.

Guinness himself had been nominated once before *Kwai,* for *The Lavender Hill Mob.*

Knighted by Queen Elizabeth in 1958, in appreciation of his talents, Guinness was told repeatedly that he "had no talent" in the days when he was struggling to gain a foothold in the theatre. Guinness had enough faith in himself not to quit and return to his former job as an advertising copywriter. But he came close to starving before he made his mark on the British stage, Broadway and in the movies.

Some recent Guinness films: *Tunes of Glory, A Majority of One, Fall of the Roman Empire, Situation Hopeless, but Not Serious, Hotel Paradiso, The Comedians, Cromwell.*

OTHER NOMINEES:
MARLON BRANDO, Sayonara
ANTHONY FRANCIOSA, A Hatful of Rain
CHARLES LAUGHTON, Witness for the Prosecution
ANTHONY QUINN, Wild is the Wind

1957
best actress

Joanne Woodward
THE THREE FACES OF EVE

JOANNE WOODWARD was just 23 and had made only two movies when she was handed one of the most difficult roles ever given a young actress— the psychotic heroine in *Three Faces of Eve.*

The movie's basis was a medically authenticated case of split personality, and Joanne Woodward, as its plagued heroine, proved equal to the demands of being three highly different personalities dwelling in one body.

Nevertheless, the picture did only modest business at the box office until the Academy saw fit to acknowledge the young actress's tour-de-force performance with an Oscar. After that, the receipts boomed gratifyingly, and Woodward's stock went up accordingly.

The Georgia-born blonde had wanted to be an actress as long as she could remember, and she finally broke down her family's opposition after being fired from a secretarial job.

She landed in that mecca of the stage-struck, New York; studied at the Neighborhood Playhouse and the Actor's Studio, and made her Broadway debut as an understudy in *Picnic,* then went into *The Lovers.*

Those were the days when TV emanated out of New York and the young actress with the undeniable spark appeared in some 100 live TV shows. A 20th Century-Fox scout caught her on TV, and she was invited to Hollywood.

Her early days in the film capital were not the happiest. She was not a conventional Hollywood beauty, and she had the independence to turn down the roles she didn't want, even if she didn't get those she did. *Eve* changed all that.

Since marrying Paul Newman in 1958, she has teamed with him most of the time. Some exceptions were *The Fugitive Kind,* with Marlon Brando, *A Big Hand for the Little Lady,* with Henry Fonda, and *They Might Be Giants,* with George C. Scott.

Once tabbed a "Plain Jane," her first "glamour" part was in *From the Terrace* (1960). *The Stripper* (1963) saw her in a role meant for Marilyn Monroe. But she won her second Oscar bid as the love-hungry, spinster-schoolteacher in *Rachel, Rachel,* which marked Newman's debut as a director.

Some Woodward-Newman films: *The Long, Hot Summer, Rally Round the Flag, Boys, A New Kind of Love, Winning.*

OTHER NOMINEES:
DEBORAH KERR, Heaven Knows, Mr. Allison
ANNA MAGNANI, Wild is the Wind
ELIZABETH TAYLOR, Raintree County
LANA TURNER, Peyton Place

137

1957
best supporting actor and actress

Red Buttons
SAYONARA

In *Sayonara,* as Sgt. Joe Kelly of the American Army of Occupation in Japan, Red Buttons chose to die with his Japanese wife, rather than leave her behind when the Army pulls out. He brought a tear to the eyes and was rewarded with an Oscar. Born in New York in 1919, Red Buttons acquired that name as a singing bellboy. He is a "graduate" of Minsky's Burlesque and was TV's Mr. Ho, Ho, Ho. His most recent films are *Stagecoach* and *They Shoot Horses, Don't They?*

OTHER NOMINEES:
VITTORIO DE SICA, A Farewell to Arms
SESSUE HAYAKAWA, The Bridge on the River Kwai
ARTHUR KENNEDY, Peyton Place
RUSS TAMBLYN, Peyton Place

Miyoshi Umeki
SAYONARA

The pert Japanese whose Oscar-winning role in *Sayonara* was her American movie debut was just 22 at the time, and an established radio, TV and movie star in her homeland. On a visit to the U.S., she had the chance to appear on the *Arthur Godfrey Show* on TV, and this led, in turn, to *Sayonara.* Since then, she's been in *Cry for Happy* and *Flower Drum Song.* Now married to an American TV producer, she hopes to "play a bad girl someday, just for a change."

OTHER NOMINEES:
CAROLYN JONES, The Bachelor Party
ELSA LANCHESTER, Witness for the Prosecution
HOPE LANGE, Peyton Place
DIANE VARSI, Peyton Place

Miyoshi Umeki makes Red Buttons a loving wife.

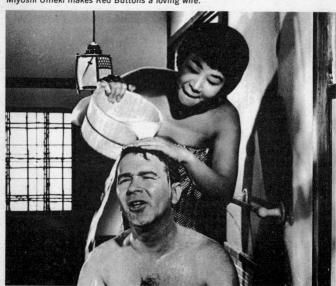

1948-57
oscar winners
in other categories

1948

DIRECTOR
JOHN HUSTON, Treasure Of
Sierra Madre

WRITING
THE SEARCH, Richard Schweizer,
David Wechsler
(Motion Picture Story)
TREASURE OF SIERRA MADRE,
John Huston (Screenplay)

CINEMATOGRAPHY
THE NAKED CITY, William Daniels
(Black and White)
JOAN OF ARC, Joseph Valentine,
William V. Skall, Winton Hoch
(Color)

ART DIRECTION-SET DECORATION
HAMLET, Roger K. Furse; Carmen
Dillon (Black and White)
THE RED SHOES, Hein Heckroth
Arthur Lawson (Color)

SOUND RECORDING
THE SNAKE PIT,
20th Century-Fox Sound Dept.

SHORT SUBJECTS
THE LITTLE ORPHAN,
M-G-M (Cartoons)
SYMPHONY OF A CITY,
20th Century-Fox (One-reel)
SEAL ISLAND, Walt Disney,
RKO Radio (Two-reel)

DOCUMENTARY
TOWARD INDEPENDENCE,
U.S. Army (Short Subjects)
THE SECRET LAND, U.S. Navy,
M-G-M (Features)

MUSIC
BUTTONS AND BOWS (The Paleface)
Jay Livingston, Ray Evans (Song)
THE RED SHOES, Brian Easdale
(Scoring of a Dramatic or
Comedy Picture)
EASTER PARADE, Johnny Green,
Roger Edens (Scoring of a
Musical Picture)

FILM EDITING
THE NAKED CITY, Paul Weatherwax
SPECIAL EFFECTS
PORTRAIT OF JENNIE, Paul Eagler,
J. McMillan Johnson, Russell
Shearman, Clarence Slifer,
Charles Freeman, James G. Stewart

COSTUME DESIGN
HAMLET, Roger K. Furse
(Black and White)
JOAN OF ARC, Dorothy Jeakins,
Karinska (Color)

**IRVING G. THALBERG
MEMORIAL AWARD**
Jerry Wald

HONORARY AND OTHER AWARDS
MONSIEUR VINCENT (French)—
voted by the Academy Board of
Governors as the most outstanding
foreign language film released
in the United States during
1948. (statuette)

IVAN JANDL, for the outstanding
juvenile performance of 1948 in
"The Search."
(miniature statuette)
SID GRAUMAN, master showman,
who raised the standard of
exhibition of motion pictures.
(statuette)
ADOLPH ZUKOR, a man who has
been called the father of the
feature film in America, for his
services to the industry over a
period of forty years. (statuette)
WALTER WANGER, for distinguished
service to the industry in adding
to its moral stature in the world
community by his production
of the picture "Joan Of Arc."
(statuette)

SCIENTIFIC OR TECHNICAL

CLASS II
VICTOR CACCIALANZA, MAURICE
AYERS and PARAMOUNT STUDIO
SET CONSTRUCTION DEPT.
NICK KALTEN, LOUIS J. WITTI
and 20TH CENTURY-FOX STUDIO
MECHANICAL EFFECTS DEPT.

CLASS III
MARTY MARTIN, JACK LANNON,
RUSSELL SHEARMAN and
RKO RADIO STUDIO
SPECIAL EFFECTS DEPT.
A. J. MORAN and WARNER BROS.
STUDIO ELECTRICAL DEPT.

1949

DIRECTOR
JOSEPH L. MANKIEWICZ,
A Letter To Three Wives

WRITING
THE STRATTON STORY, Douglas
Morrow (Motion Picture Story)
A LETTER TO THREE WIVES, Joseph
L. Mankiewicz (Screenplay)
BATTLEGROUND, Robert Pirosh
(Story and Screenplay)

CINEMATOGRAPHY
BATTLEGROUND, Paul C. Vogel
(Black and White)
SHE WORE A YELLOW RIBBON,
Winton Hoch (Color)

ART DIRECTION-SET DECORATION
THE HEIRESS, John Meehan,
Harry Horner; Emile Kuri
(Black and White)
LITTLE WOMEN, Cedric Gibbons,
Paul Groesse; Edwin B. Willis,
Jack D. Moore (Color)

SOUND RECORDING
TWELVE O'CLOCK HIGH,
20th Century-Fox Sound Dept.

SHORT SUBJECTS
FOR SCENT-IMENTAL REASONS,
Warner Bros. (Cartoons)
AQUATIC HOUSE-PARTY,
Paramount (One-reel)
VAN GOGH, Canton-Weiner
(Two-reel)

DOCUMENTARY
A CHANCE TO LIVE,
20th Century-Fox (Short Subjects)
SO MUCH FOR SO LITTLE,
Warner Bros. Cartoons, Inc.
(Short Subjects)
DAYBREAK IN UDI, British
Information Services (Features)

MUSIC
BABY, IT'S COLD OUTSIDE,
(Neptune's Daughter) Frank
Loesser (Song)
THE HEIRESS, Aaron Copland
(Scoring of a Dramatic or
Comedy Picture)
ON THE TOWN, Roger Edens,
Lennie Hayton (Scoring of a
Musical Picture)

FILM EDITING
CHAMPION, Harry Gerstad

SPECIAL EFFECTS
MIGHTY JOE YOUNG,
ARKO, RKO Radio

COSTUME DESIGN
THE HEIRESS, Edith Head,
Gile Steele (Black and White)
ADVENTURES OF DON JUAN, Leah
Rhodes, Travilla, Marjorie Best
(Color)

HONORARY AND OTHER AWARDS
THE BICYCLE THIEF (Italian)—
voted by the Academy Board of
Governors as the most outstanding
foreign language film released in
the United States during 1949.
(statuette)
BOBBY DRISCOLL, as the
outstanding juvenile actor of
1949. (miniature statuette)
FRED ASTAIRE for his unique
artistry and his contributions to
the technique of musical pictures.
(statuette)
CECIL B. DEMILLE, distinguished
motion picture pioneer, for 37
years of brilliant showmanship.
(statuette)
JEAN HERSHOLT, for distinguished
service to the motion picture
industry. (statuette)

SCIENTIFIC OR TECHNICAL

CLASS I
EASTMAN KODAK CO.
CLASS III
LOREN L. RYDER, BRUCE H.
DENNEY, ROBERT CARR and
PARAMOUNT STUDIO
SOUND DEPT.
M. B. PAUL
HERBERT BRITT
ANDRE COUTANT,
JACQUES MATHOT
CHARLES R. DAILY, STEVE CSILLAG
and PARAMOUNT STUDIO
ENGINEERING, EDITORIAL
and MUSIC DEPTS.
INTERNATIONAL PROJECTOR CORP.
ALEXANDER VELCOFF

1948-57 cont'd.

1950

DIRECTOR
JOSEPH L. MANKIEWICZ,
All About Eve

WRITING
PANIC IN THE STREETS, Edna
Anhalt, Edward Anhalt (Motion
Picture Story)
ALL ABOUT EVE, Joseph L.
Mankiewicz (Screenplay)
SUNSET BOULEVARD, Charles
Brackett, Billy Wilder,
D. M. Marshman, Jr.
(Story and Screenplay)

CINEMATOGRAPHY
THE THIRD MAN, Robert Krasker
(Black and White)
KING SOLOMON'S MINES,
Robert Surtees (Color)

ART DIRECTION-SET DECORATION
SUNSET BOULEVARD, Hans Dreier,
John Meehan, Sam Comer,
Ray Moyer (Black and White)
SAMSON AND DELILAH, Hans
Dreier, Walter Tyler, Sam Comer,
Ray Moyer (Color)

SOUND RECORDING
ALL ABOUT EVE, 20th Century-Fox
Sound Dept.

SHORT SUBJECTS
GERALD McBOING-BOING,
Columbia (Cartoons)
GRANDAD OF RACES,
Warner Bros. (One-reel)
IN BEAVER VALLEY, Walt Disney,
RKO Radio (Two-reel)

DOCUMENTARY
WHY KOREA? 20th Century-Fox
Movietone (Short Subjects)
THE TITAN: STORY OF
MICHELANGELO, Classics
Pictures, Inc. (Features)

MUSIC
MONA LISA (Captain Carey, USA)
Ray Evans, Jay Livingston (Song)
SUNSET BOULEVARD, Franz Waxman
(Scoring of a Dramatic or
Comedy Picture)
ANNIE GET YOUR GUN, Adolph
Deutsch, Roger Edens (Scoring of
a Musical Picture)

FILM EDITING
KING SOLOMON'S MINES, Ralph E.
Winters, Conrad A. Nervig

SPECIAL EFFECTS
DESTINATION MOON, George Pal

COSTUME DESIGN
ALL ABOUT EVE, Edith Head,
Charles LeMaire (Black and White)
SAMSON AND DELILAH, Edith
Head, Dorothy Jeakins, Elois
Jenssen, Gile Steele,
Gwen Wakeling (Color)

**IRVING G. THALBERG
MEMORIAL AWARD**
Darryl F. Zanuck

HONORARY AND OTHER AWARDS
GEORGE MURPHY for his services
in interpreting the film industry
to the country at large. (statuett?)
LOUIS B. MAYER for distinguished
service to the motion picture
industry. (statuette)
THE WALLS OF MALAPAGA
(Franco-Italian)—voted by the
Board of Governors as the most
outstanding foreign language
film released in the United States
in 1950. (statuette)

SCIENTIFIC OR TECHNICAL
CLASS II
JAMES B. GORDON and
20TH CENTURY-FOX STUDIO
CAMERA DEPT.
JOHN PAUL LIVADARY, FLOYD
CAMPBELL, L. W. RUSSELL
and COLUMBIA STUDIO
SOUND DEPT.
LOREN L. RYDER and PARAMOUNT
STUDIO SOUND DEPT.

1951

DIRECTOR
GEORGE STEVENS, A Place In
The Sun

WRITING
SEVEN DAYS TO NOON, Paul Dehn,
James Bernard (Motion
Picture Story)
A PLACE IN THE SUN, Michael
Wilson, Harry Brown (Screenplay)
AN AMERICAN IN PARIS, Alan Jay
Lerner (Story and Screenplay)

CINEMATOGRAPHY
A PLACE IN THE SUN, William C.
Mellor (Black and White)
AN AMERICAN IN PARIS, Alfred
Gilks, John Alton (Color)

ART DIRECTION-SET DECORATION
A STREETCAR NAMED DESIRE,
Richard Day, George James
Hopkins (Black and White)
AN AMERICAN IN PARIS, Cedric
Gibbons, Preston Ames, Edwin B.
Willis, Keogh Gleason (Color)

SOUND RECORDING
THE GREAT CARUSO, M-G-M

SHORT SUBJECTS
TWO MOUSEKETEERS,
M-G-M (Cartoons)
WORLD OF KIDS, Warner Bros.
(One-reel)
NATURE'S HALF ACRE, Walt Disney,
RKO Radio (Two-reel)

DOCUMENTARY
BENJY, Fred Zinnemann
(Short Subjects)
KON-TIKI, RKO Radio (Features)

MUSIC
IN THE COOL, COOL, COOL OF
THE EVENING (here Comes
The Groom) Hoagy Carmichael,
Johnny Mercer (Song)
A PLACE IN THE SUN, Franz
Waxman (Scoring of a Dramatic
or Comedy Picture)
AN AMERICAN IN PARIS, Johnny
Green, Saul Chaplin (Scoring of
a Musical Picture)

FILM EDITING
A PLACE IN THE SUN,
William Hornbeck

SPECIAL EFFECTS
WHEN WORLDS COLLIDE, Paramount

COSTUME DESIGN
A PLACE IN THE SUN, Edith Head
(Black and White)
AN AMERICAN IN PARIS,
Orry-Kelly, Walter Plunkett,
Irene Sharaff (Color)

**IRVING G. THALBERG
MEMORIAL AWARD**
Arthur Freed

HONORARY AND OTHER AWARDS
GENE KELLY in appreciation of his
versatility as an actor, singer,
director and dancer, and
specifically for his brilliant
achievements in the art of
choreography on film. (statuette)
RASHOMON (Japanese)—voted by
the Board of Governors as the
most outstanding foreign language
film released in the United
States during 1951. (statuette)

SCIENTIFIC OR TECHNICAL
CLASS II
GORDON JENNINGS, S. L.
STANCLIFFE and PARAMOUNT
STUDIO SPECIAL PHOTOGRAPHIC
and ENGINEERING DEPTS.
OLIN L. DUPY
RADIO CORPORATION OF AMERICA,
VICTOR DIVISION
CLASS III
RICHARD M. HAFF, FRANK P.
HERRNFELD, GARLAND C.
MISENER and ANSCO FILM
DIVISION OF GENERAL ANILINE
AND FILM CORP.
FRED PONEDEL, RALPH AYRES and
GEORGE BROWN of
Warner Bros. Studio
GLEN ROBINSON and M-G-M
STUDIO CONSTRUCTION DEPT.
JACK GAYLORD and M-G-M STUDIO
CONSTRUCTION DEPT.
CARLOS RIVAS

1952

DIRECTOR
JOHN FORD, The Quiet Man

WRITING
THE GREATEST SHOW ON EARTH,
Frederic M. Frank, Theodore
St. John, Frank Cavett
(Motion Picture Story)
THE BAD AND THE BEAUTIFUL,
Charles Schnee (Screenplay)
THE LAVENDER HILL MOB,
(British), T. E. B. Clarke
(Story and Screenplay)

CINEMATOGRAPHY
THE BAD AND THE BEAUTIFUL,
Robert Surtees (Black and White)
THE QUIET MAN, Winton C. Hoch
Archie Stout (Color)

ART DIRECTION-SET DECORATION
THE BAD AND THE BEAUTIFUL,
Cedric Gibbons, Edward Carfagno;
Edwin B. Willis, Keogh Gleason
(Black and White)
MOULIN ROUGE, Paul Sheriff;
Marcel Vertes (Color)

SOUND RECORDING
BREAKING THE SOUND BARRIER,
London Film Sound Dept.

SHORT SUBJECTS
JOHANN MOUSE, M-G-M (Cartoons)
LIGHT IN THE WINDOW,
20th Century-Fox (One-reel)
WATER BIRDS, Walt Disney,
RKO Radio (Two-reel)

DOCUMENTARY
NEIGHBOURS National Film Board
of Canada (Short Subjects)
THE SEA AROUND US,
RKO Radio (Features)

MUSIC
HIGH NOON (DO NOT FORSAKE
ME, OH MY DARLIN'), High Noon
Dimitri Tiomkin, Ned Washington
(Song)
HIGH NOON, Dimitri Tiomkin
(Scoring of a Dramatic or
Comedy Picture)
WITH A SONG IN MY HEART,
Alfred Newman (Scoring of a
Musical Picture)

FILM EDITING
HIGH NOON, Elmo Williams,
Harry Gerstad

SPECIAL EFFECTS
PLYMOUTH ADVENTURE, M-G-M

COSTUME DESIGN
THE BAD AND THE BEAUTIFUL,
Helen Rose (Black and White)
MOULIN ROUGE, Marcel Vertes
(Color)

**IRVING G. THALBERG
MEMORIAL AWARD**
Cecil B. DeMille

HONORARY AND OTHER AWARDS
GEORGE ALFRED MITCHELL for the
design and development of the
camera which bears his name
and for his continued and
dominant presence in the field of
cinematography. (statuette)
JOSEPH M. SCHENCK for long and
distinguished service to the
motion picture industry.
(statuette)
MERIAN C. COOPER for his many
innovations and contributions to
the art of motion pictures.
(statuette)
HAROLD LLOYD, master comedian
and good citizen. (statuette)
BOB HOPE, for his contribution to
the laughter of the world, his
service to the motion picture
industry, and his devotion to
the American premise. (statuette)
FORBIDDEN GAMES (French)—Best
Foreign Language Film first
released in the United States
during 1952. (statuette)

SCIENTIFIC OR TECHNICAL
CLASS I
EASTMAN KODAK CO.
ANSCO DIVISION, GENERAL
ANILINE AND FILM CORP.
CLASS II
TECHNICOLOR MOTION
PICTURE CORP.

CLASS III
PROJECTION, STILL PHOTOGRAPHIC
and DEVELOPMENT ENGINEERING
DEPTS. OF M-G-M STUDIO
JOHN G. FRAYNE, R. R. SCOVILLE,
WESTREX CORP.
PHOTO RESEARCH CORP.
GUSTAV JIROUCH
CARLOS RIVAS of M-G-M Studio

1953

DIRECTOR
FRED ZINNEMANN, From Here
To Eternity

WRITING
ROMAN HOLIDAY, Ian McLellan
Hunter (Motion Picture Story)
FROM HERE TO ETERNITY,
Daniel Taradash (Screenplay)
TITANIC, Charles Brackett,
Walter Reisch, Richard Breen
(Story and Screenplay)

CINEMATOGRAPHY
FROM HERE TO ETERNITY, Burnett
Guffey (Black and White)
SHANE, Loyal Griggs (Color)

ART DIRECTION-SET DECORATION
JULIUS CAESAR, Cedric Gibbons,
Edward Carfagno; Edwin B. Willis,
Hugh Hunt (Black and White)
THE ROBE, Lyle Wheeler, George W.
Davis; Walter M. Scott, Paul
S. Fox (Color)

SOUND RECORDING
FROM HERE TO ETERNITY,
Columbia Sound Dept.

SHORT SUBJECTS
TOOT, WHISTLE, PLUNK and
BOOM, Walt Disney, Buena Vista
Film Distribution Co., Inc.
(Cartoons)
THE MERRY WIVES OF WINDSOR
OVERTURE, M-G-M (One-reel)
BEAR COUNTRY, Walt Disney,
RKO Radio (Two-reel)

DOCUMENTARY
THE ALASKAN ESKIMO, Walt
Disney, RKO Radio
(Short Subjects)
THE LIVING DESERT, Walt Disney,
Buena Vista (Features)

MUSIC
SECRET LOVE (Calamity Jane),
Sammy Fain, Paul Francis
Webster (Song)
LILI, Bronislau Kaper (Scoring of a
Dramatic or Comedy Picture)
CALL ME MADAM, Alfred Newman
(Scoring of a Musical Picture)

FILM EDITING
FROM HERE TO ETERNITY,
William Lyon

SPECIAL EFFECTS
THE WAR OF THE WORLDS,
Paramount

COSTUME DESIGN
ROMAN HOLIDAY, Edith Head
(Black and White)
THE ROBE, Charles LeMaire,
Emile Santiago (Color)

**IRVING G. THALBERG
MEMORIAL AWARD**
George Stevens

HONORARY AND OTHER AWARDS
PETE SMITH for his witty and
pungent observations on the
American scene in his series of
''Pete Smith Specialties.''
(statuette)
20TH CENTURY-FOX FILM CORP.
in recognition of their
imagination, showmanship and
foresight in introducing the
revolutionary process known as
CinemaScope. (statuette)
JOSEPH I. BREEN for his
conscientious, open-minded and
dignified management of the
Motion Picture Production Code.
(statuette)
BELL AND HOWELL CO. for their
pioneering and basic achievements
in the advancement of the motion
picture industry. (statuette)

SCIENTIFIC OR TECHNICAL
CLASS I
PROFESSOR HENRI CHRETIEN and
EARL SPONABLE, SOL HALPRIN,
LORIN GRIGNON, HERBERT
BRAGG and CARL FAULKNER of
20th Century-Fox Studios
FRED WALLER
CLASS II
REEVES SOUNDCRAFT CORP.
CLASS III
WESTREX CORP.

1954

DIRECTOR
ELIA KAZAN, On The Waterfront

WRITING
BROKEN LANCE, Philip Yordan
(Motion Picture Story)
THE COUNTRY GIRL, George Seaton
(Screenplay)
ON THE WATERFRONT, Budd
Schulberg (Story and Screenplay)

CINEMATOGRAPHY
ON THE WATERFRONT, Boris
Kaufman (Black and White)
THREE COINS IN THE FOUNTAIN,
Milton Krasner (Color)

ART DIRECTION-SET DECORATION
ON THE WATERFRONT, Richard Day
(Black and White)
20,000 LEAGUES UNDER THE SEA,
John Meehan; Emile Kuri (Color)

SOUND RECORDING
THE GLENN MILLER STORY,
Leslie I. Carey

SHORT SUBJECTS
WHEN MAGOO FLEW,
Columbia (Cartoons)
THIS MECHANICAL AGE,
Warner Bros. (One-reel)
A TIME OUT OF WAR,
Carnival Prods. (Two-reel)

DOCUMENTARY
THURSDAY'S CHILDREN,
British Information Services
(Short Subjects)
THE VANISHING PRAIRIE, Walt
Disney, Bunea Vista (Features)

1948-57 cont'd.

MUSIC

THREE COINS IN THE FOUNTAIN (Three Coins In The Fountain) Jule Styne, Sammy Cahn (Song)

THE HIGH AND THE MIGHTY, Dimitri Tiomkin (Scoring of a Dramatic or Comedy Picture)

SEVEN BRIDES FOR SEVEN BROTHERS, Adolph Deutsch, Saul Chaplin (Scoring of a Musical Picture)

FILM EDITING

ON THE WATERFRONT, Gene Milford

SPECIAL EFFECTS

20,000 LEAGUES UNDER THE SEA, Walt Disney

COSTUME DESIGN

SABRINA, Edith Head (Black and White)

GATE OF HELL, (Japanese) Sanzo Wada (Color)

HONORARY AND OTHER AWARDS

BAUSCH & LOMB OPTICAL COMPANY for their contributions to the advancement of the motion picture industry. (statuette)

KEMP R. NIVER for the development of the Renovare Process which has made possible the restoration of the Library of Congress Paper Film Collection. (statuette)

GRETA GARBO for her unforgettable screen performances. (statuette)

DANNY KAYE for his unique talents, his service to the Academy, the motion picture industry, and the American people. (statuette)

JON WHITELEY for his outstanding juvenile performance in "The Little Kidnappers." (miniature statuette)

VINCENT WINTER for his outstanding juvenile performance in "The Little Kidnappers." (miniature statuette)

GATE OF HELL (Japanese)—Best Foreign Language Film first released in the United States during 1954. (statuette)

SCIENTIFIC OR TECHNICAL

CLASS I

PARAMOUNT PICTURES, INC., LOREN L. RYDER, JOHN R. BISHOP

CLASS III

DAVID S. HORSLEY and UNIVERSAL-INTERNATIONAL STUDIO SPECIAL PHOTOGRAPHIC DEPT.

KARL FREUND and FRANK CRANDALL

WESLEY C. MILLER, J. W. STAFFORD, K. M. FRIERSON and M-G-M STUDIO SOUND DEPT.

JOHN P. LIVADARY, LLOYD RUSSELL and COLUMBIA STUDIO SOUND DEPT.

ROLAND MILLER and MAX GOEPPINGER

CARLOS RIVAS, G. M. SPRAGUE and M-G-M STUDIO SOUND DEPT.

FRED WILSON, P. C. YOUNG

FRED KNOTH, ORIEN ERNEST

1955

DIRECTOR

DELBERT MANN, Marty

WRITING

LOVE ME OR LEAVE ME, Daniel Fuchs (Motion Picture Story)

MARTY, Paddy Chayefsky (Best Screenplay)

INTERRUPTED MELODY, William Ludwig, Sonya Levien (Story and Screenplay)

CINEMATOGRAPHY

THE ROSE TATTOO, James Wong Howe (Black and White)

TO CATCH A THIEF, Robert Burks (Color)

ART DIRECTION-SET DECORATION

THE ROSE TATTOO, Hal Pereira, Tambi Larsen; Sam Comer, Arthur Krams (Black and White)

PICNIC, William Flannery, Joe Mielziner; Robert Priestly (Color)

SOUND RECORDING

OKLAHOMA!, Fred Hynes

SHORT SUBJECTS

SPEEDY GONZALES, Warner Bros. Cartoons, Inc. (Cartoons)

SURVIVAL CITY, 20th Century-Fox (One-reel)

THE FACE OF LINCOLN, Cavalcade Pictures, Inc. (Two-reel)

DOCUMENTARY

MEN AGAINST THE ARCTIC, Walt Disney, Buena Vista (Short Subjects)

HELEN KELLER IN HER STORY, Nancy Hamilton Presentation, (Features)

MUSIC

LOVE IS A MANY-SPLENDORED THING (Love Is A Many-Spendored Thing) Sammy Fain, Paul Francis Webster (Song)

LOVE IS A MANY-SPLENDORED THING, Alfred Newman (Scoring of a Dramatic or Comedy Picture)

OKLAHOMA!, Robert Russell Bennett, Jay Blackton, Adolph Deutsch (Scoring of a Musical Picture)

FILM EDITING

PICNIC, Charles Nelson, William A. Lyon

SPECIAL EFFECTS

THE BRIDGES AT TOKO-RI, Paramount

COSTUME DESIGN

I'LL CRY TOMORROW, Helen Rose (Black and White)

LOVE IS A MANY-SPLENDORED THING, Charles LeMaire (Color)

HONORARY AND OTHER AWARDS

SAMURAI, The legend of Musashi (Japanese)—Best Foreign Language Film first released in the United States during 1955. (statuette)

SCIENTIFIC OR TECHNICAL

CLASS I

NATIONAL CARBON CO.

CLASS II

EASTMAN KODAK CO.

FARCIOT EDOUART, HAL CORL and PARAMOUNT STUDIO TRANSPARENCY DEPT.

CLASS III

20TH CENTURY-FOX STUDIO and BAUSCH & LOMB CO.

WALTER JOLLEY, MAURICE LARSON and R. H. SPIES

STEVE KRILANOVICH

DAVE ANDERSON

LOREN L. RYDER, CHARLES WEST, HENRY FRACKER and PARAMOUNT STUDIO

FARCIOT EDOUART, HAL CORL and PARAMOUNT STUDIO TRANSPARENCY DEPT.

1956

DIRECTOR

GEORGE STEVENS, Giant

WRITING

THE BRAVE ONE, (writer credit not established) (Motion Picture Story)

AROUND THE WORLD IN 80 DAYS, James Poe, John Farrow, S. J. Perelman (Best Screenplay—adapted)

THE RED BALLOON (French) Albert Lamorisse (Best Screenplay—original)

CINEMATOGRAPHY

SOMEBODY UP THERE LIKES ME, Joseph Ruttenberg (Black and White)

AROUND THE WORLD IN 80 DAYS, Lionel Lindon (Color)

ART DIRECTION-SET DECORATION

SOMEBODY UP THERE LIKES ME, Cedric Gibbons, Malcolm F. Brown; Edwin B. Willis, F. Keogh Gleason (Black and White)

THE KING AND I, Lyle R. Wheeler, John DeCuir; Walter M. Scott, Paul S. Fox (Color)

SOUND RECORDING

THE KING AND I, Carl Faulkner

SHORT SUBJECTS

MISTER MAGOO'S PUDDLE JUMPER, Columbia (Cartoons)

CRASHING THE WATER BARRIER, Warner Bros. (One-reel)

THE BESPOKE OVERCOAT, George K. Arthur (Two-reel)

DOCUMENTARY

THE TRUE STORY OF THE CIVIL WAR, Camera Eye Pictures, Inc. (Short Subjects)

THE SILENT WORLD, Columbia (French), Jacques-Yves Cousteau (Features)

MUSIC

WHATEVER WILL BE, WILL BE (QUE SERA, SERA) (The Man Who Knew Too Much) Jay Livingston, Ray Evans (Song)

AROUND THE WORLD IN 80 DAYS, Victor Young (Scoring of a Dramatic or Comedy Picture)

THE KING AND I, Alfred Newman, Ken Darby (Scoring of a Musical Picture)

FILM EDITING

AROUND THE WORLD IN 80 DAYS, Gene Ruggiero, Paul Weatherwax

SPECIAL EFFECTS
THE TEN COMMANDMENTS,
John Fulton

COSTUME DESIGN
THE SOLID GOLD CADILLAC, Jean
Louis (Black and White)
THE KING AND I, Irene Sharaff
(Color)

**IRVING G. THALBERG
MEMORIAL AWARD**
Buddy Adler

**JEAN HERSHOLT
HUMANITARIAN AWARD**
Y. Frank Freeman

FOREIGN LANGUAGE FILM AWARD
LA STRADA (Italy)
Previously an Honorary Award

HONORARY AND OTHER AWARDS
EDDIE CANTOR for distinguished
service to the film industry.
(statuette)

SCIENTIFIC OR TECHNICAL

CLASS III
RICHARD H. RANGER

TED HIRSCH, CARL HAUGE,
EDWARD REICHARD

THE TECHNICAL DEPTS. OF
PARAMOUNT PICTURES CORP.

ROY C. STEWART AND SONS,
DR. C. R. DAILY and

TRANSPARENCY DEPT. of
PARAMOUNT PICTURES CORP.

THE CONSTRUCTION DEPT. of
M-G-M STUDIO

DANIEL J. BLOOMBERG, JOHN
POND, WILLIAM WADE and
ENGINEERING and CAMERA
DEPTS. of REPUBLIC STUDIO

1957

DIRECTOR
DAVID LEAN, The Bridge On The
River Kwai

WRITING
THE BRIDGE ON THE RIVER KWAI,
Pierre Boulle (Best Screenplay—
Based on material from
another medium)
DESIGNING WOMAN, George Wells
(Best Story and Screenplay—
written directly for the screen)

CINEMATOGRAPHY
THE BRIDGE ON THE RIVER KWAI,
Jack Hildyard

ART DIRECTION-SET DECORATION
SAYONARA, Ted Haworth;
Robert Priestly

SOUND*
SAYONARA, George Groves

SHORT SUBJECTS
BIRDS ANONYMOUS,
Warner Bros. (Cartoons)
THE WETBACK HOUND, Walt Disney,
Buena Vista (Live Action Subjects)

DOCUMENTARY
ALBERT SCHWEITZER, Louis
de Rochemont (Features)

MUSIC
ALL THE WAY (The Joker Is Wild)
James Van Heusen,
Sammy Cahn (Song)
THE BRIDGE ON THE RIVER KWAI,**
Malcolm Arnold (Scoring)

FILM EDITING
THE BRIDGE ON THE RIVER KWAI,
Peter Taylor

SPECIAL EFFECTS
THE ENEMY BELOW, Walter Rossi

COSTUME DESIGN**
LES GIRLS, Orry-Kelly

**JEAN HERSHOLT
HUMANITARIAN AWARD**
Samuel Goldwyn

FOREIGN LANGUAGE FILM AWARD
THE NIGHTS OF CABIRIA (Italy)

HONORARY AND OTHER AWARDS
CHARLES BRACKETT for outstanding
service to the Academy (statuette)
B. B. KAHANE for distinguished
service to the motion picture
industry. (statuette)
GILBERT M. ("Broncho Billy")
ANDERSON, motion picture
pioneer, for his contributions to
the development of motion
pictures as entertainment.
(statuette)
THE SOCIETY OF MOTION PICTURE
AND TELEVISION ENGINEERS for
their contributions to the
advancement of the motion
picture industry. (statuette)

SCIENTIFIC OR TECHNICAL

CLASS I
TODD-AO CORP. and
WESTREX CORP.
MOTION PICTURE
RESEARCH COUNCIL

CLASS II
SOCIETE D'OPTIQUE ET DE
MECANIQUE DE HAUTE
PRECISION
HARLAN L. BAUMBACH, LORAND
WARGO, HOWARD M. LITTLE and
UNICORN ENGINEERING CORP.

CLASS III
CHARLES E. SUTTER, WILLIAM B.
SMITH, PARAMOUNT PICTURES
CORP. and GENERAL
CABLE CORP.

*Previously called
"Sound Recording"
**Rules changed to one Award

1958-67
introduction to the fourth decade

THE 31st Annual Academy Awards presentation, the first in Oscar's fourth decade, came off on April 6, 1959, without problems or crises. But some of the later ceremonies—notably in 1967 and 1968—were heavy with drama.

The top picture of 1958 was *Gigi,* and the main acting honors went to five-time nominee Susan Hayward (*I Want to Live*) *and* David Niven (*Separate Tables*) who made it his first time at bat.

April 4, 1960, saw the long-time Awards champion—*Gone with the Wind*—with ten Oscars, yield to *Ben-Hur,* which carried off 11 of the 1959 golden statuettes.

As Ben-Hur, Charlton Heston was the first performer to be Os-cared in a Biblical role, and Simone Signoret became the first actress honored for a British-made film (*Room at the Top*).

Oscar moved approximately 20 miles west of Hollywood and Vine to the Santa Monica Auditorium for its 1961 Awards ceremony. The Pantages Theatre's capacity, already too small for the annual event, was further reduced that year to permit installing a new wide screen. The Academy wanted to remain in Hollywood, but no auditorium was available there with facilities comparable to the Santa Monica site.

Drama ran high on this Oscar night. Elizabeth Taylor, still weak after a critical illness, clung shakily to Eddie Fisher on her way to the podium for her *Butterfield 8* accolade, and a special Oscar went to Gary Cooper, nearing his end.

Her 1960 Oscar perked up the spirits of Elizabeth Taylor, still not fully recovered from a serious illness.

Gregory Peck gets his 1962 Oscar from Sophia Loren, a winner the year before.

144

His 1963 win makes Sidney Poitier the proud possessor of his first Oscar.

When the time came to take note of 1961's achievements, a musical, *West Side Story,* danced away with Oscar, and Sophia Loren widened his horizon as the first thespian to win for a foreign-language film *(Two Women).* Maximilian Schell carried off the top male honor *(Judgment at Nuremberg).*

The 1963 presentation saw a five-time nominee, Gregory Peck, finally walk away with an Oscar, for *To Kill a Mockingbird,* with Anne Bancroft, of *The Miracle Worker,* lucky on her first try. The picture for 1962 was *Lawrence of Arabia.*

With the distribution of the 1963 accolades, on April 13, 1964, Oscar broke through the color line for the first time in 24 years when Sidney Poitier claimed his *Lilies of*

Julie Andrews, Rex Harrison and Lila Kedrova are a joyous threesome, as winners in the 1964 Oscar sweepstake.

Anne Bancroft picks up Elizabeth Taylor's "Virginia Woolf" Oscar for her from Lee Marvin, himself a winner in 1965.

the Field Oscar. Poitier was also the only winner present that year. Best Actress Patricia Neal *(Hud)*, supporting players Margaret Rutherford *(The V.I.P.s)* and Melvin Douglas *(Hud)* were all in Europe. The picture of the year, *Tom Jones*, was a British import.

When *My Fair Lady*, Rex Harrison, and MFL director George Cukor all merited Awards for 1964, with Julie Andrews getting the Best Actress citation for *Mary Poppins*, the controversy over the casting of Eliza Doolittle broke out anew. Gossip had it her win was as much for not playing Eliza as for her fine performance in the Disney film.

The Oscarcast was in color in 1966 for the first time, and approximately 62 million Americans watched *The Sound of Music*, Lee

Julie Christie presents the Best Actor Oscar to Wendy Hiller, standing in for Paul Scofield.

Marvin *(Cat Ballou)* and Julie Christie *(Darling)* win for 1965.

When Shelley Winters came up for her *A Patch of Blue* Oscar, she became the only actress to be twice honored in the "supporting" category.

The Academy presented the first gold medal in its history. Appropriately, it went to the Oscar ceremonies' long-time emcee, Bob Hope. It was his fifth honorary citation.

A national network performers' strike was on at Oscartime, in 1967, and the Academy faced substantial loss if the presentation were not televised. Nevertheless, the Board of Directors decided that the importance of its merit awards transcended all other considera-

The Oscar given him by Shelley Winters for 1966 helped soothe the bruises of an accident-battered Walter Matthau.

tions. The 1966 Oscars would be given out "as scheduled, with or without television."

The strike was settled less than two hours before the April 10th presentation was set to get underway. Instead of a "private" audience of 2,800 at the Santa Monica Auditorium, the Oscarcast drew the largest TV audience ever to watch a live telecast over a single network. An estimated 65 million viewers in the U.S. alone saw *A Man for All Seasons* declared the Best Picture. They did not see three of the four actors honored—Paul Scofield *(A Man for All Seasons)*, Elizabeth Taylor and Sandy Dennis (both for *Who's Afraid of Virginia Woolf?*) were elsewhere. Only Walter Matthau made it for his supporting Oscar *(The Fortune Cookie)*.

Rod Steiger's wife, actress Claire Bloom, shares a proud moment with him after the 1967 honors were distributed.

The Academy postponed its awards for the first time in its history in 1968, and canceled the banquet entirely, when the April 10th date also became the funeral day of the assassinated Civil Rights leader, Dr. Martin Luther King.

The ceremony took place two days later, with *In the Heat of the Night,* its star, Rod Steiger, and Katharine Hepburn *(Guess Who's Coming to Dinner)* the winners. The TV audience was estimated at approximately 52 million.

With Oscar now at the fifth decade mark, the Academy hopes presentations and Oscarcasts will go on without any untoward events in the next ten years, but is prepared to meet all emergencies.

1958
best picture
Gigi
M-G-M

CAST: Leslie Caron, Louis Jourdan, Maurice Chevalier, Hermione Gingold, Eva Gabor, Jacques Bergerac, Isabel Jeans, John Abbott

CREDITS: Producer, Arthur Freed; Director, Vincente Minnelli; Screenplay, Alan Jay Lerner; from a novel by Colette; music and lyrics by Frederick Loewe, Alan Jay Lerner; Costumes, Cecil Beaton; Cinematographer. Joseph Ruttenberg. Metrocolor

Maurice Chevalier is Leslie Caron's advisor; Louis Jourdan, the man with dishonorable intentions.

THE COLETTE STORY on which *Gigi* was based had been made into a French non-musical picture almost a decade before, and Audrey Hepburn's Broadway debut was in the play (also non-musical) in 1951.

But the story of *Gigi* was close kin to *My Fair Lady*. MFL was the smash stage hit of the day and movie-makers knew it would not be available to the screen for several years. So M-G-M hired Alan Jay Lerner and Frederick Loewe, the team responsible for MFL, to create a movie musical from *Gigi*. The movie they turned out was, if not quite a MFL, a delight in itself, and Leslie Caron made an enchanting Gigi.

Set in Paris at the turn of the century, the story's slyly wicked, tongue-in-cheek plot concerned a charming young Parisienne being brought up in a highly unconventional way. The women of her family specialized in being courtesans, not wives, and the family had a "protector" all picked out for her. But Gigi double-crossed them by going respectable, and so enchanted her supposed-to-be protector (Louis Jourdan) that he ends up as her husband instead.

The score sent the audience away humming *Gigi, Thank Heaven for Little Girls,* and other songs; the costumes (by Cecil Beaton who designed the MFL wardrobes) were handsome, the sets opulent.

Maurice Chevalier, as a charmingly naughty oldster, was presented with a "Special Oscar." He was the only one of the cast to be Academy-recognized, though the film itself was awarded nine of the little golden men in all.

OTHER NOMINEES:
AUNTIE MAME, Warner Bros.
CAT ON A HOT TIN ROOF, M-G-M
THE DEFIANT ONES, UA
SEPARATE TABLES, UA

1958
best actor
David Niven
SEPARATE TABLES

DAVID NIVEN was so in love with the role of Phileas Fogg, he would have made *Around the World in 80 Days* without a penny of compensation. But his well-earned Oscar came for the touching *Separate Tables*. As the phony British major, fearful of sex and afraid of people, Niven etched an unforgettable character.

He showed his joy in winning when he stumbled on the way to the podium to accept his award and quipped, "I'm so loaded down with good-luck charms I could hardly make the steps!"

Born in Scotland, Niven is a graduate of Britain's famed military academy, Sandhurst, but found army life a bore.

Coming to the U.S., he failed in a number of vocations, turning to Hollywood "as a last resort," he says.

Listed by Central Casting as "Anglo-Saxon Type 2008," he caught the public's eye in the 1937 *Prisoner of Zenda* and continued building a following with *Dodsworth, Dawn Patrol, Wuthering Heights,* and other fine films until World War II.

Returning to Hollywood after serving with distinction in the British army and rising to the rank of colonel, he helped make movie history in *The Moon Is Blue,* the first film to become a box-office smash without the Code Seal.

Co-owner of the successful TV producing firm, Four Star, Niven appears on their shows from time to time, but movies continue to engage most of his time and interest.

Some of his recent films are: *The Guns of Navarone, 55 Days at Peking, The Pink Panther, Lady L, Casino Royale, Prudence and the Pill, The Impossible Years, Before Winter Comes, The Extraordinary Seaman, The Brain.*

OTHER NOMINEES:
TONY CURTIS, The Defiant Ones
PAUL NEWMAN, Cat On a Hot Tin Roof
SIDNEY POITIER, The Defiant Ones
SPENCER TRACY, The Old Man and The Sea

1958
best actress

Susan Hayward
I WANT TO LIVE

SULTRY-VOICED, redheaded, with a provocative figure and not a smidgeon of acting experience, Susan Hayward came west as one of the many beautiful young hopefuls to try for the role of Scarlett O'Hara in *Gone with the Wind*.

Losing out, the Brooklyn-born ex-photographer's model stayed on in Hollywood, where for some eight years she played a succession of ingenues and spoiled society types. She hit her stride in 1947 with *Smash-Up,* which brought her first Oscar nomination.

She was to win three more *(My Foolish Heart, With a Song in My Heart, I'll Cry Tomorrow)* before making the picture that was to finally earn her an Oscar.

She won her Best Actress designation for *I Want to Live.* The story of Barbara Grahame, the convicted murderess executed at San Quentin in 1953 after a long, bitter fight to spare her life, was a virtuoso role, and she made the most of it. But Hayward herself believes her finest hour was as Lillian Roth in the filmed version of that star-crossed actress's frank autobiography, *I'll Cry Tomorrow*. Most critics agree with her.

Now in her late forties, Susan Hayward lives in virtual retirement in Florida. She can only be lured away from her beloved deep-sea fishing and painting by an occasional plum role, such as *Valley of the Dolls'* aging actress waging a desperate battle to maintain her place in the theatrical sun against the younger, fresher, more beautiful competition.

Some of her more recent films: *Back Street, Where Love Has Gone, I Thank a Fool, The Stolen Hours, The Honey Pot.*

OTHER NOMINEES:
DEBORAH KERR, Separate Tables
SHIRLEY MacLAINE, Some Came Running
ROSALIND RUSSELL, Auntie Mame
ELIZABETH TAYLOR, Cat On a Hot Tin Roof

1958
best supporting actor

Burl Ives
THE BIG COUNTRY

IN *The Big Country,* a sweeping tale of cattle barons fighting for control, Burl Ives found a role as big as his abilities and was Oscared for it. His "Big Daddy" in the same year's *Cat on a Hot Tin Roof* was just as memorable. One of today's most versatile entertainers, Ives came to fame as, to quote Carl Sandburg, "the mightiest ballad singer of any century."

OTHER NOMINEES:
THEODORE BIKEL, The Defiant Ones
LEE J. COBB, The Brothers Karamazov
ARTHUR KENNEDY, Some Came Running
GIG YOUNG, Teacher's Pet

best supporting actress

Wendy Hiller
SEPARATE TABLES

WENDY HILLER, one of England's most gifted actresses, got her Oscar for *Separate Tables.* But to a whole generation, Wendy Hiller is, above all, Eliza Doolittle. Long before Julie Andrews or Audrey Hepburn were *My Fair Lady,* Wendy Hiller was creating Eliza in G. B. Shaw's *Pygmalion,* the play which is the basis for the musical. That was in 1936. Two years later, she played Eliza in the movie, getting a Best Actress bid for it.

OTHER NOMINEES:
PEGGY CASS, Auntie Mame
MARTHA HYER, Some Came Running
MAUREEN STAPLETON, Lonelyhearts
CARA WILLIAMS, The Defiant Ones

151

1959
best picture

Ben-Hur
M-G-M

CAST: Charlton Heston, Jack Hawkins, Hugh Griffith, Haya Harareet, Stephen Boyd, Martha Scott, Cathy O'Donnell, Sam Jaffe, Finlay Currie, Frank Thring
CREDITS: Producer, Sam Zimbalist; Director, William Wyler; Screenplay, Karl Tunberg, from the novel by General Lew Wallace; Cinematographer, Robert L. Surtees. Technicolor

Ben-Hur was not new to the screen. General Lew Wallace's huge Biblical novel, first published in 1880, had been a silent film, and also a stage play, before M-G-M made its $15 million spectacle, which has grossed $38 million to date.

Ben-Hur earned a record number of Oscars—eleven in all—including Best Picture and the two male acting categories (Charlton Heston, Hugh Griffith).

One of the most massive spectacles ever to crowd the screen, *Ben-Hur* was surprisingly successful in not losing its people among its trapperies. They live; you care what happens to them.

The hero is the rich Jew, Ben-Hur (Heston) who falls on evil days. Through the perfidy of a Roman friend, Messala (Stephen Boyd), he winds up as a galley slave and his mother and sister are sent to prison where they contract leprosy. Reprieved when he saves the life of a Roman dignitary, Ben-Hur again rises to wealth and position and bests his erstwhile friend in a bitterly fought chariot race. But his own bitterness is exorcised only after a meeting with Christ, on His way to Calvary, after which Ben-Hur finds his womenfolk miraculously restored to health.

The big highlight of the film came with the chariot race—eleven minutes of almost unbearable tension and excitement.

Ten months in the making, *Ben-Hur* was filmed in Rome, with a cast numbering more than 8,000.

OTHER NOMINEES:
ANATOMY OF A MURDER, Columbia
THE DIARY OF ANNE FRANK, 20th Century-Fox
THE NUN'S STORY, Warner Bros.
ROOM AT THE TOP, Continental

Charlton Heston's chariot flashes past his downed enemy, Stephen Boyd.

1959
best actor
Charlton Heston
BEN-HUR

CHARLTON HESTON "explains" his being consistently cast in films heroic in mold, and most often set in past centuries, with "Producers seem to feel I have a medieval face."

Producers have also known his ability to handle epic roles since Cecil B. DeMille had the foresight to cast the powerfully built, promising young actor — seen previously in just one unimportant movie — in *The Greatest Show on Earth*.

His Academy-acclaimed title role as the Jewish hero of *Ben-Hur* was a true tour-de-force—a character so beautifully limned it was never over-shadowed by the magnitude of the spectacle.

Born in Evanston, Illinois, Heston began his career on daytime radio in Chicago while still a student at Northwestern University's School of Speech. He took time out for World War II service, then went on to become one of the first Broadway actors to achieve success on TV.

A 16-mm, amateur version of *Julius Caesar,* made on campus at Northwestern, brought him a Holly-wood bid in 1949.

Hollywood has kept him especially busy since—in everything from Moses in *The Ten Commandments* and Michelangelo in *The Agony and the Ecstasy* to the astronaut who crash-lands into a man-hating ape civilization 2,000 years in the future, in *Planet of the Apes*.

A perfectionist who believes in keeping on learning and feels the stage the greatest teacher, Heston manages to take time out almost every year for a stage role.

Among his other recent films: *El Cid, 55 Days at Peking, The Greatest Story Ever Told, Khartoum, Counterpoint, Will Penny, Number One, Julius Caesar.*

OTHER NOMINEES:
LAURENCE HARVEY, Room at the Top
JACK LEMMON, Some Like It Hot
PAUL MUNI, The Last Angry Man
JAMES STEWART, Anatomy of a Murder

1959
best actress
Simone Signoret
ROOM AT THE TOP

IN *Room at the Top,* her "older woman," married but tragically in love with a cynical young opportunist to whom she was just an affair, tore at the heartstrings and earned Simone Signoret an Oscar.

The British-made film introduced Signoret—one of the great ladies of the French screen and stage—to the American movie-goer. It also brought the fascinating star, who has sensuous mature appeal, a flock of flattering offers from Hollywood.

She turned all of them down, and it was not until 1965 that she found a script and a role exciting enough to bring her to the film capital. It was the drug-addicted, pathetic Contessa in the star-studded filmization of Katherine Anne Porter's *Ship of Fools.*

Signoret calls herself "a lazy actress" and maintains she is much more interested in her real-life role

as the wife of singer-actor Yves Montand.

Born in 1921 in Wiesbaden, Germany, where her father was part of the army of occupation after World War I, she grew up in Paris. During the Nazi hold on the French capital in World War II, she supported two younger brothers while her father served with the Free French Forces in England.

Before the war ended, and as the result of her friendship with a group of young players, she was playing bit parts in the movies.

Her French-language *La Ronde, Diabolique* and *The Sleeping Car Murders* have been widely shown in the U.S. Her English-language films include: *Term of Trial, The Deadly Affair, Games, The Sea Gull.*

OTHER NOMINEES:
DORIS DAY, Pillow Talk
AUDREY HEPBURN, The Nun's Story
KATHARINE HEPBURN, Suddenly, Last Summer
ELIZABETH TAYLOR, Suddenly, Last Summer

Simone Signoret loves Laurence Harvey too much for her own good.

1959
best supporting actor

Hugh Griffith
BEN-HUR

HIS COLORFUL Sheik Ildeerim in *Ben-Hur* had Academy members marking their X's beside his name intent on electing him Best Supporting Actor. A specialist in flamboyant roles, Griffith was also the florid squire in *Tom Jones* (1963), and contributed some of its most amusing and memorable moments. The picture won a Best Picture citation, and the actor from Wales—once a mundane bank clerk—was rewarded with his second nomination.

OTHER NOMINEES:
ARTHUR O'CONNELL, Anatomy of a Murder
GEORGE C. SCOTT, Anatomy of a Murder
ROBERT VAUGHN, The Young Philadelphians
ED WYNN, The Diary of Anne Frank

best supporting actress

Shelley Winters
THE DIARY OF ANNE FRANK

SHELLEY WINTERS has become the screen's leading exponent of unpleasant mothers. As Richard Beymer's whining parent in *The Diary of Anne Frank,* she not only added more than her share to the tensions besetting the pathetic group of Jewish refugees hiding out from the Nazis, but won the first of her two well-deserved Oscars. She had been nominated once before, in 1951, for *A Place in the Sun,* and would win again in 1965.

OTHER NOMINEES:
HERMIONE BADDELEY, Room at the Top
SUSAN KOHNER, Imitation of Life
JUANITA MOORE, Imitation of Life
THELMA RITTER, Pillow Talk

155

1960
best picture

The Apartment
MIRISCH-UNITED ARTISTS

CAST: Jack Lemmon, Shirley MacLaine, Fred Mac-Murray, Ray Walston, Edie Adams, Jack Kruschen, David Lewis, Joan Shawlee, Joyce Jameson, Hope Holiday
CREDITS: Producer-Director, Billy Wilder; Screenplay, Billy Wilder, I.A.L. Diamond; Cinematographer, Joseph LaShelle.

THE YEAR 1960 was not a particularly good year as far as movies went; nothing of real distinction appeared. At the same time, there was a relaxing of the production code as to what could and could not be shown on the screen, and Billy Wilder, who produced, directed and wrote the screenplay for *The Apartment,* took full advantage of it.

An off-beat movie that swung between wry comedy and near-tragedy and at times approached the lewd, *The Apartment* had received only lukewarm critical approval. It was a box-office triumph, however, and came up the picture of the year.

In it, an ambitious insurance clerk furthers his business career by lending his little apartment in a marginal New York neighborhood to four of his firm's executives for clandestine trysts. When his married boss's girlfriend, with whom he happens to be in love, too, makes a suicide attempt there, he remorsefully bows out of the firm.

One of the picture's great assets was its excellent cast. Jack Lemmon was the clerk out to make a quick business success; Shirley MacLaine, the girl who tried to kill herself, and Fred MacMurray, the heel who drove her to it. Lemmon, Shirley MacLaine, and Jack Kruschen in a supporting role, all won Academy nominations.

The Apartment also boasted a slick production and a genuinely funny script, and with it, Bill Wilder became one of the few directors whose name is as well known as most stars, and brings out the movie-going crowd.

Jack Kruschen and Jack Lemmon come to the assistance of Shirley MacLaine after her suicide attempt.

OTHER NOMINEES:
THE ALAMO, UA
ELMER GANTRY, UA
SONS AND LOVERS, 20th Century-Fox
THE SUNDOWNERS, Warner Bros.

1960
best actor
Burt Lancaster
ELMER GANTRY

RUGGEDLY HANDSOME Burt Lancaster can be considered a Hollywood phenomenon. With an acting background of just three weeks in a Broadway flop that brought him exceptionally fine notices, Lancaster became a movie star with his first picture, *The Killers,* made in 1946.

What's more, within the next couple of years, he formed his own production company, Hecht-Lancaster, in partnership with his agent, Harold Hecht.

Until its dissolution some ten years later, Hecht-Lancaster turned out a dazzling number of box-office successes, including *Elmer Gantry,* for which Lancaster, as its flashy, spell-binding, conscienceless revivalist, rated an Oscar.

The flamboyant Lancaster, born in New York in 1913 had a colorful career pre-films. He was a circus athlete for five years; spent three years in the Army during World War II, and tried a variety of occupations, from boiler stoker to department-store floorwalker, before becoming a major Hollywood luminary at the age of 32.

In the movies, too, he refuses to be typed. His roles have ranged from a Sicilian Prince in *The Leopard* to a Nazi in *Judgment at Nuremberg.* He also has the distinction of being the man who charmed Deborah Kerr out of her former screen respectability into a blazing illicit affair in *From Here to Eternity.* He won an Oscar nomination for *Eternity* and *Birdman of Alcatraz,* but was skipped for *Separate Tables.*

Lancaster's other films include: *The Rainmaker, Come Back, Little Sheba, Seven Days in May, The Train, The Hallelujah Trail, The Professionals, The Scalphunters, The Swimmer, Castle Keep, The Gypsy Moths, Airport.*

OTHER NOMINEES:
TREVOR HOWARD, Sons and Lovers
JACK LEMMON, The Apartment
LAURENCE OLIVIER, The Entertainer
SPENCER TRACY, Inherit the Wind

1960
best actress
Elizabeth Taylor
BUTTERFIELD 8

OF *Butterfield 8,* for which she got her first Oscar, Elizabeth Taylor says contemptuously, "I think it stinks."

Liz Taylor had fought hard against playing its fast-living hard-dying call-girl heroine at all. In the end she had taken it only to write finis to her MGM contract and be able to accept 20th Century-Fox's tempt-ing $1,000,000 offer to play *Cleopatra.*

Certainly an Oscar could hardly have been in her calculations in connection with *Butterfield 8,* when she missed out on the coveted little gold man in much better pictures the three previous years. She was up for "Best Actress" in 1957 for *Raintree County;* in 1958 for *Cat on a Hot Tin Roof,* and in 1959 for *Suddenly, Last Summer.*

Despite her feelings about the worth of the picture, she was on hand, pale and shaky after her near-fatal bout with pneumonia, to pick up her Oscar.

An actress since early childhood, Elizabeth Taylor gave her first memorable performance in 1944 in *National Velvet.* She was 12 at that time.

In 1951, in *A Place in the Sun,* she showed evidence of becoming an adult performer of stature; then followed up with fine performances in *Rhapsody* and *Giant.*

Her *Cleopatra* garnered little praise but produced a flock of sensational headlines and led to her well-publicized, fifth marriage to flamboyant co-star Richard Burton, who was Antony.

Other pre-1960 films: *Love Is Better than Ever, Ivanhoe, Elephant Walk, Rhapsody, The Last Time I Saw Paris.*

OTHER NOMINEES:
GREER GARSON, Sunrise at Campobello
DEBORAH KERR, The Sundowners
SHIRLEY MacLAINE, The Apartment
MELINA MERCOURI, Never On Sunday

1960

best supporting actor

Peter Ustinov
SPARTACUS

IT SEEMS particularly fitting that after being nominated for *Quo Vadis* and appearing in *The Egyptian*, Ustinov won his first Oscar for another epic, *Spartacus*. The London-born thespian with the Russian name made his debut on the English stage at the age of 17, playing old men. "It was a mistake," says Peter Ustinov, now in his forties. "For years I played nothing but old men."

OTHER NOMINEES:
PETER FALK, Murder, Inc.
JACK KRUSCHEN, The Apartment
SAL MINEO, Exodus
CHILL WILLS, The Alamo

best supporting actress

Shirley Jones
ELMER GANTRY

SHIRLEY JONES was so grateful to have her Oscar, it was the first thing she rescued when her house caught fire in the big Bel-Aire blaze of a few years back. Pre-*Elmer Gantry*, she starred in *Oklahoma* and *Carousel* and was typed as a musical ingenue. Her portrayal of the young prostitute in *Gantry* was a challenge she met by giving a fine performance.

OTHER NOMINEES:
GLYNIS JOHNS, The Sundowners
SHIRLEY KNIGHT, The Dark at the Top of the Stairs
JANET LEIGH, Psycho
MARY URE, Sons and Lovers

159

1961
best picture

West Side Story
MIRISCH-UNITED ARTISTS

CAST: Natalie Wood, Richard Beymer, Rita Moreno, George Chakiris, Russ Tamblyn, Simon Oakland, William Bramley, John Austin, David Winters

CREDITS: Producer, Robert Wise; Directors, Robert Wise, Jerome Robbins; Screenplay, Ernest Lehman; from a musical play by Arthur Laurents; Choreography, Jerome Robbins; Music and Lyrics, Leonard Bernstein, Stephen Sondheim; Cinematographer, Daniel L. Fapp. Technicolor

THAT much overworked word "milestone" can truly be applied to *West Side Story*, the stage musical that became a movie the Academy membership voted the outstanding picture of 1961. Its story is somber, and each fiery dance number is integrated into the story and car-

Exuberant Russ Tamblin and other "Jets" own the street.

ries it forth in a way never before done in a film musical.

The tale the movie tells is pure *Romeo and Juliet*, with the feud between the Montagues and the Capulets, and its tragic aftermath, translated into terms of today and set in New York's seething Puerto-Rican jungle.

Its hero is the leader of the "Jets," a Puerto-Rican-baiting gang; its heroine, a Puerto-Rican girl. In classic Shakespearean style, they and their star-crossed romance become casualties of gang warfare.

Natalie Wood, emerging out of the juvenile ranks, was Maria, the heroine (with Marnie Nixon doing her singing). As the hero, Rick, Richard Beymer was considered by many critics to be too-clean-cut a type to make a completely convincing gang leader.

Maria, I Feel Pretty, Tonight and the rest of the much lauded Leonard Bernstein-Stephen Sondheim songs, came over on the screen with stunning impact, and the fast and furious dancing was the movie's most discussed feature, both for itself and in the way it was used to further the story.

Jerome Robbins, who had choreographed and directed the magnificent dancing in the stage original performed the same chore for the film, and was rewarded with a special Oscar for it.

The picture collected ten Oscars only two of which went to actors, both in supporting roles. George Chakiris, who headed the "Sharks," the Puerto-Rican gang that clashed so savagely with Beymer's "Jets," got one; Rita Moreno, his volatile girlfriend, got the other.

OTHER NOMINEES:
FANNY, Warner Bros.
THE GUNS OF NAVARONE, Columbia
THE HUSTLER, 20th Century-Fox
JUDGMENT AT NUREMBERG, UA

As THE German lawyer passionately defending the Nazi generals on trial in *Judgment at Nuremberg,* for wartime crimes, tall, handsome Maximilian Schell got an Oscar for a role he first created on TV.

In real life, Vienna-born Schell was just eight when his family fled to Switzerland in 1938, after the Nazi take-over of Austria.

He once wanted to be a priest. Instead, he is one of four brothers and sisters in the theatre. Maria Schell was the best known until Maximilian caught up with her.

Acting financed his way through Zurich University, and he became a full-fledged professional upon completing his education.

He has starred in German-language plays throughout Europe and in several German movies. His English-speaking debut took place on Broadway in 1958 in *Interlock,* to excellent notices.

Back again in Europe, he was playing in Paris when 20th Century-Fox decided to take a chance on "Maria Schell's brother" and cast him in *The Young Lions,* with Marlon Brando and Montgomery Clift.

It was Schell who garnered most of the fan mail, but he didn't appear again on the American screen until *Judgment at Nuremberg,* three years later.

Not that there was a dearth of

offers. Schell refuses any part he feels is not right for him. His first directorial effort, *First Love,* won an Oscar nomination for Best Foreign Language Film of 1970.

His films include: *The Condemned of Altoona, Topkapi, Return from the Ashes, Counterpoint, The Desperate Ones.*

OTHER NOMINEES:
CHARLES BOYER, Fanny
PAUL NEWMAN, The Hustler
SPENCER TRACY, Judgment at Nuremberg
STUART WHITMAN, The Mark

1961
best actress
Sophia Loren
TWO WOMEN

WITH HER earthy tormented mother futilely trying to protect her young daughter against the horrors of war in *Two Women,* Sophia Loren became the first actress to win an Academy Best Actress citation for a foreign-language film.

With *Two Women,* too, the lushly beautiful Italian proved she was much more than a sex symbol; she was an actress of fire and power second to none.

The role must have evoked many memories of her own unhappy childhood as a scrawny girl, born of natural union and growing up amid grueling poverty in war-torn Italy.

Incredibly, she emerged into a breathtakingly lovely, voluptuous 14-year-old who came out second in a Rome beauty contest. She also caught the attention of movie producer Carlo Ponti.

Now her husband, the much-older Ponti guided her to stardom in Italian films such as *Gold of Naples.*

"Learn English!" he kept urging, and by the time she made *Boy On a Dolphin* in 1957, and came to Hollywood, her English was near-perfect. She made a series of movies — *The Pride and the Passion, Desire Under the Elms, The Key, Heller in Pink Tights* and one solid success, *Houseboat,* with Cary Grant, then returned to Italy.

Oscar-nominated for the second time for another Italian-language film, *Marriage Italian Style,* super star Sophia continues to make her movies abroad. But these days they are usually in English and for American film companies. Among her most recent: *Judith, Arabesque, A Countess from Hong Kong, Sunflower, The Priest's Wife.*

OTHER NOMINEES:
AUDREY HEPBURN, Breakfast at Tiffany's
PIPER LAURIE, The Hustler
GERALDINE PAGE, Summer and Smoke
NATALIE WOOD, Splendor in the Grass

1961
best supporting actor

George Chakiris
WEST SIDE STORY

OF GREEK ANCESTRY and darkly handsome, George Chakiris scored as a Puerto Rican gang leader in *West Side Story,* both on the London stage and in the Award-winning film. Earlier, the ambitious young man who broke into show business dancing in Broadway choruses, had spent a discouraging couple of years in Hollywood. This time, the fiery Chakiris — most recently seen in *The Day the Hot Line Got Hot* (1968) — was found to be Oscar material.

OTHER NOMINEES:
MONTGOMERY CLIFT, Judgment at Nuremberg
PETER FALK, Pocketful of Miracles
JACKIE GLEASON, The Hustler
GEORGE C. SCOTT, The Hustler (Nomination refused)

best supporting actress

Rita Moreno
WEST SIDE STORY

RITA MORENO was 17 when she played her first Latin role in the movies. The Puerto-Rican-born actress hoped her *West Side Story* Oscar would help her to other roles. Instead, she was still offered only Latin or exotic parts, and after making a minor picture, in which she was a Filipino, the former child actress—who was in some 18 films before her Oscar win—left Hollywood. In 1968, she reactivated her movie career, making *The Night of the Following Day* with Marlon Brando.

OTHER NOMINEES:
FAY BAINTER, The Children's Hour
JUDY GARLAND, Judgment at Nuremberg
LOTTE LENYA, The Roman Spring of Mrs. Stone
UNA MERKEL, Summer and Smoke

1962
best picture
Lawrence of Arabia
HORIZON-COLUMBIA

CAST: Peter O'Toole, Alec Guinness, Anthony Quinn, Omar Sharif, Jack Hawkins, Jose Ferrer, Anthony Quayle, Claude Rains, Arthur Kennedy, Donald Wolfit, Michel Rey
CREDITS: Producer, Sam Spiegel; Director, David Lean; Screenplay, Robert Bolt; Cinematographer, F. A. Young. Technicolor

FIVE YEARS after their *Bridge on the River Kwai* was the Oscar-winner, producer Sam Spiegel and director David Lean came up with another Best Picture, *Lawrence of Arabia.*

Lawrence was a colossal undertaking, and its sweep of desert pageantry and history-in-the-making was magnificent. The movie was made mainly in the Sudanese desert, an inhospitable region of burning daytime heat and chilling night cold. The camera caught its harsh, repellent beauty so brilliantly that the scenery seemed to be the star at times, and one of the picture's seven Oscars was for photography.

The film seemed overlong, however, chiefly because the mysterious Lawrence of Arabia was too remote a character to hold interest for four hours.

An inordinately complex man who has been labeled everything from hero, to charlatan, to sadist, Thomas Edward Lawrence blazed his way to glory in the desert, then sought anonymity as a common soldier under an assumed name, and died in a motorcycle crash in London in 1935.

The film made no attempt to explain his baffling personality, but concentrated on his military exploits in bringing the Arabs into the Allied camp in World War I, and his key role in helping British General Allenby destroy the infamous Ottoman Empire.

As Lawrence, Irish actor Peter O'Toole, who had previously made a few minor British movies, rated an Oscar nomination. Another bid went to a handsome Egyptian actor, known only to the Arab world to that point, Omar Sharif.

Two *Kwai* veterans were prominent in the cast: Alec Guinness, as Prince Feisel, and Jack Hawkins, as General Allenby, and such stars as Anthony Quinn and Jose Ferrer were seen in lesser roles.

The desert proves a treacherous foe to Omar Sharif and Peter O'Toole.

OTHER NOMINEES:
THE LONGEST DAY,
   20th Century-Fox
THE MUSIC MAN,
   Warner Bros.
MUTINY ON THE BOUNTY,
   M-G-M
TO KILL A MOCKINGBIRD,
   Universal-International

1962
best actor
Gregory Peck
TO KILL A MOCKINGBIRD

NO NATIVE CALIFORNIAN won the top movie award until Gregory Peck caught the elusive little fellow in *To Kill a Mockingbird.*

In that excellent study of Southern small-town mores, his Lincolnesque lawyer—more successful in raising his motherless children than in defending a Negro wrongfully accused of raping a white girl—is beautifully underplayed for maximum impact.

Peck hit Hollywood in 1944, after several years on the stage. He was a star in his first movie, won his first Academy bid with his second, *The Keys to the Kingdom.*

In those days, ruggedly good-looking young men in their twenties were hard to find out of uniform. So the back injury that had ended his days as a college athlete and kept him out of service was a Hollywood godsend.

But Peck was no wartime make-do. The actor who started his career as a barker at the New York World's Fair is still a top star. In addition, he often is the producer, or co-producer, of his films, including *Mockingbird* and *Captain Newman.*

His other Oscar nominations were for *The Yearling, Duel in the Sun, Gentlemen's Agreement,* and *Twelve O'Clock High.*

A member of the National Council of Arts and active in numerous civic and charitable organizations, tall, soft-spoken Peck is also president of the Motion Picture Academy and was the recipient of its 1967 Jean Hersholt Humanitarian Award "for his untiring devotion to humanitarian causes."

His some 30 films include: *The Paradine Case, The Guns of Navarone, Behold a Pale Horse, Arabesque, The Stalking Moon, McKenna's Gold, The Chairman, Marooned.*

OTHER NOMINEES:
BURT LANCASTER, Bird Man of Alcatraz
JACK LEMMON, Days of Wine and Roses
MARCELLO MASTROIANNI, Divorce—Italian Style
PETER O'TOOLE, Lawrence of Arabia

1962
best actress

Anne Bancroft
THE MIRACLE WORKER

In 1952, Hollywood first called the New York TV actress, born Anna Maria Italiano, promptly changed her name to Anne Bancroft, then relegated her to a dreary bunch of B pictures.

She stuck it out for five years, but the last film, something called *The Girl in Black Stockings,* was just too much. She fled back to Gotham, and New Yorkers loved her in the two-person play (with Henry Fonda), *Two for the Seesaw.* Nevertheless, Hollywood used Shirley MacLaine, for the film.

But *Seesaw's* stage director, William Penn, and its author, William Gibson, had another play up their sleeves, *The Miracle Worker,* based on Helen Keller's childhood. They never even considered anyone else beside Bancroft for the half-blind Annie Sullivan who waged such a determined battle to get the wild, rebellious child, who had been left deaf, blind and mute by an illness, to communicate with others.

Bancroft gave them a performance that made her a star and in the play's long climactic scene, in which she finally got young Helen (Patty Duke, 14 at the time), to utter the one word "water" both the audience and the players were wrung dry emotionally.

This time, the Penn-Gibson team were so determined Bancroft would not be robbed of the chance to put that marvelous performance on film that they produced the picture themselves. The result was a movie of rare power and inspiration, and both Bancroft and young Miss Duke, who also repeated her original role, were Oscar-honored.

Hollywood was still in no hurry to break down the Bancroft door, so she took off for England, where she made *The Pumpkin Eater.* This brought another Oscar nomination her way, and the movie capital decided to take notice of her again.

Her latest Hollywood film, *The Graduate,* meant a third nomination for her, for her stunning performance as the older woman who seduces her daughter's boyfriend.

Bancroft believes in mixing theatre and film, and in 1963 she returned to Broadway as Berthold Brecht's *Mother Courage,* and the 1966-67 season saw her co-starred with Jason Robards in the New York production of *The Devils.*

Her other recent films were *Seven Women* and *The Slender Thread.*

OTHER NOMINEES:
BETTE DAVIS, What Ever Happened to Baby Jane?
KATHARINE HEPBURN, Long Day's Journey Into Night
GERALDINE PAGE, Sweet Bird of Youth
LEE REMICK, Days of Wine and Roses

1962
best supporting actor

Ed Begley
SWEET BIRD OF YOUTH

ED BEGLEY claimed life started for him with his *Sweet Bird of Youth* Oscar, but he did a lot of living and acting before. He had earned his living at fairs, carnivals, in circuses and on Broadway. He was the voice of Franklin Delano Roosevelt on radio's famed *State of the Union* program, and he won national recognition on TV in *Twelve Angry Men,* later repeating his role in the movie. Among his films are: *Sorry, Wrong Number* and *The Unsinkable Molly Brown.* He died April 28, 1970, at 69.

OTHER NOMINEES:
VICTOR BUONO, What Ever Happened to Baby Jane?
TELLY SAVALAS, Bird Man of Alcatraz
OMAR SHARIF, Lawrence of Arabia
TERENCE STAMP, Billy Budd

best supporting actress

Patty Duke
THE MIRACLE WORKER

WITH HER portrayal of the animal-like young Helen Keller in *The Miracle Worker,* Patty Duke, then 14, became the youngest person to win an Academy Award in competition with adults. It was her first movie, too. Firsts were nothing new to the girl who could act up such a storm. In the play on which the movie was based, she earned the distinction of becoming the youngest thespian ever to be elevated to Broadway stardom.

OTHER NOMINEES:
MARY BADHAM, To Kill a Mockingbird
SHIRLEY KNIGHT, Sweet Bird of Youth
ANGELA LANSBURY, The Manchurian Candidate
THELMA RITTER, Bird Man of Alcatraz

1963
best picture

Tom Jones
UNITED ARTISTS-LOPERT

CAST: Albert Finney, Susannah York, Hugh Griffith, Diane Cilento, Dame Edith Evans, Joan Greenwood, David Tomlinson, George Devine, George A. Cooper, Joyce Redman, Peter Bull
CREDITS: Producer-Director, Tony Richardson; Screenplay, John Osborne, from the novel by Henry Fielding; Cinematographer, Walter Lassally. Eastmancolor

THE 18th century was an earthy era, and one of its most uninhibited literary works was Henry Fielding's *Tom Jones,* which was turned into the best film of 1963.

Tom, the adopted son of a British country squire, is a love-'em-and-leave-'em lady charmer who goes blithely from bed to bed, while managing to get into enough other mischief to come within moments of being hanged.

Director Tony Richardson and the skillful screenplay pulled out all the moral stops in this British-made production, and Richardson kept his bawdy material moving at as fast and funny a clip as has been seen. He won an Oscar for his efforts.

The acting, too, was topnotch, and though none of the actors was a final winner, five of the cast were nominated: Albert Finney, a most engaging Tom; Hugh Griffith, a delight as his lusty adoptive father, and grubby, too-free-with-her-love Diane Cilento. The others were Dame Edith Evans and Joyce Redman, Finney's gross eating companion in one of the film's most outrageously hilarious sequences. Susannah York was the squire's daughter, with whom Tom finally winds up.

Even more than its general excellence as a film, its unrestrained sexiness brought patrons on the run, and *Tom Jones* became a box-office champion.

OTHER NOMINEES:
AMERICA AMERICA, Warner Bros.
CLEOPATRA, 20th Century-Fox
HOW THE WEST WAS WON, M-G-M; Cinerama
LILIES OF THE FIELD, UA

Albert Finney's gallantry meets the approval of Susannah York and Hugh Griffith.

1963
best actor
Sidney Poitier
LILIES OF THE FIELD

and excellent diction are much admired. But in his first bid to become an actor, after a hitch in the U.S. Army, New York's American Negro Theatre turned him down flat because of his thick West Indian accent. The Miami-born, Bahamas-raised young man became the thea-

Sidney Poitier and Lilia Skala learn much from each other.

OTHER NOMINEES:
ALBERT FINNEY,
  Tom Jones
RICHARD HARRIS,
  This Sporting Life
REX HARRISON,
  Cleopatra
PAUL NEWMAN,
  Hud

"IT'S BEEN a long journey to this moment." In that short, emotion-charged speech, Sidney Poitier summed up the hard road that led to the second Oscar ever to be awarded to a member of his race. (Hattie McDaniel was the first to win).

His foot-loose, light-hearted G.I. in *Lilies of the Field*, who virtually adopted five bewildered German nuns trying to resettle in Arizona, is memorable for more than his fine performance. It was the breakthrough in films for a Negro in a role in which his color was purely incidental.

He also broke precedent in *A Patch of Blue* and *Guess Who's Coming to Dinner*. In both, he romanced a white girl, in the first by implication; in the second, openly.

Today, Poitier's resonant voice

tre's janitor, in exchange for lessons in acting and diction.

After success on Broadway in *Lysistrata, Anna Lucasta* and *A Raisin in the Sun,* he made his first movie, *No Way Out,* in 1949, and won his first Oscar nomination in 1958 for *The Defiant Ones.*

In 1967, despite high acclaim for his roles in *To Sir, with Love, In the Heat of the Night,* and *Guess Who's Coming to Dinner,* he was passed over in the Academy nominations. Scuttlebut has it that the votes for him were so split between his three excellent performances that none got enough votes by itself.

Other Poitier films include: *Duel at Diablo, Porgy and Bess, The Slender Thread, For Love of Ivy, The Lost Man, They Call Me Mr. Tibbs, Brother John.*

1963
best actress
Patricia Neal
HUD

AN ACTRESS of great power and perception, Patricia Neal never really hit her stride in films until *Hud*.

In that hard-hitting, modern-day Western from Paramount, she had a role she could really sink her teeth into, and tore into its earthy, hurt-by-life housekeeper, who repulsed the advances of Paul Newman, her employer's charming wastrel of a son.

Oscar night, however saw her in England, awaiting the birth of her fourth child, rather than at the Santa Monica Auditorium.

The Kentucky-born tawny blonde came to Hollywood as the result of fine notices in her first Broadway play, Lillian Hellman's *Another Part of the Forest*. She made one inconsequential movie, followed by *The Fountainhead,* which did little for her career.

The Breaking Point, based on Hemingway's *To Have and To Hold,* and *A Face in the Crowd* drew critical raves for both pictures and their star, but audiences were scant.

Hud was a pick-up for her sagging career. It brought her the meaty role of the nurse in *In Harm's Way*. But soon after, three massive strokes almost wrote "the end" to Pat Neal's life as well as her career.

Her own determination and that of her devoted husband, British writer Roald Dahl, pulled her through. Early in 1968, at the age of 42, she was able to resume her career, in the film version of the Pulitzer Prize play, *The Subject Was Roses,* and won another nomination.

Among her films are: *The Hasty Heart, Breakfast at Tiffany's, The Washington Story, The Road Builder.*

Patricia Neal is wise enough to know Paul Newman is not serious.

1963
best supporting actor

Melvyn Douglas
HUD

THE TALL, gray-haired actor who, as the father in *Hud,* was dubbed best of the supporting fraternity in 1962, has been one of the country's best actors for some 40 years whether the medium be the theatre, movies or TV. Over the years, too, he has made a smooth transition from romantic lead to distinguished character actor. His 1970 picture, *I Never Sang for My Father,* earned him a Best Actor nomination.

OTHER NOMINEES:
NICK ADAMS, Twilight of Honor
BOBBY DARIN, Captain Newman, M.D.
HUGH GRIFFITH, Tom Jones
JOHN HUSTON, The Cardinal

best supporting actress

Margaret Rutherford
THE V.I.P.'S

Margaret Rutherford was 72 when Oscar smiled on her for *The V.I.P.'s.* She was 74 when Queen Elizabeth bestowed an even greater honor on her — Dame of the British Empire. Having things happen at a late age was usual for the spritely oldster. She started to act at 33, didn't marry until 52. She was in her 70s when she established herself as Agatha Christie's elderly sleuth, Miss Marple, in the "Murder" series: *Murder She Said, Murder on the Gallop, Murder Most Foul, Murder Ahoy.*

Dame Margaret Rutherford died, aged 80, on May 22, 1972 from complications suffered after a hip fracture.

OTHER NOMINEES:
DIANE CILENTO, Tom Jones
DAME EDITH EVANS, Tom Jones
JOYCE REDMAN, Tom Jones
LILIA SKALA, Lilies of the Field

1964
best picture
My Fair Lady
WARNER BROS.

CAST: Rex Harrison, Audrey Hepburn, Stanley Holloway, Wilfred Hyde-White, Gladys Cooper, Jeremy Britt, Theodore Bikel, Mona Washbourne.
CREDITS: Producer, Jack L. Warner; Director, George Cukor; Screenplay, Alan Jay Lerner, from the play "Pygmalion" by George Bernard Shaw; Music and Lyrics by Frederick Loewe, Alan Jay Lerner; Costumes and scenery, Cecil Beaton; Cinematography, Harry Stradling. Technicolor

FROM the moment *My Fair Lady* premiered almost simultaneously in New York, Chicago and Los Angeles, it was evident that Warner Bros. need have no worry about its $17 million investment paying off.

The film had a great deal to live up to. The stage's MFL ran some six and a half years in New York, more than five years in London, and *Why Can't the English, The Rain in Spain* and the 16 other enchanting Alan Lerner-Frederick Loewe musical numbers were world famous.

Jack Warner's signing of Rex Harrison to recreate his marvelous stage Professor Higgins on film met with universal approval. There was much dissension when he turned down Julie Andrews, a screen unknown then, who had created the part on stage, for the well-known film star, Audrey Hepburn. Practically the only quarrel with the picture the critics had was with Hepburn's opening scenes as the Cockney guttersnipe. Everyone agreed she was just fine once Eliza Doolittle began her conversion into a lady. (Hepburn was not even nominated by the Academy that year, though MFL got eight Oscars in all.)

As practically everybody must know by now, MFL stems back to George Bernard Shaw's *Pygmalion* and is a combination of the Cinderella and Svengali themes. A crisply irascible professor of phonetics makes a wager he can turn a Cockney flowergirl into a lady who can pass as a duchess, and while doing so, loses his locked-up heart to her charms.

Filmed entirely in Hollywood, MFL's costumes and sets were breathtaking, the color photography spectacular, and they accounted for three of the film's Oscars.

OTHER NOMINEES:
BECKET, Paramount
DR. STRANGELOVE OR: HOW I LEARNED TO STOP WORRYING AND LOVE THE BOMB, Columbia
MARY POPPINS, Disney
ZORBA THE GREEK, 20th Century-Fox

Rex Harrison is fascinated by Audrey Hepburn's Cockney English.

1964
best actor
Rex Harrison
MY FAIR LADY

REX HARRISON had had plenty of practice for his Oscar-winning role in the film version of *My Fair Lady.* He played the querulous perfectionist, Professor Higgins, on the stage in the smash London and New York musical sensation more than a thousand times.

One of the legitimate theatre's most distinguished sons, Harrison had made a number of British films before his American screen debut in 1949. The picture was *Anna and the King of Siam,* later to become the basis for another marvelous stage and screen musical, *The King and I.*

Despite the picture's success, and the nickname he acquired—"Sexy Rexy"—he didn't really catch the movie-goer's unqualified approbation until his regal, yet very human, Caesar in *Cleopatra.* That role also brought him his first Oscar nomination.

The following year, at 56—an age when few players who haven't been there before climb the pinnacle of screen eminence—his Professor Higgins was to make him a major film star. It also earned him the coveted Oscar, and was responsible for his becoming the number one candidate for one of the most eagerly sought-after roles in years—the doctor who talks to the animals in *Dr. Dolittle.*

The tall, handsome Britisher with the elegant air began his career some 44 years ago on a Liverpool stage. He made his British movie debut in 1929; was a flight lieutenant in the Royal Air Force during World War II, and resumed his career after that unhappy period passed into history.

Recent Harrison films include: *The Yellow Rolls Royce; The Agony and the Ecstasy, The Honey Pot, A Flea in Her Ear, Staircase.*

OTHER NOMINEES:
RICHARD BURTON, Becket
PETER O'TOOLE, Becket
ANTHONY QUINN, Zorba the Greek
PETER SELLERS, Dr. Strangelove

1964
best actress
Julie Andrews
MARY POPPINS

THAT SUPERSTAR Julie Andrews won filmdom's highest accolade with her first picture, *Mary Poppins,* is small wonder. The big wonder is that it took so long for hip movie makers to discover her potential.

The daughter of show-business parents, she has been a performer since the age of 12. At 19, she was a Broadway star the day after she opened in Gotham in *The Boyfriend.*

After more than three years on Broadway as Eliza Doolittle in *My Fair Lady,* and an additional 18 months with it in London, she returned to the Great White Way in *Camelot.*

Walt Disney saw her, and on the spot offered her the part of Mary Poppins, the flying governess with the magical bag of tricks, and she proved simply "superfragilaceous."

Julie Andrews next raised her lovely voice, with its amazing, five-octave range, as another famous governess, the girl who found the religious life was not for her, in *The Sound of Music.* It has been making sweet sounds at the box office for more than three years, and there are no complaints about her *Thoroughly Modern Milly,* either.

The Theatre Owners of America showed their appreciation of her box-office pull by crowning her No. 1 box-office star for 1968. After *Sound* came *Star!,* in which she plays Gertrude Lawrence, the fabulous English musical-comedy star of the 1920s and '30s. In *Darling Lili,* she portrays a World War I spy.

Julie Andrews' non-musical films —all successes—include: *The Americanization of Emily, Hawaii,* and *Torn Curtain.*

OTHER NOMINEES:
ANNE BANCROFT, The Pumpkin Eater
SOPHIA LOREN, Marriage Italian Style
DEBBIE REYNOLDS, The Unsinkable Molly Brown
KIM STANLEY, Seance on a Wet Afternoon

1964
best supporting actor

Peter Ustinov
TOPKAPI

PETER USTINOV's second Oscar came his way for his not-too-bright, small-time con man duped by a much shrewder pair of sharpies in that sly comedy, *Topkapi*. Ustinov's credits read like the accomplishments of several men: starring roles in 14 plays and more than a score of movies; author of some 31 plays, movies and books; movie and stage director; TV and radio star; book illustrator. He claims it's easy. "One relaxes me from the other."

OTHER NOMINEES:
JOHN GIELGUD, Becket
STANLEY HOLLOWAY, MY Fair Lady
EDMOND O'BRIEN, Seven Days in May
LEE TRACY, The Best Man

best supporting actress

Lila Kedrova
ZORBA THE GREEK

ANYONE who can steal a scene from Anthony Quinn has to be good. Lila Kedrova, *Zorba the Greek*'s disreputable Madame Hortense, almost stole the picture, and was Oscared for the feat. The Russian-born redhead, raised in Paris, was a piano prodigy at eight. At 15, she made her stage debut as an ingenue with a Russian company in Paris. She made three post-Zorba American films—*Wild Wind in Jamaica, Torn Curtain, Penelope*—then went back home and is now making movies in Europe.

OTHER NOMINEES:
GLADYS COOPER, My Fair Lady
DAME EDITH EVANS, The Chalk Garden
GRAYSON HALL, The Night of the Iguana
AGNES MOOREHEAD, Hush...Hush, Sweet Charlotte

175

1965
best picture
The Sound Of Music
20TH CENTURY-FOX

CAST: Julie Andrews, Christopher Plummer, Eleanor Parker, Richard Haydn, Charmian Carr, Peggy Wood, Anna Lee, Portia Nelson, Daniel Truhitte, Norma Varden, Marni Nixon, Angela Cartwright.
CREDITS: Producer-Director, Robert Wise; Screenplay, Ernest Lehman; from the musical play by Howard Lindsay, Russel Crouse; Music and Lyrics, Richard Rodgers, Oscar Hammerstein II; Cinematographer, Ted McCord. DeLuxe Color

TO DATE, *The Sound of Music* has racked up a world-wide box-office return of more than $115 million. This makes it the all-time moneymaker, and the picture is still nowhere near the end of its run.

Interest in *Sound* was high from the moment it was announced 20th Century-Fox would make it into a movie. With Mary Martin as its star, it had been one of the greatest Broadway hits on record. The lilting Rodgers-Hammerstein musical numbers were long familiar, and the Von Trapp Singers, whose true-life experiences were the story's basis, were known to millions.

But most of all, after the heat that was generated over the *My Fair Lady* Eliza Doolittle casting, moviegoers were looking forward avidly to seeing and hearing the center of the controversy, Julie Andrews.

As the postulant obviously unsuited to nunnery life who becomes the beloved governess of the motherless Von Trapp children, coaxes their father out of his military stiffness, and winds up as the Baroness Von Trapp, Julie Andrews lived up to expectations.

Christopher Plummer's Captain Von Trapp combined the necessary good looks and aristocratic standoffishness, and the picture gave Marnie Nixon the opportunity to be seen as well as heard, after ghosting the singing for the likes of Natalie Wood and Audrey Hepburn.

Brought in at a cost of $8 million, *Sound* has toppled *Gone with the Wind* from its longtime position as box-office champion.

OTHER NOMINEES:
DARLING, Embassy Pictures
DOCTOR ZHIVAGO, M-G-M
SHIP OF FOOLS, Columbia
A THOUSAND CLOWNS, UA

Julie Andrews passes on her own love of life to her young charges.

1965
best actor
Lee Marvin
CAT BALLOU

IF EVER A CAREER illustrates what an Oscar can mean to an actor, it is Lee Marvin's.

The tall (6'-3"), lean, prematurely-grey-haired actor had been around Hollywood some 13 years. Never top-billed, but a dependable character man, he had wrought havoc and mayhem over the years in *Donovan's Reef, The Big Heat, Bad Day at Black Rock, Hangman's Noose, Raintree County, The Caine Mutiny, The Killers,* and dozens of other films.

Comedy was not his forte, but in 1965, Columbia Pictures had the inspiration to cast him in a double role in a hilarious Western spoof, *Cat Ballou.* He was the "good" gunman—a drunk whose gun arm needed a hefty slug of booze to work right —hired by a former schoolteacher now an outlaw (Jane Fonda) to help avenge her father's death.

Marvin was also the desperado he was out to kill—The Kid's evil twin, Ted Strawn, who wore an awesome artificial nose because his own had been bitten off in a fight.

The duel between the brothers, with The Kid temporarily sobered up and corseted into trim uprightness, was a highlight of the movie.

Cat turned out to be the year's big sleeper, a quickie that became a major box-office attraction and rewarded Marvin with that all-important Oscar.

His stock had been bolstered that year, too, in one of its biggest films, the all star *Ship of Fools,* where he played the bigoted, has-been ball-player who made a drunken pass at Vivien Leigh and was clobbered with her shoe for it.

Marvin is a New Yorker of distinguished heritage who had been kicked out of some of the East's best private schools, studied acting under the G.I. Bill, debuted on Broadway in *Billy Budd,* and appeared during TV's "golden era" in some 250 small-screen dramatic productions.

He's a hard working actor who considers acting a profession for the disciplined. Since his Oscar win, he's been in the enviable position of being able to write his own ticket and terms.

He's also able to wait, these days, for the right role. He read scripts for a year after *Cat* and *Ship* before going into *The Professionals.* His latest starring films are: *The Dirty Dozen, Point Blank, Sergeant Ryker, Hell in the Pacific, Paint Your Wagon.*

OTHER NOMINEES:
RICHARD BURTON, The Spy Who Came in From the Cold
LAURENCE OLIVIER, Othello
ROD STEIGER, The Pawnbroker
OSKAR WERNER, Ship of Fools

1965
best actress
Julie Christie
DARLING

THE SECOND English Julie to become a superstar overnight in the 1960's, Julie Christie was so thrilled she burst into tears when she was given her Oscar.

The beautiful and talented Miss Christie makes no bones about enjoying success.

"Being so sought after is an enviable situation," says the girl who got there by her stunning performance as *Darling*'s ruthless model, who scratches her way to the social heights, then finds life at the top meaningless.

Daughter of an English tea planter, Julie was born in Assam, India, April 14, 1941, and educated in England and France.

She is unconventional, definitely a part of the "now" generation, and picked up her Oscar in a dress as eye-poppingly mini as her streaming blonde hair was long.

She started with a small provincial repertory theatre, played in a couple of minor movies, did a stint on British TV.

Then came *Billy Liar*. She was on screen for just eleven minutes. But they were electric and brought her a flock of movie offers, which she eyed enviously, but turned down to acquire more stage experience.

Nevertheless, *Billy Liar* proved her touchstone to film fame.

Two years later, when its director, David Lean, was casting *Dr. Zhivago*, he remembered Julie and entrusted her with the key role of Zhivago's great love, Lara.

For her performance in *McCabe and Mrs. Miller* in 1971, Julie Christie won a second Best Actress nomination.

Her other films are: *Young Cassidy, Fahrenheit 451, Far from the Madding Crowd, Petulia, The Go Between, The Presbyterian Church Wager*.

OTHER NOMINEES:
JULE ANDREWS, The Sound of Music
SAMANTHA EGGAR, The Collector
ELIZABETH HARTMAN, A Patch of Blue
SIMONE SIGNORET, Ship of Fools

1965
best supporting
actor

Martin Balsam
A THOUSAND CLOWNS

NATIVE New Yorker Martin Balsam won his Oscar as the very conventional brother of oddball Jason Robards in an unconventional comedy, *A Thousand Clowns*. But the top character man is equally at home in drama. He gave stand-out performances in *On the Waterfront, 12 Angry Men, Psycho, Seven Days in May, Cape Fear*. Balsam moves easily between stage and screen, but prefers Broadway to Hollywood.

OTHER NOMINEES:
IAN BANNEN, The Flight of the Phoenix
TOM COURTENAY, Doctor Zhivago
MICHAEL DUNN, Ship of Fools
FRANK FINLAY, Othello

best supporting
actress

Shelley Winters
A PATCH OF BLUE

HER SECOND OSCAR came to Shelley Winters for what was a virtuoso performance in *Patch of Blue*. She was a despicable mother once again— an amoral shrew who had blinded her daughter in one of her rages. Here, the very embodiment of ignorance, bigotry and self-righteousness, she makes every outraged effort to keep that daughter away from her one friend, an understanding young Negro. Some other recent films: *Wild in the Streets, Buena Sera, Mrs. Campbell, Bloody Mama*.

OTHER NOMINEES:
RUTH GORDON, Inside Daisy Clover
JOYCE REDMAN, Othello
MAGGIE SMITH, Othello
PEGGY WOOD, The Sound of Music

1966
best picture

A Man For All Seasons
COLUMBIA

CAST: Paul Scofield, Wendy Hiller, Leo McKern, Robert Shaw, Orson Welles, Susannah York, Nigel Davenport, John Hurt, Corin Redgrave
CREDITS: Producer-Director, Fred Zinnemann; Screenplay, Robert Bolt, Cinematographer, Ted Moore. Technicolor

WHEN the original Robert Bolt drama—which he later fashioned into the screenplay—opened in London in the summer of 1960, most critics were quick to emphasize that though *A Man for All Seasons* leads inexorably to death, it is actually a paean to life and an inspiration.

A Man takes place in 16th century England. But men like Sir Thomas More, who love life yet have the moral fiber to lay down their lives for their principles, are found in every century.

The film concentrates on the last seven years of More's life. The struggle between More and his King, Henry VIII, hinges on Henry's determination to break with Rome so he can wed again, and good Catholic More's inability to go along with such heresy. More resigns as chancellor, hoping to be able to live out his life as a private citizen. But Henry will settle for nothing less than that the much respected More give public approval to his headstrong course. When More stubbornly refuses to compromise he is beheaded.

The picture took six Oscars, with Paul Scofield, who also appeared as More on the London and New York stages, named Best Actor. Robert Shaw won a "supporting" nomination for his young, virile Henry VIII, not yet the victim of his own excesses. So did Wendy Hiller, as Sir Thomas's practical, yet warmly tender wife.

Made with loving care as a prestige film, *A Man* became a surprise box-office bonanza as well.

OTHER NOMINEES:
ALFIE, Paramount
THE RUSSIANS ARE COMING THE RUSSIANS ARE COMING, UA
THE SAND PEBBLES, 20th Century-Fox
WHO'S AFRAID OF VIRGINIA WOOLF?, Warner Bros

The King (Robert Shaw) visits the Mores (Susannah York, Paul Scofield, Wendy Hiller).

1966
best actor

Paul Scofield
A MAN FOR ALL SEASONS

ONE OF THE GIANTS of the British stage, Paul Scofield had made only three films—only *The Train* is known on this side of the Atlantic — before *A Man for All Seasons* brought him an Oscar with his first nomination.

It is typical of Scofield that Academy Awards night found him playing Shakespeare in London, instead of in Santa Monica, accepting the Oscar. Tall, distinguished-looking Scofield is, basically, a man of the theatre.

He first brought his Oscar winning Sir Thomas More—one of history's most heroic men of the cloth —to life on a London stage in 1960, for a smash run; then came with it to Broadway, where it was as great a success.

Born in Hurstpierpoint near Brighton, January 21, 1922, Scofield was the son of the village schoolmaster, but no scholar himself. Instead, from the moment he stepped on stage at 13, as Juliet in a boy's school production of *Romeo and Juliet,* his sights were set on the theatre.

He made his London debut in two bit parts in John Drinkwater's *Abraham Lincoln,* each with the same one line to speak. It was, "Yes Sir." He polished his famed Shakespearean interpretations razor-sharp with Britain's esteemed Birmingham Repertory Theatre, at Stratford-on-Avon, and as one of the Royal Shakespeare Company's most eminent members.

When Scofield brought his *Hamlet* to the Moscow Art Theatre during the darkest days of the Cold War, he "single-handedly kept the Iron Curtain lifted for two weeks."

The stage-oriented Scofield was not seen on the big screen again until 1971 when he transferred his magnificent *King Lear* to film.

OTHER NOMINEES:
ALAN ARKIN, The Russians Are Coming
   The Russians Are Coming
RICHARD BURTON, Who's Afraid of Virginia Woolf?
MICHAEL CAINE, Alfie
STEVE McQUEEN, The Sand Pebbles

1966
best actress

Elizabeth Taylor
WHO'S AFRAID OF VIRGINIA WOOLF?

A VIOLENT storm of criticism broke over superstar Elizabeth Taylor's beauteous head when she sidestepped the 1966 Academy Awards ceremonies after winning a nomination and was not on hand to pick up her second Oscar.

But her bravura portrayal of Martha, the sloppy, foul-mouthed, graying voluptuary in *Who's Afraid of*

Richard Burton blossomed so explosively during their on-screen affair in *Cleopatra,* the Burtons have rarely appeared in a picture that doesn't provide a first-rate showcase for both of them, as did *The Taming of the Shrew.*

Occasionally, however, Taylor will accept what is in reality a secondary role, so long as the vehicle offers Burton the acting scope he looks for. *The Comedians* is this type of picture.

Recently, Taylor has been seen in several films without her adored Richard, who has yet to win an Oscar, despite his towering talent and six nominations. In *Reflections in a Golden Eye,* Marlon Brando was

Virginia Woolf? cannot be faulted, and her willingness to submerge her famed good looks for it was admirable.

Never out of the headlines, both in her personal life and as an actress, Elizabeth Taylor, now in her mid-thirties, is not only one of the world's richest actresses, but one of the most independent.

Since her off-screen romance with

opposite her; in *Secret Ceremony* it was Robert Mitchum, and in *The Only Game in Town,* Warren Beatty.

Other recent Taylor-Burton films are: *The VIP's, The Sandpiper, Dr. Faustus, Boom!*

OTHER NOMINEES:
ANOUK AIMEE, A Man and a Woman
IDA KAMINSKA, The Shop on Main Street
LYNN REDGRAVE, Georgy Girl
VANESSA REDGRAVE, Morgan

1966
best supporting actor

Walter Matthau
THE FORTUNE COOKIE

WHEN WALTER MATTHAU sounded off to the press about nominees not present on Oscar Night, nobody had a better right. Despite multiple bruises sustained in an auto accident a day or so before, Matthau was there when his own name rang out, honoring him for his screamingly funny shyster-lawyer in *The Fortune Cookie*. He won a 1971 Best Actor bid for his touching old man in *Kotch*. His many movies include *Hello, Dolly!*, *A New Leaf*, *Plaza Suite*.

OTHER NOMINEES:
MAKO, The Sand Pebbles
JAMES MASON, Georgy Girl
GEORGE SEGAL, Who's Afraid of Virginia Woolf?
ROBERT SHAW, A Man for All Seasons

best supporting actress

Sandy Dennis
WHO'S AFRAID OF VIRGINIA WOOLF?

THOUGH Sandy Dennis feels her reasons for not picking up her Oscar in person were valid — she was making *Sweet November* in New York at the time and she hates to fly—she'll be on hand if she's ever nominated again. "It's much easier to go than raise a storm of criticism," says the shy star who won her Oscar as the young wife in *Virginia Woolf*. Her other films are: *Up the Down Staircase*, *The Fox*, *That Cold Day in the Park*, *Thank You All Very Much*, *The Out-of-Towners*.

OTHER NOMINEES:
WENDY HILLER, A Man for All Seasons
JOCELYN LaGARDE, Hawaii
VIVIEN MERCHANT, Alfie
GERALDINE PAGE, You're a Big Boy Now

183

1967
best picture

In the Heat of the Night
UNITED ARTISTS

CAST: Sidney Poitier, Rod Steiger, Warren Oates, Lee Grant, James Patterson, Quentin Dean, Larry Gates, William Schallert, Beah Richards
CREDITS: Producer, Walter Mirisch; Director, Norman Jewison; Screenplay, John Ball; Cinematographer, Haskell Wexler. DeLuxe Color

THE BEST PICTURE of 1967 is excellent entertainment. It also makes a definite statement about our time, and Hollywood would not have touched it in an earlier day.

The crux of the story is prejudice, both white and black, and it concerns a Northern Negro detective (Sidney Poitier) and a small-town chief of police (Rod Steiger) in the deep South who are thrown together on a case by chance.

Poitier is just passing through Sparta at the time one of its wealthiest citizens is discovered murdered. So naturally, as a black man suspiciously affluent-looking and unknown in town, he immediately becomes the prime suspect. Steiger jails him until a phone call to the Philadelphia police establishes he is indeed what he professes to be—one of their top homicide men.

Steiger is new at his job, has never been on a murder case, and his knowledge of scientific methods of detection is sketchy. He is smart enough to know he must take advantage of Poitier's know-how to make himself look good. So he goads Poitier into staying on to help him. By the time the case is closed, each man has grown to like and respect the other.

The racial angle is prominent throughout. One of the most exciting sequences centers around an attack on Poitier by white youths armed with chains and headed by the brother of a sexy teen-ager (Quentin Dean) whose habit of posing nude in her window holds the key to the murder.

OTHER NOMINEES:
BONNIE AND CLYDE, Warner Bros.-Seven Arts
DOCTOR DOLITTLE, 20th Century-Fox
THE GRADUATE, Embassy
GUESS WHO'S COMING TO DINNER, Columbia

Sidney Poitier is set on leaving, Rod Steiger determined to make him stay.

1967
best actor

Rod Steiger
IN THE HEAT OF THE NIGHT

IN HIS THANK-YOU, Rod Steiger, Oscar in hand, paid Sidney Poitier, who shares marquee honors with him in *In the Heat of the Night,* one of the most gracious compliments ever heard in an acceptance speech.

Steiger said, "I want to thank Mr. Sidney Poitier, whose friendship gave me the knowledge to enhance my performance—and we shall overcome."

Obviously excited, the 42-year-old star also found his win "unbelievable . . . overwhelming." Not so Hollywood. He'd been the year's front runner as *Heat*'s small-town sheriff who finds repugnant the superior know-how of a Northern Negro detective (Poitier), equally contemptuous of him, when chance teams them up to solve a murder.

Many felt Steiger should have got the Oscar in 1965, as well as a nomination, for his poignant portrayal in *The Pawnbroker* of a Jew living a Zombi-like existence since the horrors of Nazi Germany.

Steiger is probably the only top movie personality who can walk down Fifth Avenue or Hollywood Boulevard without being mobbed. Fans simply don't recognize the dark-haired, full-faced actor who has an almost uncanny ability to change his appearance.

In his 1968 comic-suspenser, *No Way to Treat a Lady,* he wears a variety of disguises, from a mincing wig designer to a brawny plumber, as he goes about strangling middle-aged women who remind him of his mother.

When the 25-year-old New York-er, fresh from a five-year Navy hitch, joined the amateur dramatic group at the division of the Veteran's Administration where he was working, his reason was that the girls he wanted to date belonged.

Instead, he got so interested in acting he soon quit Washington to study for the theatre in New York. His much-praised Broadway debut, in a revival of Clifford Odet's *Night Music,* set the pattern that was to bring movie stardom later. In his 20s, Steiger played a 55-year-old detective, and looked it.

His first Academy nomination was in the supporting category, in 1954's *On the Waterfront,* his second film.

An Emmy winner, too, Steiger, who is divorced from actress Claire Bloom, divides his time between movies, TV and the stage.

Other recent Steiger films: *The Loved One, Dr. Zhivago, The Girl and the General, The Sergeant, The Illustrated Man, Three into Two Won't Go, Waterloo.*

OTHER NOMINEES:
WARREN BEATTY, Bonnie and Clyde
DUSTIN HOFFMAN, The Graduate
PAUL NEWMAN, Cool Hand Luke
SPENCER TRACY, Guess Who's Coming to Dinner

1967
best actress
Katharine Hepburn
GUESS WHO'S COMING TO DINNER

THIRTY-FIVE YEARS were to elapse between Katharine Hepburn's two Oscars.

In 1967, after five years of complete professional inactivity, she returned to the screen for what was to be the last of the Tracy-Hepburn films, *Guess Who's Coming to Dinner.*

As the parents of a 21-year-old daughter (her niece, Katharine Houghton) who brings an outstanding young Negro (Sidney Poitier) home with the announcement they want to marry, she and Tracy come face to face with a social problem that tests their liberal beliefs. Both stars came through with Academy quality portrayals and were nominated, Tracy posthumously, as he died June 20, 1967.

Hepburn had been second only to Bette Davis as the most nominated thespian. With *Dinner* she caught up with Davis in nominations. When the Academy picked her performance for the Oscar itself, she and Davis—both among the screen's longest-lasting luminaries—were running neck-and-neck in the Oscar race. Each had been honored by her peers with two Oscars and ten nominations.

Rumor has it that Hepburn came back to the screen for *Dinner* chiefly because Tracy, in ill health and also retired for some years, wanted to do it.

But once Hepburn made up her mind to make the move, she got back into the swing of movie-making with all the energy and luster of her youth. The following year she was to become the most-Oscared star in Academy history, with *The Lion in Winter.*

OTHER NOMINEES:
ANNE BANCROFT, The Graduate
FAYE DUNAWAY, Bonnie and Clyde
DAME EDITH EVANS, The Whisperers
AUDREY HEPBURN, Wait Until Dark

1967
best supporting actor

George Kennedy
COOL HAND LUKE

OSCAR gave the nod to George Kennedy's sharply delineated character of the *Cool Hand Luke* convict who starts out battling Paul Newman to keep his leadership of the chain gang, only to wind up as Newman's admiring second in command. Reaching "starring" stature via the character-actor route is doing it the long, hard way, but big George Kennedy—six-feet-four and weighing 210 pounds—says, "Now, I'm going to let Oscar keep me!"

OTHER NOMINEES:
JOHN CASSAVETES, The Dirty Dozen
GENE HACKMAN, Bonnie and Clyde
CECIL KELLAWAY, Guess Who's Coming to Dinner
MICHAEL J. POLLARD, Bonnie and Clyde

best supporting actress

Estelle Parsons
BONNIE AND CLYDE

ESTELLE PARSONS caused a wave of laughter to ripple through Santa Monica Auditorium when she gasped, "Oh, boy, it's heavy!" as presenter Walter Matthau passed the Oscar to her. Her Broadway play, *The Seven Descents of Myrtle,* had shut down for the night, so she could fly to the Coast to pick up her award. *Bonnie and Clyde* was her first movie. Her second, *Rachel, Rachel,* brought her another nomination.

OTHER NOMINEES:
CAROL CHANNING, Thoroughly Modern Millie
MILDRED NATWICK, Barefoot in the Park
BEAH RICHARDS, Guess Who's Coming to Dinner
KATHARINE ROSS, The Graduate

1958-67
oscar winners in other categories

1958

DIRECTOR
VINCENTE MINNELLI, Gigi

WRITING
GIGI, Alan Jay Lerner (Best Screenplay—based on material from another medium)
THE DEFIANT ONES, Nathan E. Douglas, Harold Jacob Smith (Best Story and Screenplay—written directly for the screen)

CINEMATOGRAPHY
THE DEFIANT ONES, Sam Leavitt (Black and White)
GIGI, Joseph Ruttenberg (Color)

ART DIRECTION-SET DECORATION
GIGI, Wiliam A. Horning, Preston Ames; Henry Grace, Keogh Gleason

SOUND
SOUTH PACIFIC, Todd-AO Sound Dept.

SHORT SUBJECTS
KNIGHTY KNIGHT BUGS, Warner Bros. (Cartoons)
GRAND CANYON, Walt Disney, Buena Vista (Live Action Subjects)

DOCUMENTARY
AMA GIRLS, Walt Disney, Buena Vista (Short Subjects)
WHITE WILDERNESS, Walt Disney, Buena Vista (Features)

MUSIC
GIGI (Gigi) Frederick Loewe, Alan Jay Lerner (Song)
THE OLD MAN AND THE SEA, Dimitri Tiomkin (Scoring of a Dramatic or Comedy Picture)
GIGI, Andre Previn (Scoring of a Musical Picture)

FILM EDITING
GIGI, Adrienne Fazan

SPECIAL EFFECTS
tom thumb, Tom Howard

COSTUME DESIGN
GIGI, Cecil Beaton

IRVING G. THALBERG MEMORIAL AWARD
Jack L. Warner

FOREIGN LANGUAGE FILM AWARD
MY UNCLE, (France)

HONORARY AND OTHER AWARDS
MAURICE CHEVALIER for his contributions to the world of entertainment for more than half a century. (statuette)

SCIENTIFIC OR TECHNICAL

CLASS II
DON W. PRIDEAUX, LEROY G. LEIGHTON and LAMP DIVISION of GENERAL ELECTRIC CO. PANAVISION, INC.

Class III
WILLY BORBERG
FRED PONEDEL, GEORGE BROWN, CONRAD BOYE

1959

DIRECTOR
WILLIAM WYLER, Ben-Hur

WRITING
ROOM AT THE TOP, Neil Paterson (Best Screenplay—based on material from another medium)
PILLOW TALK, Russell Rouse, Clarence Greene; Stanley Shapiro, Maurice Richlin (Best Story and Screenplay—written directly for the screen)

CINEMATOGRAPHY
THE DIARY OF ANNE FRANK, William C. Mellor (Black and White)
BEN-HUR, Robert L. Surtees (Color)

ART DIRECTION-SET DECORATION
THE DIARY OF ANNE FRANK, Lyle R. Wheeler, George W. Davis; Walter M. Scott, Stuart A. Reiss (Black and White)
BEN-HUR, William A. Horning, Edward Carfagno; Hugh Hunt (Color)

SOUND
BEN-HUR, MGM Studio Sound Dept.

SHORT SUBJECTS
MOONBIRD, Storyboard, Inc. (Cartoons)
THE GOLDEN FISH, (French) Columbia (Live Action Subjects)

DOCUMENTARY
GLASS, George K. Arthur—Netherlands Gov't. (Short Subjects)
SERENGETI SHALL NOT DIE, (German) Transocean (Film Features)

MUSIC
HIGH HOPES (A Hole In The Head) (Song) James Van Heusen, Sammy Cahn (Song)
BEN-HUR, Miklos Rozsa (Scoring of a Dramatic or Comedy Picture)
PORGY AND BESS, Andre Previn, Ken Darby (Scoring of a Musical Picture)

FILM EDITING
BEN-HUR, Ralph E. Winters, John D. Dunning

SPECIAL EFFECTS
BEN-HUR, A. Arnold Gillespie, Robert MacDonald, Milo Lory

COSTUME DESIGN
SOME LIKE IT HOT, Orry-Kelly (Black and White)
BEN-HUR, Elizabeth Haffenden (Color)

JEAN HERSHOLT HUMANITARIAN AWARD
Bob Hope

FOREIGN LANGUAGE FILM AWARD
BLACK ORPHEUS, (France)

HONORARY AND OTHER AWARDS
LEE DE FOREST for his pioneering inventions which brought sound to the motion picture. (statuette)
BUSTER KEATON for his unique talents which brought immortal comedies to the screen. (statuette)

SCIENTIFIC OR TECHNICAL

CLASS II
DOUGLAS G. SHEARER, ROBERT E. GOTTSCHALK, JOHN R. MOORE
WADSWORTH E. POHL, WILLIAM EVANS, WERNER HOPF, S. E. HOWSE, THOMAS P. DIXON, STANFORD RESEARCH INSTITUTE, TECHNICOLOR CORP.
WADSWORTH E. POHL, JACK ALFORD, HENRY IMUS, JOSEPH SCHMIT, PAUL FASSNACHT, AL LOFQUIST, TECHNICOLOR CORP.
DR. HOWARD S. COLEMAN, DR. A. FRANCIS TURNER, HAROLD H. SCHROEDER, JAMES R. BENFORD, HAROLD E. ROSENBERGER
ROBERT P. GUTTERMAN and LIPSNER-SMITH CORP.

Class III
UB IWERKS
E. L. STONES, GLEN ROBINSON, WINFIELD HUBBARD and LUTHER NEWMAN

1960

DIRECTOR
BILLY WILDER, The Apartment

WRITING
ELMER GANTRY, Richard Brooks (Best Screenplay—based on material from another medium)
THE APARTMENT, Billy Wilder, I.A.L. Diamond (Best Story and Screenplay—written directly for the screen)

CINEMATOGRAPHY
SONS AND LOVERS, Freddie Francis (Black and White)
SPARTACUS, Russell Metty (Color)

ART DIRECTION-SET DECORATION
THE APARTMENT, Alexander Trauner; Edward G. Boyle (Black & White)
SPARTACUS, Alexander Golitzen, Eric Orbom; Russell A. Gausman, Julia Heron (Color)

SOUND
THE ALAMO, Samuel Goldwyn Studio Sound Dept., Todd-AO Sound Dept.

SHORT SUBJECTS
MUNRO, Film Representations, Inc. (Cartoons)
DAY OF THE PAINTER, Kingsiey-Union Films (Live Action Subjects)

DOCUMENTARY
GIUSEPPINA, Lester A. Schoenfeld Films (British), (Short Subjects)
THE HORSE WITH THE FLYING TAIL, Walt Disney, Buena Vista, (Features)

MUSIC
NEVER ON SUNDAY (Never On Sunday) Manos Hadjidakis (Song)
EXODUS, Ernest Gold (Scoring of a Dramatic or Comedy Picture)
SONG WITHOUT END (The Story of Franz Liszt), Morris Stoloff, Harry Sukman (Scoring of a Musical Picture)

FILM EDITING
THE APARTMENT, Daniel Mandell

SPECIAL EFFECTS
THE TIME MACHINE, Gene Warren,
Tim Baar

COSTUME DESIGN
THE FACTS OF LIFE, Edith Head,
Edward Stevenson (Black & White)
SPARTACUS, Valles, Bill Thomas
(Color)

JEAN HERSHOLT
HUMANITARIAN AWARD
Sol Lesser

FOREIGN LANGUAGE FILM AWARD
THE VIRGIN SPRING (Sweden)

HONORARY AND OTHER AWARDS
GARY COOPER for his many
memorable screen performances
and the international recognition
he, as an individual, has gained
for the motion picture industry.
(statuette)
STAN LAUREL for his creative
pioneering in the field of
cinema comedy. (statuette)
HAYLEY MILLS for "Pollyanna,"
the most outstanding juvenile
performance during 1960.
(miniature statuette)

SCIENTIFIC OR TECHNICAL
CLASS II
AMPEX PROFESSIONAL
PRODUCTS CO.

Class III
ARTHUR HOLCOMB, PETRO VLAHOS
and COLUMBIA STUDIO
CAMERA DEPT.
ANTHONY PAGLIA and
20TH CENTURY-FOX STUDIO
MECHANICAL EFFECTS DEPT.
CARL HAUGE, ROBERT GRUBEL
and EDWARD REICHARD

1961
DIRECTOR
ROBERT WISE, JEROME ROBBINS,
West Side Story

WRITING
JUDGMENT AT NUREMBERG, Abby
Mann (Best Screenplay—based on
material from another medium)
SPLENDOR IN THE GRASS, William
Inge (Best Story and Screenplay—
written directly for the screen)

CINEMATOGRAPHY
THE HUSTLER, Eugen Shuftan
(Black and White)
WEST SIDE STORY, Daniel L. Fapp
(Color)

ART DIRECTION-SET DECORATION
THE HUSTLER, Harry Horner;
Gene Callahan (Black and White)
WEST SIDE STORY, Boris Leven;
Victor A. Gangelin (Color)

SOUND
WEST SIDE STORY, Todd-AO
Sound Dept., Samuel Goldwyn
Studio Sound Dept.

SHORT SUBJECTS
ERSATZ (The Substitute), Herts-Lion
International Corp. (Cartoons)
SEAWARDS THE GREAT SHIPS,
Lester A. Schoenfeld Films
(Live Action Subjects)

DOCUMENTARY
PROJECT HOPE, Klaeger Film
(Short Subjects)
LE CIEL ET LA BOUE (Sky Above and
Mud Beneath), (French), (Features)

MUSIC
MOON RIVER (Breakfast At
Tiffany's) Henry Mancini,
Johnny Mercer (Song)
BREAKFAST AT TIFFANY'S, Henry
Mancini (Scoring of a Dramatic
or Comedy Picture)
WEST SIDE STORY, Saul Chaplin,
Johnny Green, Sid Ramin,
Irwin Kostal (Scoring of a
Musical Picture)

FILM EDITING
WEST SIDE STORY, Thomas Stanford

SPECIAL EFFECTS
THE GUNS OF NAVARONE, Bill
Warrington, Vivian C. Grenham

COSTUME DESIGN
LA DOLCE VITA (Italian),
Piero Gherardi (Black and White)
WEST SIDE STORY, Irene Sharaff
(Color)

IRVING G. THALBERG
MEMORIAL AWARD
Stanley Kramer

JEAN HERSHOLT
HUMANITARIAN AWARD
George Seaton

FOREIGN LANGUAGE FILM AWARD
THROUGH A GLASS DARKLY,
(Sweden)

HONORARY AND OTHER AWARDS
WILLIAM L. HENDRICKS for his
outstanding patriotic service in
the conception, writing and
production of the Marine Corps
film, "A Force In Readiness,"
which has brought honor to the
Academy and the motion picture
industry. (statuette)
FRED L. METZLER for his
dedication and outstanding
service to the Academy of Motion
Picture Arts and Sciences.
(statuette)
JEROME ROBBINS for his brilliant
achievements in the art of
choreography on film. (statuette)

SCIENTIFIC OR TECHNICAL
CLASS II
SYLVANIA ELECTRIC
PRODUCTS, INC.
JAMES DALE, S. WILSON, H. E.
RICE, JOHN RUDE, LAURIE
ATKIN, WADSWORTH E. POHL,
H. PEASGOOD and
TECHNICOLOR CORP.
20TH CENTURY-FOX RESEARCH
DEPT., under the direction of
E. I. SPONABLE and HERBERT E.
BRAGG, and DELUXE
LABORATORIES, INC., with the
assistance of F. D. LESLIE,
R. D. WHITMORE, A. A. ALDEN,
ENDEL POOL and
JAMES B. GORDON

CLASS III
HURLETRON, INC., ELECTRIC EYE
EQUIPMENT DIVISION
WADSWORTH E. POHL,
TECHNICOLOR CORP.

1962
DIRECTOR
DAVID LEAN, Lawrence Of Arabia

WRITING
TO KILL A MOCKINGBIRD, Horton
Foote (Best Screenplay—based on
material from another medium)
DIVORCE—ITALIAN STYLE, Ennio de
Concini, Alfredo Giannetti,
Pietro Germi (Best Story and
Screenplay—written directly for
the screen)

CINEMATOGRAPHY
THE LONGEST DAY, Jean Bourgoin,
Walter Wottitz (Black and White)
LAWRENCE OF ARABIA, Fred A.
Young (Color)

ART DIRECTION-SET DECORATION
TO KILL A MOCKINGBIRD,
Alexander Golitzen, Henry
Bumstead; Oliver Emert
(Black and White)
LAWRENCE OF ARABIA, John Box,
John Stoll; Dario Simoni (Color)

SOUND
LAWRENCE OF ARABIA, Shepperton
Studio Sound Dept.

SHORT SUBJECTS
THE HOLE, Storyboard, Inc.,
Brandon Films, Inc. (Cartoons)
HEUREUX ANNIVERSAIRE (Happy
Anniversary), Atlantic Pictures
Corp., (Live Action Subjects)

DOCUMENTARY
DYLAN THOMAS, Janus Films
(Welsh) (Short Subjects)
BLACK FOX, Heritage Films, Inc.
(Features)

MUSIC
DAYS OF WINE AND ROSES (Days
Of Wine And Roses) Henry
Mancini, Johnny Mercer (Song)
LAWRENCE OF ARABIA, Maurice
Jarre (Music Score—
substantially original)
THE MUSIC MAN, Ray Heindorf
(Scoring of Music—adaptation
or treatment)

FILM EDITING
LAWRENCE OF ARABIA, Anne Coates
SPECIAL EFFECTS
THE LONGEST DAY, Robert
MacDonald, Jacques Maumont

COSTUME DESIGN
WHAT EVER HAPPENED TO
BABY JANE?, Norma Koch
(Black and White)
THE WONDERFUL WORLD OF THE
BROTHERS GRIMM, Mary Wills
(Color)

JEAN HERSHOLT
HUMANITARIAN AWARD
Steve Broidy

FOREIGN LANGUAGE FILM AWARD
SUNDAYS AND CYBELE (France)

SCIENTIFIC OR TECHNICAL
CLASS II
RALPH CHAPMAN
ALBERT S. PRATT, JAMES L.
WASSELL, HANS C. WOHLRAB
NORTH AMERICAN
PHILIPS CO., INC.
CHARLES E. SUTTER, WILLIAM
BRYSON SMITH and
LOUIS C. KENNELL

CLASS III
ELECTRO-VOICE, INC.
LOUIS G. MACKENZIE

189

1963

DIRECTOR
TONY RICHARDSON, Tom Jones

WRITING
TOM JONES, John Osborne (Best
Screenplay—based on material
from another medium)
HOW THE WEST WAS WON, James
R. Webb (Best Story and
Screenplay—written directly for
the screen)

CINEMATOGRAPHY
HUD, James Wong Howe
(Black and White)
CLEOPATRA, Leon Shamroy (Color)

ART DIRECTION-SET DECORATION
AMERICA AMERICA, Gene Callahan
(Black and White)
CLEOPATRA, John DeCuir, Jack
Martin Smith, Hildyard Brown,
Herman Blumenthal, Elven Webb,
Maurice Pelling, Boris Juraga;
Walter M. Scott, Paul S. Fox,
Ray Moyer (Color)

SOUND
HOW THE WEST WAS WON,
MGM Studio Sound Dept.

SHORT SUBJECTS
THE CRITIC, Columbia (Cartoons)
AN OCCURRENCE AT OWL CREEK
BRIDGE, Cappagariff-Janus Films,
(Live Action Subjects)

DOCUMENTARY
CHAGALL, Auerbach-Flag Films
(Short Subjects)
ROBERT FROST: A LOVER'S
QUARREL WITH THE WORLD,
WGBH Educational Foundation
(Features)

MUSIC
CALL ME IRRESPONSIBLE (Papa's
Delicate Condition) James Van
Heusen; Sammy Cahn (Song)
TOM JONES, John Addison (Music
Score—substantially original)
IRMA LA DOUCE, Andre Previn
(Scoring of Music—adaptation
or treatment)

FILM EDITING
HOW THE WEST WAS WON,
Harold F. Kress

COSTUME DESIGN
FEDERICO FELLINI'S 8½,
Piero Gherardi (Black and White)
CLEOPATRA, Irene Sharaff, Vittorio
Nino Novarese, Renie (Color)

SOUND EFFECTS
IT'S A MAD, MAD, MAD, MAD
WORLD, Walter G. Elliott

SPECIAL VISUAL EFFECTS
CLEOPATRA, Emil Kosa, Jr.

**IRVING G. THALBERG
MEMORIAL AWARD**
Sam Spiegel

FOREIGN LANGUAGE FILM AWARD
FEDERICO FELLINI'S 8½ (Italy)

SCIENTIFIC OR TECHNICAL
CLASS III
DOUGLAS G. SHEARER,
A. ARNOLD GILLESPIE

1964

DIRECTOR
GEORGE CUKOR, My Fair Lady

WRITING
BECKETT, Edward Anhalt (Best
Screenplay—based on material
from another medium)
FATHER GOOSE, S. H. Barnett,
Peter Stone, Frank Tarloff
(Best Story and Screenplay—written
directly for the screen)

CINEMATOGRAPHY
ZORBA THE GREEK, Walter Lassally
(Black and White)
MY FAIR LADY, Harry Stradling
(Color)

ART DIRECTION-SET DECORATION
ZORBA THE GREEK, Vassilis
Fotopoulos (Black and White)
MY FAIR LADY, Gene Allen, Cecil
Beaton; George James Hopkins
(Color)

SOUND
MY FAIR LADY, Warner Bros.
Studio Sound Dept.

SHORT SUBJECTS
THE PINK PHINK, UA (Cartoons)
CASALS CONDUCTS: 1964, Thalia
Films-Beckman Film Corp.
(Live Action Subjects)

DOCUMENTARY
NINE FROM LITTLE ROCK,
U.S. Information Agency
(Short Subjects)
WORLD WITHOUT SUN,
Columbia (Features)

MUSIC
CHIM CHIM CHER-EE (Mary
Poppins) Richard M. Sherman,
Robert B. Sherman (Song)
MARY POPPINS, Richard M.
Sherman, Robert B. Sherman
(Music Score—substantially
original)
MY FAIR LADY, Andre Previn
(Scoring of Music—adaptation
or treatment)

FILM EDITING
MARY POPPINS, Cotton Warburton

COSTUME DESIGN
THE NIGHT OF THE IGUANA,
Dorothy Jeakins (Black and White)
MY FAIR LADY, Cecil Beaton (Color)

SOUND EFFECTS
GOLDFINGER, Norman Wanstall

SPECIAL VISUAL EFFECTS
MARY POPPINS, Peter Ellenshaw,
Hamilton Luske, Eustace Lycett

FOREIGN LANGUAGE FILM AWARD
YESTERDAY, TODAY AND
TOMORROW (Italy)

HONORARY AND OTHER AWARDS
WILLIAM TUTTLE for his
outstanding make-up achievement
for "7 Faces Of Dr. Lao."
(statuette)

SCIENTIFIC OR TECHNICAL
CLASS I
PETRO VLAHOS, WADSWORTH E.
POHL, UB IWERKS

CLASS II
SIDNEY P. SOLOW, EDWARD H.
REICHARD, CARL W. HAUGE,
JOB SANDERSON

PIERRE ANGENIEUX

CLASS III
MILTON FORMAN, RICHARD B.
GLICKMAN, DANIEL J. PEARLMAN

STEWART FILMSCREEN CORP.

ANTHONY PAGLIA and 20TH
CENTURY-FOX STUDIO
MECHANICAL EFFECTS DEPT.

EDWARD H. REICHARD,
CARL W. HAUGE

EDWARD H. REICHARD, LEONARD
L. SOKOLOW, CARL W. HAUGE

NELSON TYLER

1965

DIRECTOR
ROBERT WISE, The Sound Of Music

WRITING
DOCTOR ZHIVAGO, Robert Bolt
(Best Screenplay—based on
material from another medium)

DARLING, Frederic Raphael (Best
Story and Screenplay—written
directly for the screen)

CINEMATOGRAPHY
SHIP OF FOOLS, Ernest Laszlo
(Black and White)
DOCTOR ZHIVAGO, Freddie Young
(Color)

ART DIRECTION-SET DECORATION
SHIP OF FOOLS, Robert Clatworthy;
Joseph Kish (Black and White)
DOCTOR ZHIVAGO, John Box, Terry
Marsh, Dario Simoni (Color)

SOUND
THE SOUND OF MUSIC, 20th
Century-Fox Studio Sound Dept.,
Todd-AO Sound Dept.

SHORT SUBJECTS
THE DOT AND THE LINE,
M-G-M (Cartoons)

THE CHICKEN (Le Poulet),
Pathe Contemporary Films
(Live Action Subjects)

DOCUMENTARY
TO BE ALIVE!, Johnson Wax
(Short Subjects)

THE ELEANOR ROOSEVELT STORY,
American Intl. (Features)

MUSIC
THE SHADOW OF YOUR SMILE
(The Sandpiper) Johnny Mandel,
Paul Francis Webster (Song)

DOCTOR ZHIVAGO, Maurice Jarre
(Music Score—substantially
original)

THE SOUND OF MUSIC, Irwin
Kostal (Scoring of Music—
adaptation or treatment)

FILM EDITING
THE SOUND OF MUSIC,
William Reynolds

COSTUME DESIGN
DARLING, Julie Harris
(Black and White)

DOCTOR ZHIVAGO, Phyllis Dalton
(Color)

SOUND EFFECTS
THE GREAT RACE, Tregoweth Brown

SPECIAL VISUAL EFFECTS
THUNDERBALL, John Stears

**IRVING G. THALBERG
MEMORIAL AWARD**
William Wyler

**JEAN HERSHOLT
HUMANITARIAN AWARD**
Edmond L. DePatie

FOREIGN LANGUAGE FILM AWARD
THE SHOP ON MAIN STREET
(Czechoslovakia)

HONORARY AND OTHER AWARDS
BOB HOPE for unique and
distinguished service to our
industry and the Academy.
(Gold Medal)

**SCIENTIFIC OR TECHNICAL
CLASS II**
ARTHUR J. HATCH
STEFAN KUDELSKI

1966
DIRECTOR
FRED ZINNEMANN, A Man For
All Seasons

WRITING
A MAN FOR ALL SEASONS, Robert
Bolt (Best Screenplay—based on
material from another medium)
A MAN AND A WOMAN, Claude
Lelouch; Pierre Uytterhoeven,
Claude Lelouch (Best Story and
Screenplay—written directly
for the screen)

CINEMATOGRAPHY
WHO'S AFRAID OF VIRGINIA
WOOLF?, Haskell Wexler
(Black and White)
A MAN FOR ALL SEASONS,
Ted Moore (Color)

ART DIRECTION-SET DECORATION
WHO'S AFRAID OF VIRGINIA
WOOLF?, Richard Sylbert; George
James Hopkins (Black and White)
FANTASTIC VOYAGE, Jack Martin
Smith, Dale Hennesy; Walter M.
Scott, Stuart A. Reiss (Color)

SOUND
GRAND PRIX, M-G-M Studio
Sound Dept.

SHORT SUBJECTS
HERB ALPERT AND THE TIJUANA
BRASS DOUBLE FEATURE,
Paramount (Cartoons)

WILD WINGS, British Transport
Films (Live Action Subjects)

DOCUMENTARY
A YEAR TOWARD TOMORROW,
Office of Economic Opportunity
(Short Subjects)
THE WAR GAME (British), Pathe
Contemporary Film (Features)

MUSIC
BORN FREE (Born Free) John Barry,
Don Black (Song)
BORN FREE, John Barry
(Original Music Score)
A FUNNY THING HAPPENED ON
THE WAY TO THE FORUM,
Ken Thorne (Scoring of Music—
adaptation or treatment)

FILM EDITING
GRAND PRIX, Fredric Steinkamp,
Henry Berman, Stewart Linder,
Frank Santillo

COSTUME DESIGN
WHO'S AFRAID OF VIRGINIA
WOOLF?, Irene Sharaff
(Black and White)
A MAN FOR ALL SEASONS,
Elizabeth Haffenden, Joan Bridge
(Color)

SOUND EFFECTS
GRAND PRIX, Gordon Daniel

SPECIAL VISUAL EFFECTS
FANTASTIC VOYAGE, Art Cruickshank

**IRVING G. THALBERG
MEMORIAL AWARD**
Robert Wise

**JEAN HERSHOLT
HUMANITARIAN AWARD**
George Bagnall

FOREIGN LANGUAGE FILM AWARD
A MAN AND A WOMAN (France)

HONORARY AND OTHER AWARDS
Y. FRANK FREEMAN for unusual
and outstanding service to the
Academy during his thirty years
in Hollywood. (statuette)
YAKIMA CANUTT for achievements
as a stunt man and for developing
safety devices to protect stunt
men everywhere. (statuette)

**SCIENTIFIC OR TECHNICAL
CLASS II**
MITCHELL CAMERA CORP.
ARNOLD & RICHTER KG
CLASS III
PANAVISION INC.
CARROLL KNUDSON
RUBY RAKSIN

1967
DIRECTOR
MIKE NICHOLS, The Graduate

WRITING
IN THE HEAT OF THE NIGHT,
Stirling Silliphant (Best
Screenplay—based on material
from another medium)
GUESS WHO'S COMING TO
DINNER, William Rose (Best
Story and Screenplay—written
directly for the screen)

CINEMATOGRAPHY
BONNIE AND CLYDE, Burnett Guffey

ART DIRECTION-SET DECORATION
CAMELOT, John Truscott,
Edward Carrere; John W. Brown

SOUND
IN THE HEAT OF THE NIGHT,
Samuel Goldwyn Studio
Sound Dept.

SHORT SUBJECTS
THE BOX, Brandon Films (Cartoons)
A PLACE TO STAND, Ontario Dept.
of Economics & Development,
Columbia Pictures
(Live Action Subjects)

DOCUMENTARY
THE REDWOODS, King Screen
Productions (Short Subjects)
THE ANDERSON PLATOON, The
French Broadcasting System
(Features)

MUSIC
TALK TO THE ANIMALS (Doctor
Dolittle), Leslie Bricusse (Song)
THOROUGHLY MODERN MILLIE,
Elmer Bernstein (Original
Music Score)
CAMELOT, Alfred Newman, Ken
Darby (Scoring of Music—
adaptation or treatment)

FILM EDITING
IN THE HEAT OF THE NIGHT,
Hal Ashby

COSTUME DESIGN
CAMELOT, John Truscott

SOUND EFFECTS
THE DIRTY DOZEN, John Poyner

SPECIAL VISUAL EFFECTS
DOCTOR DOLITTLE, L. B. Abbott

**IRVING G. THALBERG
MEMORIAL AWARD**
Alfred Hitchcock

**JEAN HERSHOLT
HUMANITARIAN AWARD**
Gregory Peck

FOREIGN LANGUAGE FILM AWARD
CLOSELY WATCHED TRAINS
(Czechoslovakia)

HONORARY AND OTHER AWARDS
ARTHUR FREED for distinguished
service to the Motion Picture
Academy of Arts and Sciences in
the production of six top-rated
Awards telecasts. (statuette)

**SCIENTIFIC OR TECHNICAL
CLASS III**
ELECTRO-OPTICAL DIVISION
of KOLLMORGEN CORP.
PANAVISION INC.
FRED R. WILSON
WALDON O. WATSON and
UNIVERSAL CITY STUDIO
SOUND DEPT.

1968-
introduction to the fifth decade

WITH THE 41st Annual Academy Awards, Oscar started his fifth decade in a new home — the Dorothy Chandler Pavilion in the handsome Los Angeles Music Center.

Something else was new, too. Instead of one emcee, ten "Friends of Oscar" — among them Ingrid

Bob Hope was on hand to give Martha Raye the 1968 Jean Hersholt Humanitarian Award, honoring her many Vietnam tours to entertain the troops.

Veteran star John Wayne accepts his well-deserved 1969 Best Actor Oscar from Barbra Streisand who was the Best Actress Award-winner in 1968.

Bergman, Bob Hope and Frank Sinatra — announced the 1968 Awards on April 14, 1969.

With Katharine Hepburn (Lion in Winter) and Barbra Streisand (Funny Girl) tied as Best Actress, Oscar had his first co-winners since 1932. Hepburn also became the first three-time winner in either top acting category.

Cliff Robertson's Best Actor

accolade for the title role in Charly was also somewhat of a surprise, for "small" pictures like Charly rarely reap top honors.

The movie of the year was Oliver. The lavish musical version of Oliver Twist earned five Oscars and a special citation for choreographic excellence.

Jack Albertson (The Subject Was Roses) and Ruth Gordon (Rosemary's Baby) picked up "Supporting" Oscars. To Martha Raye went the Jean Hersholt Humanitarian Award for her overseas tours.

For the 42nd Annual Academy Awards, again held in the Chandler Pavilion, Oscar had 17 "Friends,"

Among those present at the 1968 ceremony were the Paul Newmans. He directed Rachel, Rachel, which won wife Joanne Woodward a nomination.

including Cliff Robertson, Clint Eastwood, Bob Hope and Elizabeth Taylor, as presenters.

The big night was April 7, 1970, and two of the top citations for 1969 were also unexpected. Best Picture *Midnight Cowboy* and Best Actress Maggie Smith had been considered very dark horses — *Cowboy* because of its "X" rating, and Miss Smith because *The Prime of Miss Jean Brodie* was shown so early in the year.

Gig Young *(They Shoot Horses, Don't They?)* and Goldie Hawn, in her first picture *(Cactus Flower)*, were the "Supporting" players very first Best Actress Oscar.

This was the night Hollywood proved its veterans have a very special place in its heart. Honorary Awards "for superlative and distinguished service in the making of motion pictures" went to Lillian Gish, who started her screen career in 1912, and Orson Welles. About "to retire" Frank Sinatra also took home the Jean Hersholt Humanitarian Award for his many charities, and screen veterans carried off both Supporting Oscars: Helen Hayes *(Airport)* and John Mills *(Ryan's Daughter.)*.

For the second year, the Best

Known as one of Hollywood's most generous stars, Frank Sinatra received the coveted Jean Hersholt Humanitarian Award for 1970 in recognition of his extensive charitable work.

Holding his own Oscar as 1969's Best Supporting Actor, Gig Young posed with Raquel Welch, who accepted for Goldie Hawn, and Fred Astaire, who showed the audience there was still magic in his feet.

Oscared. A Special Award to Cary Grant for "outstanding artistry and many memorable performances" had him close to tears.

The great and near great gathered again at the Chandler the night of April 15, 1971, this time for the 1970 Awards, Oscar's 43rd time around. Oscar's Friends now numbered 34 moviedom toppers, including Janet Gaynor, winner of the

Actress winner was British—Glenda Jackson *(Women in Love)*.

The cliff-hanger of the evening was, of course, the Best Actor Award, and the applause was thunderous when, despite his brush-off of the honor, the name in the envelope proved that of George C. Scott. Unquestionably, his was the performance of the year in the picture of the year, *Patton*.

fifth decade-cont'd.

The highlight of the 44th Annual Academy Awards, held April 10, 1972, at the Dorothy Chandler Pavilion, was the massive and affectionate tribute to Charlie Chaplin. But there were the other Oscars to be given, too, and four masters of ceremonies were on hand for the occasion.

There was Helen Hayes, who referred to herself as a "Ms of Ceremonies." There was also witty Alan King; Sammy Davis, Jr., who called himself "Archie Bunker's friend," and last, but far from least, Jack Lemmon.

The French Connection was the big winner of the evening, with five Oscars. It rated as the year's Best Picture; its star, Gene Hackman and Director William Friedkin were also honored, and it picked up the other two Oscars for Best Screenplay and Film Editing.

Today's "best"—Cloris Leachman, Ben Johnson and Gene Hackman — pay homage to the peerless Chaplin at the Governors Ball, as Oona beams.

Jane Fonda "sneaks off" with her Oscar.

Jane Fonda was Oscared most deservedly for her virtuoso performance in one of the better thrillers of 1971, *Klute.*

An oddity of the Supporting Actor and Actress categories was that all ten contestants were first-time nominees and four were from *The Last Picture Show*. The winners were *Show's* Ben Johnson and Cloris Leachman.

Assisting the four M.C.'s were a record number of well-known presenters, ranging from Ann-Margret and Liza Minnelli to yesteryear-star Betty Grable, Joe Namath and famed playwright Tennessee Williams.

Filmdom's night of nights ran two-and-a-half hours, opening with a sparkling musical production, *Lights, Camera, Action,* starring Joel Grey and spotlighting some highlights in Hollywood's history. But above all else it was the night Charlie Chaplin came back to town.

1968
best picture

Oliver!
COLUMBIA

CAST: Ron Moody, Oliver Reed, Shani Wallis, Mark Lester, Jack Wild, Harry Secombe, Hugh Griffith, Sheila White
CREDITS: Producer, John Woolf; Director, Sir Carol Reed; Screenplay, Vernon Harris; from the musical by Lionel Bart; Music and lyrics, Lionel Bart; Music Director, John Green; Cinematographer, Oswald Morris; Choreographer, Onna White

THE YEAR'S BEST PICTURE is a spectacular, multi-million-dollar movie version of the famed London and Broadway stage musical, and it had that Oscar look from the moment it hit the screen.

An instantaneous box-office winner, *Oliver!* gathered five Oscars, including the awards for best director, best scoring of a musical, and art direction, plus a special award for choreography.

Owing its inspiration to the Charles Dickens classic, *Oliver Twist*, it tells the well-known story of the orphaned, hungry young inmate of a British workhouse who commits the unpardonable sin of asking for more gruel. Sold to a heartless undertaker as a result, he runs off to London, where he falls in with Fagin's gang of young pickpockets, but is ultimately united with his long-lost, wealthy uncle.

Two of its excellent cast rated Oscar nominations — Ron Moody, who first made the despicable Fagin into a lovable old rogue in the original stage production, and Jack Wild, the 15-year-old Artful Dodger. Wild had been one of the younger boys in the stage *Oliver!*

A dedicated cast, a foot-tapping score, magnificent dance numbers, sets that bring Nineteenth-Century London glowingly alive in all its elegance and squalor, and a highly dramatic story—all point to *Oliver!* becoming not only a top money-maker, but a screen classic as well.

OTHER NOMINEES:
FUNNY GIRL, Columbia
THE LION IN WINTER, Avco-Embassy
RACHEL, RACHEL, Warner Bros.-7 Arts
ROMEO & JULIET, Paramount

Fagin (Ron Moody) is flanked by The Artful Dodger (Jack Wild), left, and Oliver (Mark Lester).

1968
best actor

Cliff Robertson
CHARLY

WHEN Cliff Robertson's name was announced as a Best Actor nominee, he was on location in the Philippines, making *Too Late the Hero*. And despite his vow that he would make it back to Los Angeles on Oscar Night, even if he had to swim, he was not on hand on April 14.

Robertson had not been able to get the time off to come, and when the good news was relayed to him, his, "It's very hard to believe," was very understandable.

Robertson had spent long, frustrating years in trying to get *Charly* onto the big screen. He first played the mentally retarded youth who is turned into a genius by an operation, then regresses to his former child-like state, in the TV drama, *The Two Worlds of Charlie Gordon*.

Twice before, Robertson had given outstanding performances in TV plays, only to lose out when they became movies. His role in *The Hustler* went to Paul Newman, and Jack Lemmon played in the movie version of *The Days of Wine and Roses*.

This time, he was taking no chances; he purchased the screen rights himself.

It took him seven years to get *Charly* financed, into production, and onto the nation's screens. Previous pictures dealing with mental retardation have been box-office bombs, and movie company after movie company said "no thanks," when Robertson approached them, until ABC's Selmur Pictures decided to take a chance.

With *Charly* (the spelling is his) proving one of Hollywood's biggest "sleepers," Robertson stands to make a fortune. He took a big share of the picture against a token salary.

Robertson is a native Californian who scored his first big acting success in the Chicago stage production of *Mr. Roberts*. He came to Hollywood in 1956, after several years on Broadway, for *Picnic*, and has been a movie regular since.

One of his most talked about screen roles was as young John F. Kennedy in *PT 109*. Like Kennedy, Robertson was a lieutenant (j.g.) in World War II, but in the Maritime Service rather than the Navy.

The handsome actor is married to glamorous society girl-actress Dina Merrill, by whom he has a baby daughter.

His films include: *Autumn Leaves, The Interns, Sunday in New York, The Best Man, 633 Squadron, The Honeypot*.

OTHER NOMINEES:
ALAN ARKIN, The Heart Is a Lonely Hunter
ALAN BATES, The Fixer
PETER O'TOOLE, The Lion in Winter
RON MOODY, Oliver!

1968
best actress
Katharine Hepburn
THE LION IN WINTER

KATHARINE HEPBURN never comes to the Oscar ceremony, and she again ran true to form. Even the prospect that her magnificent Eleanor of Aquitaine in *The Lion in Winter* would make her the Academy's first triple "Best Actress" failed to bring her.

With her third Oscar, Hepburn broke precedent in several ways. It was the first tie (with Barbra Streisand) in the Best Actress category, and only the second tie in Academy history. It was also the first time an actress won two Oscars in a row since Luise Rainer in 1936-1937. Furthermore, the *Lion* nomination was Hepburn's eleventh, making her the most nominated thespian in Oscar's 41 years.

Katharine Hepburn was a natural for the 12th Century Queen, whose husband, Henry II (played by Peter O'Toole) had to keep her locked up to control her. Hepburn herself considers Eleanor of Aquitaine one of the high spots in her long, distinguished career.

Despite the eight centuries that lie between them, Hepburn is curiously like Eleanor of Aquitaine. The richest, most powerful, most brilliant woman of her time, Eleanor was a crusading individualist whose ideas were far in advance of her time. For one thing, she believed passionately in the equality of women.

Hepburn—the daughter of a strong-minded mother who was a civil rights pioneer—is as much an individualist and intellectual rebel as Eleanor. She, too, believes passionately in the equality of the sexes, with the provision that some women are more equal than most men.

Like Eleanor, too, Hepburn is a brilliant conversationalist, has enormous physical stamina, is decisive and self-disciplined.

Her next film, *The Madwoman of Chaillot*, a disappointment, Hepburn, now in her sixties, returned to Broadway in 1970. It was her first stage appearance in some 30 years, her first musical ever, and she scored a real triumph as French designer Chanel in *Coco*.

Katharine Hepburn and Peter O'Toole

1968
best actress
Barbra Streisand
FUNNY GIRL

UNLIKE HER CO-WINNER, Barbra Streisand was very much in evidence on Oscar Night. Wearing see-through black evening pajamas, she clasped her Oscar with a heartfelt, "Hello, Gorgeous!" and paid a graceful compliment in declaring, "I am honored to be in such magnificent company as Katharine Hepburn."

The little girl from Brooklyn is somewhat of a theatrical phenomenon. Though she has never taken a singing lesson in her life and insists she is not a singer, but "an actress who sings," Streisand reached superstar status in her early 20s, as the result of one great musical role; her records sell in the millions, and her TV "Specials" get top ratings.

As a teen-ager right out of high school, she made a short-lived attempt to land a Broadway spot. Broadway proved unreceptive to the small brunette with the Queen Nefertiti profile. So she made her debut on Amateur Night at a local theatre, with the result that a nearby night club booked her. This led to a part in an off-Broadway review which lasted a single night, but landed her a Broadway role in a musical, *I Can Get It for You Wholesale.* The reviews were mixed, but as the unnoticed, unloved secretary, Streisand was a sensation. As a result, she was chosen to play Fanny Brice, the great comedienne whose private life was such a heartbreak, in *Funny Girl.*

Opening on Broadway on March 24, 1964, the musical and its young star were smash hits, and triumphed again two years later in London.

When *Funny Girl* was to be transferred to film, there was no question that Streisand would be its star.

Separated from actor Elliot Gould, by whom she has a small son, Barbra Streisand is an enormously talented, hard-working actress-singer who, as a child, set her goal to become "the best" Broadway, film and recording star in the business.

Streisand won her Oscar just ten days before her 27th birthday, and is one of today's superstars.

Her other films are: *Hello, Dolly!, On a Clear Day You Can See Forever, The Owl and the Pussycat, What's Up, Doc.*

OTHER NOMINEES:
PATRICIA NEAL, The Subject Was Roses
VANESSA REDGRAVE, Isadora
JOANNE WOODWARD, Rachel, Rachel

1968
best supporting actor

Jack Albertson
THE SUBJECT WAS ROSES

AFTER ALMOST 40 years in show business, Jack Albertson's talent is finally winning the recognition it deserves. Though he has been in vaudeville, burlesque, countless stage plays and "so many movies I can't remember them all," his name was not known to the public until his smash hit on Broadway in *The Subject Was Roses*. As its angry, frustrated husband and father, he won a Tony Award, and his repeat of the role in the movie version has brought him an Oscar. Since *Roses,* Albertson has been seen in *Changes*.

OTHER NOMINEES:
SEYMOUR CASSEL, Faces
DANIEL MASSEY, Star!
JACK WILD, Oliver!
JACK WILDER, The Producers

best supporting actress

Ruth Gordon
ROSEMARY'S BABY

"I DON'T KNOW why it took so long," quipped the spritely 72-year-old, picking up her Oscar for her role as the modern-day witch in *Rosemary's Baby*. Long one of our great stage stars, Ruth Gordon made her screen debut in 1939, as Mary Todd in *Abe Lincoln in Illinois,* and won a Supporting Actress nomination in 1965 for *Inside Daisy Clover*. With her husband, playwright-director Garson Kanin, she has won three writing nominations (*A Double Life,* 1947; *Adam's Rib,* 1950; *Pat and Mike,* 1952)

OTHER NOMINEES:
LYNN CARLIN, Faces
SONDRA LOCKE, The Heart Is a Lonely Hunter
KAY MEDFORD, Funny Girl
ESTELLE PARSONS, Rachel, Rachel

1969
best picture
Midnight Cowboy
UNITED ARTISTS

CAST: Dustin Hoffman, Jon Voight, Sylvia Miles, John McGiver, Brenda Vaccaro, Barnard Hughes, Ruth White
CREDITS: Producer, Jerome Hellman; Director, John Schlesinger; Screenplay, Waldo Salt; Musical Supervision, John Barry; Director of Photography, Adam Holender

THOUGH *Midnight Cowboy* was one of 1969's most highly praised films, the odds seemed against an X-rated film being Oscared. But in today's climate of permissiveness, on screen and off, the barred-to-all-under-17 tag proved no barrier. *Cowboy* also picked up Oscars for Best Director and Best Screenplay from Another Medium.

Cowboy is much more than just a well-made, seamy, slice-of-life drama about a male hustler (Jon Voight) and the sickly Bronx-born grifter (Dustin Hoffman) who first fleeces him, then befriends him. It is a compassionate story of human loneliness, of two friendless people groping their way to their first meaningful human contact.

Voight, a movie novice, is the "midnight cowboy," a good-looking, brash youth from Texas out to parlay his sexual prowess into fame and fortune in the Big Town. Hoffman, as "Ratzo," a New York punk, at first takes him, then teams up with him. Hoffman, as cynical and knowing as Voight is optimistic and naive, has his own dream — to get to Florida somehow and find restored health and a new life there.

In their efforts to bilk a hostile world rebuffing them at every turn, this unlikely pair progress from partners in shady business to comrades. Each has found his first real friend. Voight even manages to get bus fare to take them to Florida — but on the way, time runs out for Hoffman.

Voight and Hoffman each received a well-earned Best Actor Nomination. Sylvia Miles rated a Best Supporting Actress bid as the ex-hooker who turns the tables on a gullible Voight.

OTHER NOMINEES:
BUTCH CASSIDY AND THE SUNDANCE KID,
   20th Century-Fox
ANNE OF THE THOUSAND DAYS, Universal
HELLO DOLLY, 20th Century-Fox
Z, Cinema V

*Dustin Hoffman and "Cowboy"
Jon Voight*

1969
best actor
John Wayne
TRUE GRIT

THIS YEAR'S Best Actor is a movie legend. "Duke" Wayne has been in pictures almost as long as Oscar. His career covers some 41 years and he has been a major star since he made a sensation in John Ford's *Stagecoach* in 1939.

One of the top ten box-office attractions for the past 20 years, Wayne won only one Academy nomination before, for *Sands of Iwo Jima* (1949). No wonder he quipped, accepting his Oscar for *"Rooster"* in *True Grit,* "If I'd known, I'd have put the eye-patch on thirty-five years earlier."

What Wayne did as Rooster — the ornery, one-eyed marshal hired by a teen-ager to run down her father's murderer — was to parody himself and his usual film roles. The result was pure delight and had practically all of Hollywood rooting for him to be Oscared, not only for Rooster, but in honor of his long, distinguished career.

Now in his mid-60's, the six-foot-four Wayne — born Marion Michael Morrison in Winterset, Iowa — has starred in some 200 movies. In his early Hollywood days, he made over 200 two-reelers, and was "Singing Sam," the screen's first singing cowboy (a double did the warbling) in a whole series of B pictures.

Best known as a Western star, he was seen in 1968 in the controversial war story, *The Green Berets.* Some other non-Western Waynes were *The Quiet Man* (1952), *The High and the Mighty* (1954) and *In Harm's Way* (1965).

A blunt man who says what he thinks, Wayne refused to let his bout with lung cancer, some five years ago, slow him down. He does manage, however, to take two- and three-month vacations these days on his beloved ship, *The Wild Goose,* a 135-foot converted minesweeper.

Whether he is at home in Newport Beach, California, or on his 17,000-acre cattle ranch in Arizona, the house overflows with family. He has seven children (by two wives) ranging in age from 35 years down to five, and 18 grandchildren.

For Oscar night, Wayne returned from Mexico, where he was making *Rio Lobo,* then went on to the new location, Tucson, Arizona. He found the entire company, right down to his horse, sporting black eye-patches in celebration of his victory.

Some of his more recent films are: *The Alamo, North to Alaska, Hatari, The Man Who Shot Liberty Valance, Donovan's Reef, McLintock, Circus World, The Sons of Katie Elder, The War Wagon, Chisum, The Cowboys.*

OTHER NOMINEES:
RICHARD BURTON, Anne of the Thousand Days
DUSTIN HOFFMAN, Midnight Cowboy
PETER O'TOOLE, Goodbye, Mr. Chips
JON VOIGHT, Midnight Cowboy

1969
best actress

Maggie Smith
THE PRIME OF MISS JEAN BRODIE

ANYONE WHO missed Maggie Smith in *The Prime of Miss Jean Brodie* missed one of the greatest performances on film. Nobody who saw it will ever forget her unorthodox, self-deluding Scottish spinster-school-marm, who discovers her much-valued "prime" is over when one of her very special girls strips away her pretenses and steals her man.

Nevertheless, Maggie Smith was not considered a front runner in the Oscar race, largely because the film was shown so early in the year. This is always a handicap, so her win, deserved as it was, was rather unexpected.

Born Margaret Smith some 30-odd years ago in Illford, Essex, she chose her plain nickname "Maggie" for professional purposes. This is indicative of the brilliant, no-nonsense British star who makes no bones that the stage is her real love and movies are just her "jam money."

She's been making them on and off since 1961, when she practically stole *The VIP's* from under the noses of Elizabeth Taylor and Richard Burton. "Grand larceny," was Burton's wry description of her scene-stealing.

Red-headed, green-eyed Maggie Smith started acting in high-school plays. She was on the British stage in *Cakes and Ale* when an American producer spotted her and brought her to Broadway for the *New Faces Review*. She proved a sensation.

A former member of London's famed Old Vic Company, she has been with Sir Lawrence Olivier's prestigeous National Theatre since its inception in 1959. She played Des-demona in Olivier's stage *Othello*, and repeated the role in the film version, to win her first Oscar nomination (1965).

When the National Theatre made its American debut early in 1970 in Los Angeles, film city had an appreciative look at Maggie Smith on stage in a Restoration comedy, *The Beau Stratagem*, and Chekhov's *The Three Sisters*.

Married to actor Robert Stephens —the man she lost in *Jean Brodie*— and the mother of a young son, Maggie Smith believes in keeping her private life private. She grants few interviews and volunteers little personal information. Just so long as she keeps making those "jam-money" movies, it is enough.

Her other films are: *The Pumpkin Eater, Young Cassidy, Hot Millions.*

OTHER NOMINEES:
GENEVIEVE BUJOLD, Anne of the Thousand Days
JANE FONDA, They Shoot Horses, Don't They?
LIZA MINNELLI, The Sterile Cuckoo
JEAN SIMMONS, The Happy Ending

1969
best supporting actor

Gig Young
THEY SHOOT HORSES, DON'T THEY?

IN CHANGING his screen image from light comedian to heavy in *They Shoot Horses*, stage and screen veteran Gig Young won an Oscar as the cynical, hard-driving emcee of a brutal Depression-era dance marathon. The four-times-married, Minnesota-born thespian made his screen debut in *The Gay Sisters* (1942) with Barbara Stanwyck, and was Oscar-nominated twice before — for *Come Fill the Cup* (1951) and *Teacher's Pet* (1958). Some other films: *That Touch of Mink, Strange Bedfellows, The Shuttered Room.*

OTHER NOMINEES:
RUPERT CROSSE, The Reivers
ELLIOTT GOULD, Bob & Carol & Ted & Alice
JACK NICHOLSON, Easy Rider
ANTHONY QUAYLE, Anne of the Thousand Days

best supporting actress

Goldie Hawn
CACTUS FLOWER

BLOND GOLDIE HAWN is smart enough to parlay being "dumb" into a career that brought her, at 24, an Oscar for *Cactus Flower,* her first movie. In it, she more than held her own with Ingrid Bergman and Walter Matthau. Born in Washington, D.C., she ran a dancing school and was in the chorus of several stage musicals before becoming famous as the resident giggler on TV's zaniest show, Martin and Rowen's *Laugh In.* She missed picking up her Oscar because she was in England, making a movie, *There's a Girl In My Soup.*

OTHER NOMINEES:
CATHERINE BURNS, Last Summer
DYAN CANNON, Bob & Carol & Ted & Alice
SYLVIA MILES, Midnight Cowboy
SUSANNAH YORK, They Shoot Horses, Don't They?

1970
best picture

Patton
20TH CENTURY FOX

CAST: George C. Scott, Karl Malden, Michael Bates, Karl Michael Vogler, Ed Binns, Lawrence Dobkin
CREDITS: Producer, Frank McCarthy; Director, Franklin J. Schaffner; Screenplay, Francis Ford Coppola, Edmund H. North; Director of Photography, Fred Koenekamp. In Dimension 150, DeLuxe Color

WINNER of seven Oscars, including the coveted Best Actor and Best Director accolades, *Patton* swept through the Academy Awards for 1970 the way the General himself rolled over enemies in World War II with his tanks.

The multi-million-dollar movie, for which General of the Army Omar N. Bradley, USA, served as chief military advisor, takes a penetrating look at the man who was perhaps the most aggressive, flamboyant and controversial commander ever to wear an American uniform.

It took producer Frank McCarthy, a retired Brigadier General, 20 years to turn his dream of a movie on Patton into reality. Released as a roadshow in February, by Oscar time it already grossed $24 million.

General George S. Patton (superbly played by George C. Scott) was a man of flinty courage, big hurts and a scathing tongue. A millionaire's son who quoted Seneca and Napoleon on war and was a brilliant tactician, he could ruthlessly whip a demoralized Second Corps, decisively beaten by German Field Marshal Edwin Rommel, "the Desert Fox," into a topflight fighting unit.

He could also slap a hospitalized G.I. with shattered nerves, claiming he was nothing but a shirking coward; be demoted as a result; reach hero status again in the crucial Battle of the Bulge, yet remain an Army thorn until the day he died.

Helping to bring this exciting screen biography of a most complex man vividly alive are Karl Malden, as Bradley; Karl Michael Vogler, as Rommel, and Michael Bates, playing Patton's arch rival, British Field Marshal Bernard Montgomery.

OTHER NOMINEES
AIRPORT, Universal
FIVE EASY PIECES, Columbia
LOVE STORY, Paramount
M*A*S*H, 20th Century-Fox

General Patton (George C. Scott) slaps a hospitalized soldier (Tim Considine) whom he accuses of cowardice.

1970
best actor

George C. Scott
PATTON

THE EXPLOSIVE Mr. Scott, as he has been called, is as much a man who does not travel with the crowd as was General George S. Patton, whom he portrays so magnificently on the screen.

Nothing could make most movie people happier than to win an Oscar. Not so Scott. He tried to withdraw his name when the nominations were announced, as he had previously in 1961, on his second nomination, for *The Hustler.* (He made no such request when nominated for the first time in 1959, for *Anatomy of a Murder.*)

The Academy turned down his request for a second time, and on Oscar night proved it could pay honor to great acting, regardless of the ungraciousness of the performer.

When Scott was reached the next day in New York, where he had started filming on *The Hospital,* he claimed not to have watched the ceremonies. His only comment was that the suggestion to present the statuette to the General George S. Patton Museum in Fort Knox, Kentucky, seemed like a good idea.

The seven-Oscared *Patton* was Scott's eighth film since his movie debut in 1959 in *The Hanging Tree.* The Hollywood maverick is essentially a stage actor and regards movie-making largely as an economic necessity.

Scott scored his first stage hit in the title role of *Richard III* at the New York Shakespeare Festival in 1956. Before that, he spent several hard years trying to get a foothold on Broadway, during which time he held a variety of "eating money" odd jobs.

The scrappy, dark-haired, strong-willed six-footer was born in Wise, West Virginia, 42 years ago, grew up in Detroit and went into the Marines at 17. After a four-year hitch, he signed in at the University of Missouri, where in varsity shows he discovered he liked acting.

Among Scott's greatest successes are his rasping, vicious prosecutor in *The Andersonville Trial,* both on Broadway and TV, and his first comic role, after a series of heavies, in the Broadway smash, *Plaza Suite.*

Scott, who has been divorced three times and is the father of five children, was again nominated for Best Actor in 1971's *The Hospital.* This time, he did not ask that his name be withdrawn. He was silent.

His other pictures are: *The List of Adrian Messenger, Dr. Strangelove, The Bible, The Flim-Flam Man, Petulia, They Might Be Giants, The Last Run.*

OTHER NOMINEES:
MELVYN DOUGLAS, I Never Sang for My Father
JAMES EARL JONES, The Great White Hope
JACK NICHOLSON, Five Easy Pieces
RYAN O'NEAL, Love Story

1970
best actress

Glenda Jackson
WOMEN IN LOVE

THIS ENORMOUSLY talented English actress was virtually unknown to American moviegoers before her electrifying performance as the strong-willed, emancipated sculptress in *Women in Love,* which brought her a well-earned Oscar.

The next year the Academy again looked her way, honoring her beautifully restrained performance in *Sunday Bloody Sunday* — one of the acting highlights of the year — with another Best Actress nomination.

Yet Glenda Jackson, at 36, regards her career as infinitely less important than being the mother of two-year-old Daniel Hodges, who is "nearing the age when he needs a full-time mother." She wouldn't hesitate to quit her career, she says, "If the time comes when he asks me to stay at home."

Meanwhile, Glenda Jackson's busy work schedule kept her away from Hollywood at Oscar time. She was appearing on British TV in the title role of the series, *Elizabeth R,* and she was also playing the Virgin Queen in the film, *Mary Queen of Scots,* in production at the time.

While she didn't think an Oscar would go to an English actress twice in a row, she "couldn't help hoping just a little," and she admits it was "such a thrill" to win.

Born near Liverpool, she originally planned on becoming a ballerina, then switched to acting when she became too tall for ballet.

She graduated with honors from London's prestigious Royal Academy of Dramatic Arts, then spent six lean years in various repertory companies. The going was so rough that she and her husband, stage director Roy Hodges, often found themselves waiting on tables or working in factories to keep from going hungry.

Her break came with acceptance into the Royal Shakespeare Company's Theatre of Cruelty.

Her Ophelia in the Royal Shakespeare's 1965 production of *Hamlet* won her much acclaim. Her New York debut, as murderess Charlotte Corday, in *The Persecution and Assassination of Jean Paul Marat as Performed by the Inmates of the Asylum at Charenton under the Direction of the Marquis de Sade,* resulted in her being named as Broadway's most promising newcomer.

She repeated her role in the film version of the 23-word-titled play. It was her first movie.

Her other films are: *Negatives; The Music Lovers.*

OTHER NOMINEES:
JANE ALEXANDER, The Great White Hope
ALI MACGRAW, Love Story
SARAH MILES, Ryan's Daughter
CARRIE SNODGRESS, Diary of a Mad Housewife

1970
best supporting actor

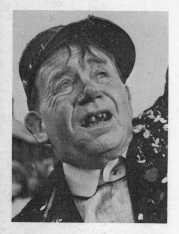

John Mills
RYAN'S DAUGHTER

ONE OF Britain's most distinguished stage and screen stars, John Mills has concentrated on character roles for the past ten years and earned his Oscar in the difficult role of a mute, misshapen cretin whose eyes talked for him. The father of actresses Hayley and Juliet Mills was born in Felixstowe, Suffolk, in 1908, started as a chorus boy and became known for his many military roles. Among his notable films are: *In Which We Serve, Great Expectations, Hobson's Choice, Tunes of Glory, The Family Way, Oh! What a Lovely War.*

OTHER NOMINEES:
RICHARD CASTELLANO, Lovers and Other Strangers
CHIEF DAN GEORGE, Little Big Man
GENE HACKMAN, I Never Sang for My Father
JOHN MARLEY, Love Story

best supporting actress

Helen Hayes
AIRPORT

FORTY YEARS after winning her first Oscar, this spritely septuagenarian was honored by her peers for her marvelous little old lady stowaway in *Airport*, her first film in 14 years. As a result of the part, this great lady of stage and screen finds she cannot step on a plane now without being the subject of some wisecrack. With a career spanning more than 60 years, Helen Hayes has decided that "I must refrain from making any more statements about my dream of retirement. It's beginning to sound absurd."

OTHER NOMINEES:
KAREN BLACK, Five Easy Pieces
LEE GRANT, The Landlord
SALLY KELLERMAN, M*A*S*H
MAUREEN STAPLETON, Airport

1971
best picture
The French Connection
20TH CENTURY-FOX

CAST: Gene Hackman, Fernando Rey, Roy Scheider, Marcel Bozzuffi, Frederic De Pasquale, Bill Hickman.
CREDITS: Producer, Philip D'Antoni; Director, William Friedkin; Screenplay, Ernest Tidyman; Director of Photography, Owen Roizman. DeLuxe Color

THE FRENCH CONNECTION's total of eight nominations brought five Oscars, including the much-coveted Best Picture, Best Actor and Best Director accolades.

A highly entertaining thriller with overtones of a social documentary on the drug trade, *Connection* is based on the real life exploits of a tough-as-nails, dedicated, two-man team of New York City narcotics squad detectives. Theirs is the violent, no-quarter-given world of cold-blooded mobsters and calloused cops vieing to outwit and out-shoot each other for a shipment of pure heroin with a street value of $32 million.

The narcotics squadmen are Best Actor Gene Hackman, who plays a longshot hunch that puts him bull-doggedly on the trail of the massive shipment, and his sidekick, Roy Scheider. (Scheider won a Best Supporting Actor nomination for his fine work.)

The pair's grim determination to crack one of the biggest dope smuggling operations ever to rise out of the shadowy depths of the international drug traffic climaxes in one of the most spine-tingling and unusual car chases ever filmed.

Hackman commandeers a car to pursue a wildly speeding Brooklyn elevated train where a French killer holds a gun at the engineer's head as it flashes past station after station.

Shot on location on the streets of New York and in Marseilles, France, *Connection's* international cast includes French star Marcel Bozzuffi, as the killer, with Spain's polished Fernando Rey as the brains behind the narcotics racket.

OTHER NOMINEES:
A CLOCKWORK ORANGE, Warner Bros.
FIDDLER ON THE ROOF, United Artists
THE LAST PICTURE SHOW, Columbia
NICHOLAS AND ALEXANDRA, Columbia

Detective Gene Hackman (bottom of stairs) catches up with his quarry, gunman Marcel Bozzuffi.

1971
best actor
Gene Hackman
THE FRENCH CONNECTION

A JUBILANTLY emotional Gene Hackman, close to tears, picked up his Oscar for his outstanding portrayal of a cop as uncompromisingly tough as the dope ring he was out to smash.

Hackman is in virtually every scene in 1971's Best Picture. He even insisted on handling much of the stunt-driving in the dramatic and dangerous "chase" sequences, as he is a motorcycle and sprint-car enthusiast.

A year ago, Hackman won a nomination in a vastly different role. He was the loving son vainly seeking his father's affection in *I Never Sang for My Father.* That nomination, like his first, for *Bonnie and Clyde,* was in the Supporting Actor category.

A native Californian born a bare hour away from Hollywood, in San Bernardino, Hackman was a stage and TV actor before coming to movies. His brilliant performance opposite Sandy Dennis in *Any Wednesday* won him a big Broadway hand, and his face was familiar on the nation's TV screens as a guest-star on such shows as CBS *Playhouse, The F.B.I.* and *The Invaders.*

Hackman got his start toward a theatrical career after a five-year hitch in the Marines, when he signed up under the G.I. Bill for a radio and TV course. He worked behind the cameras on stations in Florida and Illinois, then came to New York and studied with a dramatic coach and appeared on Broadway in several comedies.

Hackman made his screen debut in *Lilith,* which starred Warren Beatty, and Beatty remembered him when *Bonnie and Clyde* was being cast.

Despite his screen success, Hackman professes not to like himself much on film. He has formed his own production company and looks forward to producing and acting as well as directing.

He followed *The French Connection* by co-starring with Lee Marvin in *Kansas City Prime,* and expects to make another film based on the career of Eddie Egan, the narc-squad cop whose exploits he portrays in *The French Connection.* (Egan himself played a small role in *Connection* and is now a screen actor.)

Hackman and his wife are the parents of three children and call Beverly Hills home.

Hackman's films include: *The Gypsy Moths, Marooned, Downhill Racer,* and *Doctor's Wives.*

OTHER NOMINEES
PETER FINCH, Sunday Bloody Sunday
WALTER MATTHAU, Kotch
GEORGE C. SCOTT, The Hospital
TOPOL, Fiddler on the Roof

1971
best actress
Jane Fonda
KLUTE

JANE FONDA's Bree Daniel, the stylish and intelligent call girl who almost becomes the victim of a pathological killer, was a stunning performance.

In recognizing its excellence and ignoring the controversy surrounding her as a political activist, the Academy proved its only standards for Oscar-honors are professional expertise and talent.

The first of her distinguished acting family to be Oscared, Jane Fonda was as adept as the Academy in separating her professional life from her political life. She said, accepting the Award, "There is a great deal to say, but I'm not going to say it. Thank you."

Henry Fonda's outspoken daughter, who won a previous Best Actress bid for 1969's *They Shoot Horses, Don't They?*, didn't intend to become an actress. "I was consciously trying to avoid an acting career," she says, and two years of playing summer stock with her father didn't change her mind.

That was done by her father's next-door neighbor at Malibu — Lee Strasberg, director of the famed Actor's Studio.

Before he managed to do so, Jane spent two years at Vassar, quitting there "because I was wasting my father's money." She next studied art in Paris and at New York's Art Student's League; worked in the offices of the *Paris Review*, and was a high-fashion model, appearing on the covers of magazines like *Vogue*.

When she decided to become an actress, she studied with Strasberg. A screen test given her by her godfather, producer Josh Logan, led to her Hollywood screen debut in 1960, in *Tall Story* with Anthony Perkins.

The New York-born actress, who lost her mother when she was ten, is a true cosmopolite. She speaks several languages and is as much at home abroad as in Brentwood, the posh Los Angeles suburb where she spent a good part of her childhood.

Separated from French director Roger Vadim, whom she met when she played in his *Circle of Love (La Ronde)* and married in 1965, she has a daughter, Vanessa, born three years later.

Jane Fonda's movies include: *Sunday in New York, The Chase, Hurry Sundown, Any Wednesday, Barefoot in the Park, Cat Ballou,* and *Barbarella*.

OTHER NOMINEES:
JULIE CHRISTIE, McCabe and Mrs. Miller
GLENDA JACKSON, Sunday Bloody Sunday
VANESSA REDGRAVE, Mary, Queen of Scots
JANET SUZMAN, Nicholas and Alexandra

1971
best supporting actor

Ben Johnson
THE LAST PICTURE SHOW

THE ACTOR who said, "Ain't it purty," when he accepted his Oscar, and then opined, "It couldn't have happened to a nicer fellah!" originally turned down his Award-winning role of Sam, the Lion. His old friend, Director John Ford, got him to reconsider. An Oklahoma cowboy used to earning a dollar a day and keep, Johnson's first Hollywood check brought him $300, and after that, "you couldn't have driven me back to Oklahoma with a club." His films include: *Wagon Master, Rio Grande, Shane, One-Eyed Jacks, Chisum,* and *Dime Box.*

OTHER NOMINEES:
JEFF BRIDGES, The Last Picture Show
LEONARD FREY, Fiddler on the Roof
RICHARD JAECKEL, Sometimes a Great Notion
ROY SCHEIDER, The French Connection

best supporting actress

Cloris Leachman
THE LAST PICTURE SHOW

TO CLORIS LEACHMAN her Academy-Awarded lonely, passionate wife in a small Texas town in the 1950s was her "most difficult role." One of Oscar's most excited honorees, she exclaimed, "I've fought against cliches all my life, and look at me, I'm a hopeless cliche!" A regular on TV's *Mary Tyler Moore Show,* she is the wife of producer-director George Englund and mother of five lively youngsters. Her films include *Butch Cassidy and the Sundance Kid,* and *Lovers and Other Strangers.*

OTHER NOMINEES:
ANN-MARGRET, Carnal Knowledge
ELLEN BURSTYN, The Last Picture Show
BARBARA HARRIS, Who Is Harry Kellerman and
    Why Is He Saying Those Terrible Things About Me?
MARGARET LEIGHTON, The Go-Between

211

1972
best picture

The Godfather
PARAMOUNT PICTURES

CAST: Marlon Brando, Al Pacino, Jame Caan, Richard Castellano, Robert Duvall, Sterling Hayden, John Marley, Richard Conte, Diane Keaton.

CREDITS: Producer, Albert S. Ruddy; Director, Francis Ford Coppola; Screenplay, Mario Puzo and Francis Ford Coppola; Director of Photography, Gordon Willis; Technicolor.

NATIONWIDE SPECULATION as to who would play the venerable Don Corleone in "The Godfather" began as soon as Paramount Pictures acquired screen rights to the best-selling Mario Puzo novel.

With each copy sold, a new casting director was self-created and in barber shops, beauty parlors and barrooms across the country millions of "experts" were explaining why their favorites were the only ones equipped to play the title role.

Because director Francis Ford Coppola (who won a 1972 Oscar for best screenplay, along with Puzo) wanted the role portrayed by a distinguished and versatile actor, his first choice was Marlon Brando. There was much skepticism since in the book Don Corleone was a man in his sixties, short, stocky and with greying hair. Brando, on the other hand, in his mid-forties, retained a youthful demeanor. The decision was finalized when Coppola invited several executives to see an anonymous screen test. A few moments after the test ended, there were shouts of approval as everyone questioned the actor's identity. Brando was signed immediately to portray the Godfather.

Three supporting players, Al Pacino, James Caan and Robert Duvall were also nominated for acting Awards for their "Godfather" roles.

Filming "The Godfather" was no easy task since some 90 per cent of the scenes were shot in the busy thoroughfares of New York City and its suburbs. So that Brando's unique makeup would not be revealed prematurely to the press and public, producer Al Ruddy maintained a veil of secrecy around the filming. For the three months of location shooting, daily crowds of onlookers were disappointed because they couldn't get close to members of the cast.

The most troublesome scenes of all were those shot on Mott Street where Little Italy borders on Chinatown. The narrow sidewalks were cluttered with pushcarts. Windows and fire escapes were jammed with spectators elbowing each other for a better view of the scene where Don Corleone emerges from his olive oil factory and is gunned down by a rival "family." It was a scene that was repeated endlessly during three full days of filming.

In all, more than 120 exterior locations around Manhattan, the Bronx, Brooklyn and Staten Island were used. Quieter and more controlled were the interior scenes which were made at the old Filmways Studio in the Bronx.

The music for "The Godfather" was created by the renowned Italian composer, Nino Rota.

Best Picture: Marlon Brando poses with family for daughter's wedding in "The Godfather."

OTHER NOMINEES:
CABARET, Allied Artists
DELIVERANCE, Warner Bros.
THE EMIGRANTS, Warner Bros
SOUNDER, 20th Century-Fox

1972
best actor

Marlon Brando
THE GODFATHER

TYPICAL OF Marlon Brando's unorthodox career was his refusal to accept his Best Actor Oscar for "The Godfather." First of the post-war rebels, Brando set a new and very different style in leading men from the moment he burst onto the nation's screens as the brutish Stanley Kowalski in "A Streetcar Named Desire."

Long an outspoken sympathizer and active worker for minority groups, and American Indians in particular, the unconventional actor sent a young Apache woman known as Sacheen Littlefeather, attractively dressed in Indian dress, to the Oscar ceremonies as his representative.

She told a stunned audience that Brando felt he "could not accept the Oscar because of the film industry's treatment of Indians, and on television in re-runs, and also because of the recent happenings at Wounded Knee."

Miss Littlefeather's announcement drew a mixed reaction of boos and cheers from the audience.

Brando did win and accept an Oscar in 1954 for his performance in "On the Waterfront."

Born in Omaha, Nebraska, and educated at the Shattuck Military Academy in Faribault, Minn., Brando studied at the Dramatic Workshop of the New School for Social Research with acting coach Stella Adler. The following year, 1944, he made his professional acting debut on Broadway in a supporting role in "I Remember Mama."

In February, 1946, he appeared in Maxwell Anderson's "Truckline Cafe," which led to the role of Marchbanks in George Bernard Shaw's "Candida," opposite Katharine Cornell. This was followed by a lead in Ben Hecht's "A Flag Is Born," after which he starred opposite Tallulah Bankhead in Jean Cocteau's "An Eagle Has Two Heads."

At this point, Brando took off for a year of travel and study, returning to the Broadway stage in 1947 as Stanley Kowalski in Tennessee Williams' "A Streetcar Named Desire." His performance made him an international celebrity overnight.

Among his other best known pictures are "Viva Zapata!" which won him the Best Actor's Award at the Cannes Film Festival, "Julius Caesar," "On The Waterfront," for which he won the 1954 Academy Award, "The Wild Ones," "Guys and Dolls," "Teahouse of the August Moon," "One-Eyed Jacks," "The Fugitive Kind" and "The Ugly American." His most recent film is the controversial "Last Tango in Paris."

Brando's refusal to accept the Oscar marked the second time such an incident took place. George C. Scott turned down the 1970 Best Actor Oscar for his performance in "Patton."

OTHER NOMINEES:
MICHAEL CAINE, Sleuth
LAURENCE OLIVIER, Sleuth
PETER O'TOOLE, The Ruling Class
PAUL WINFIELD, Sounder

1972
best actress

Liza Minnelli
CABARET

LIZA MINNELLI, WHO WON an Academy Award nomination as Best Actress in 1970 for her touching performance as Pookie Adams in "The Sterile Cuckoo," was this year's choice of Best Actress for her first screen musical, "Cabaret," in which she portrayed Berlin singer Sally Bowles. The Allied Artists-ABC Pictures presentation, also starring Michael York and Joel Grey, authentically recalls the synthetic gaiety and decadence of Germany in the early 1930's.

Liza, an accomplished singer, dancer and actress, is equally at home on a nightclub floor, a legitimate stage, a motion picture sound stage or a television studio. That she comes by her talent naturally is questioned by no one. Daughter of the fabulous Judy Garland and distinguished Academy Award winning director Vincent Minnelli, Liza was born in Los Angeles on March 10, 1946. She attended school in Beverly Hills, Switzerland and Paris, but she knew she wanted to be a performer from the time she was 16 years old. She toured in repertory, portraying leads in "The Diary of Anne Frank," "The Fantasticks," "Carnival," and "The Pajama Game." At 19 she made her Broadway debut in "Flora the Red Menace," and promptly walked off with the theater's coveted Antoinette Perry ("Tony") Award. Her nightclub debut at the Shoreham Hotel in Washington later that year broke all attendance records and won acclaim from nitery critics.

The young actress launched her first album ("Liza Minnelli") in 1968 for A&M Records, and her initial single "You Are For Loving," hit the high-mark sale of 500,000 copies. A second album for A&M was "Come Saturday Morning." Her other albums include "It Amazes Me," "Judy and Liza at the Palladium," "There Is A Time," and "New Feeling." Her most recent album is Capitol Records' "Maybe This Time."

In June, 1970, she starred in her own television special, "Liza," for NBC.

Among her other motion pictures are "The Sterile Cuckoo" and "Tell Me That You Love Me, Junie Moon."

OTHER NOMINEES:
DIANA ROSS, Lady Sings The Blues
MAGGIE SMITH, Travels With My Aunt
CICELY TYSON, Sounder
LIV ULLMANN, The Emigrants

1972
best supporting actor

Joel Grey
CABARET

"DON'T LET ANYONE TELL you this isn't a terrific thrill," a beaming Joel Grey told the audience at the 1972 Academy Awards in accepting his Oscar for his role as the sardonic master of ceremonies in the Allied Artists release, "Cabaret."

In the movie, Joel re-created the role he played on Broadway in the stage production which won him the 1967 Antoinette Perry ("Tony") award. Two years later, he was similarly nominated for "Best Star Actor," in the Broadway musical, "George M!". These two New York productions established him as one of the most sought after song and dance stars on Broadway. It was producer-director Hal Prince who raised him to movie star billing in "Cabaret."

OTHER NOMINEES:
EDDIE ALBERT, The Heartbreak Kid
JAMES CAAN, The Godfather
ROBERT DUVALL, The Godfather
AL PACINO, The Godfather

best supporting actress

Eileen Heckart
BUTTERFLIES ARE FREE

EILEEN HECKART, WHO starred with Goldie Hawn and Edward Albert in "Butterflies Are Free," a Frankovich production for Columbia Pictures release, has an almost incredible record for her more than 25 years as an actress: 32 plays, 10 movies and 20 different TV shows. She has played comedy and drama, tragedy and musical comedy.

In "Butterflies Are Free," she re-created the part she played in the original Broadway and the London stage production. Her other movies include "Miracle in the Rain," "The Bad Seed," "Bus Stop," "Somebody Up There Likes Me," "Up the Down Staircase" and "No Way to Treat a Lady."

OTHER NOMINEES:
JEANNIE BERLIN, The Heartbreak Kid
GERALDINE PAGE, Pete 'n' Tillie
SUSAN TYRELL, Fat City
SHELLEY WINTERS, The Poseidon Adventure

1973
best picture

The Sting
UNIVERSAL

CAST: Paul Newman, Robert Redford, Robert Shaw, Charles Durning, Eileen Brennan, John Heffernan, Jack Kehoe, Ray Walston, Harold Gould, Dana Elcar, Dimitra Arliss.

CREDITS: Producers, Tony Bill, Michael and Julia Phillips; Director, George Roy Hill; Screenplay by David S. Ward; Director of Photography, Robert Surtees; Richard D. Zanuck/David Brown Presentation.

IN *THE STING*, a Zanuck/Brown presentation for Universal Studios, Paul Newman and Robert Redford play a pair of daring con men in Chicago's underworld of the '30s. The Bill/Phillips production of a George Roy Hill film also starred England's Robert Shaw as the formidable adversary who is their mark.

Produced by Tony Bill and Julia and Michael Phillips, *The Sting*, written by David S. Ward, also won the Oscar for Best Original Story and Screenplay. Filming of *The Sting* lasted 12 weeks and took place in various Los Angeles and Chicago locations, as well as the sound stages of Universal Studios.

The Golden Age of the Big Con — Chicago of the Thirties, its heroes, its exploits and its language — provides the theme of the film. While the same decade produced the bloody violence of gangland wars, professionals of the "Big Con" disdained brutality. Their methods were more subtle, taking their mark solely by means of the skilled hand or sharp wit. Paul Newman and Robert Redford play two such con men, pitting their wits against Robert Shaw as a classy but vicious New York racketeer.

To complete the assemblage of grifters, flunkies and thugs, director George Roy Hill flew to New York for additional casting. *The Sting* is thus peppered with some of the finest character actors in the country: Charles During, Ray Walston, John Heffernan, Harold Gould, Dana Elcar, Ed Bakey, Leonard Barr, Sally Kirkland and many others. Their fine performances undoubtedly helped win the film's best picture Oscar.

OTHER NOMINEES:
AMERICAN GRAFFITI, Universal
CRIES AND WHISPERS, New World Pictures
THE EXORCIST, Warner Bros.
A TOUCH OF CLASS, Avco Embassy

Best Picture: Robert Shaw, Robert Redford and Paul Newman in "The Sting."

1973
best actor

Jack Lemmon
SAVE THE TIGER

"THIS IS ONE HELLUVA honor, and I am thrilled," a jubilant Jack Lemmon said, in accepting his Oscar for the role of Harry Stoner in *Save The Tiger.*

"I had a speech prepared - in 1959," he added, "but I've forgotten it.

He was nominated for Best Actor for *Some Like It Hot* in 1959. He also received the nomination in 1960 for *The Apartment,* and received an earlier Oscar in 1955 for Best Supporting Actor for Mr. Roberts. This makes him the first actor to win both Best Supporting and Best Actor Oscars.

Lemmon is married to actress Felicia Farr. They have a daughter, Courtney, age 8.

OTHER NOMINEES:
MARLON BRANDO, Last Tango In Paris
JACK NICHOLSON, The Last Detail
AL PACINO, Serpico
ROBERT REDFORD, The Sting

1973
best actress

Glenda Jackson
A TOUCH OF CLASS

MELVIN FRANK, producer of *A Touch of Class,* accepted the Best Actress award for Glenda Jackson, whose busy work schedule kept her in England during the presentations. She thus joined the small group of two-time winners, having received an Oscar in 1970 for *Women In Love.* She also received a nomination in 1971 for *Sunday Bloody Sunday.*

Her other pictures include *The Music Lovers, Mary, Queen of Scots, Triple Echo* and *The Nelson Affair.* She is also remembered for her remarkable television portrayal of the title role in the BBC series, *Elizabeth R.*

She is married to Roy Hodges, a London stage director. They have one son, Daniel, aged 6.

OTHER NOMINEES:
ELLEN BURSTYN, The Exorcist
MARSHA MASON, Cinderella Liberty
BARBRA STREISAND, The Way We Were
JOANNE WOODWARD, Summer Wishes,
    Winter Dreams

1973
best supporting actor

best supporting actress

1968-1973 Oscar Winners in other categories on pages 6-7

John Houseman
THE PAPER CHASE

BEST SUPPORTING ACTOR, John Houseman, a legendary Hollywood and Broadway writer and producer, made his screen acting debut as the brilliant, methodical professor, in Twentieth Century-Fox's *The Paper Chase*. The film about Harvard law students is based on the popular John Jay Osborn, Jr. novel published in 1971.

Houseman co-founded the famed Mercury Theater with Orson Welles in 1937. Throughout the 1940's and 50's he commuted between New York and Los Angeles producing 18 feature films, including *The Bad and the Beautiful, Julius Caesar* and *Lust For Life*.

OTHER NOMINEES:
VINCENT GARDENIA, Bang The Drum Slowly
JACK GILFORD, Save The Tiger
JASON MILLER, The Exorcist
RANDY QUAID, The Last Detail

Tatum O'Neal
PAPER MOON

TATUM O'NEAL, who co-starred with her father, Ryan O'Neal, in *Paper Moon*, is 10 years old and was born in Los Angeles.

Director Peter Bogdanovich convinced O'Neal to allow Tatum to play his daughter in the film, and O'Neal agreed with the provision that this be the only acting she do until she is old enough to make her own decision about a career.

Tatum's mother is the former Joanna Moore. She has a brother Griffin, 8, and a step-brother, Patrick, 5, whose mother is Leigh Taylor-Young.

OTHER NOMINEES:
LINDA BLAIR, The Exorcist
CANDY CLARK, American Graffiti
MADELINE KAHN, Paper Moon
SYLVIA SIDNEY, Summer Wishes, Winter Dreams